*May the good Lord bless and keep you!*

*Jim Brooks*

# Adam & Eve
# Were Real
## Forgotten History
## of Mankind

By Dr. N. James Brooks, Jr.

ADAM & EVE WERE REAL
Forgotten History of Mankind
Copyright © 2017, Dr. N. James Brooks, Jr.

All Scripture quotations, unless otherwise specified are from The Holy Bible, King James Version, Copyright © 1977, 1984, Thomas Nelson Inc. Publishers.

ISBN:
978-0-9990892-0-0

Library of Congress Number:
2017910813

To order additional copies, visit:
http://www.AdamAndEveWereReal.com

**For more information please contact:**

Newton Publishing Co.

http://www.NewtonPublishingCo.com

# Dedication

This book, "Adam and Eve Were Real," is dedicated to all those who have encouraged me thru the years. My grandparents and my parents, all of whom taught me to believe the Bible and who gave me an interest in and a love of history.

I must thank my grandfather Brooks, who taught me that truth can stand being questioned and examined.

Most of all I wish to thank my beloved wife for her continued love and support during all the years I have worked on this book. She has believed in the importance of this research from its very beginning and has never ceased to encourage me.

To all of you, I dedicate this book, the fruit of 20 years of research and a lifetime of seeking after the truth.

- Dr. N. James Brooks, Jr.

# TABLE OF CONTENTS

# PREFACE

This book, titled "Adam & Eve Were Real: Forgotten History Of Mankind," began as a personal research project of mine. I grew up in a family with an interest in history. Over the years, in the course of my personal reading I came across occasional references to ancient writings that mentioned Adam and Eve and other people and events that I had previously only heard about in the Bible. This intrigued me. It was especially intriguing since those references were from sources outside of the Bible and sources that were very old, ancient in fact.

Nearly twenty years ago, I decided to begin researching historical records that reference people and events mentioned in the Bible. I was astounded to discover that the Bible does not have to be accepted solely by faith. If ancient legends and histories found around the world are true, then people and events mentioned in the Bible are true also.

There are stories about Creation, some of them in writing, that reference Adam and Eve, sometimes by name. Some of these written accounts long predate the Bible. There are also ancient histories that speak of gods and goddesses who of course are not in the Bible, but along with them Adam and Eve are mentioned.

There are accounts in many ancient legends, oral histories, and sometimes ancient written records that speak of people and events mentioned in Genesis.

To me this said, "Yes, the Bible is true." Out of this personal research came the book you are about to read. I spent some fifteen years researching it. I have thousands of pages of notes. From that research came this book, with others hopefully to follow.

I spent many long days and hours in my research. Quite a bit of money went into my research as well, for some of the books I reference have been long out of print and copies are often very hard to locate. What I have discovered has astounded me. I think anyone who reads this book will be astounded too.

This book is offered to everyone who believes the stories in the book of Genesis and who would like proof that those stories are true. This book is also offered to any and everyone who has an open and an inquiring mind, and who is interested in the truth.

I think everyone who reads this book will then want to go back to the Book of Genesis (which means the Book of Beginnings) and read and read again of the beginnings of mankind, for the information there is true.

As you read, remember, if that book is true then you can be certain that the rest of the Bible is also true. You are therefore enjoined to read it all and to practice what you read.

Hurry and do it, for one of the things that the ancient Jewish and early Christian teachers said was that after six thousand years the stage of Creation in which we live would be replaced with a new heaven and a new earth that the prophet Isaiah spoke of.

According to them that six thousand years is about up. Are you ready? If you haven't already done so, turn to God as revealed thru His son, Jesus Christ, and let Him make you into a new person, perfectly fitted for the new heavens and the new earth that He has promised us.

- Dr. N. James Brooks, Jr.

## All That Is Good Is Thine

If there be good in that which I have wrought,
I wrought it not, the work alone is Thine,
If I have failed to write what Thou hast planned,
The fault alone is mine, an over eager son of man,
The good is Thine, all failure mine,
Only what Thou conceivest would I do,
And one stone the more be shaped to its place,
For step by step in the pathway of right,
Will make me a stone in Thy temple of light.

-   Dr. N. James Brooks, Jr.

# WHERE TO BEGIN:
# The Introduction

Every book needs an introduction, a given reason for its existence. A book without an introduction is like a child without a heritage, a child with no history, a child of unknown origin. Sadly, that is what most of the world's peoples today are like, definitely those who live in the Western World.

Our true heritage has been stripped from us and we have been left with a false heritage, a false history, one that is not ours, but one that we have been told to claim. No people can be greater than they believe their forebears to have been. A people who believe their forebears to have been a great people, who strove against great odds and prevailed, will be willing to strive themselves against great odds, believing that they too will prevail.

A people though who have been taught that they come from worthless stock, that their forebears were worthless people who never accomplished anything, will likewise think that they, their ancestors' descendants, are worthless and can never accomplish anything.

Unfortunately, the young people of the Western World are growing up thinking and being taught that they come from worthless stock. They increasingly think they are worthless, because they are being taught that their ancestors were worthless.

When Hitler was seeking converts, he found that his most likely followers were young people with feelings of worthlessness and low self-esteem. The Nazis took those young converts and destroyed their lives. Young people today are again looking for something that will give them a personal feeling of value and self-worth. Like the youth of the past, they will gain their feelings of self-worth from God, or they will fall prey to another manmade ideology that promises fulfillment, but in the end, destroys those who believe in it.

Any ideology or belief system that is without God is like an edifice, a building, built on shifting sand. Such an edifice will surely fall.

Come with me now and let us look at the past, the far distant past of our ancestors, and the ancestors of all people. Let us see where we really come from, for if we know where we come from, we will know where we are going.

Our story begins with the origin of our ancestors. It begins a long time ago, though not as long ago as many would have us believe, for our origin is not what most tell us, nor what most would have us think. Our origin is much more exalted than that of a monkey or a half human caveman, spending millions of years evolving to the status of a man.

We began as created man, as fully alert, alive, and as intelligent as any man or woman today. We were created by God, in His own image. It is that story, the story of mankind, that you are now about to read.

Though far we wander from the scenes of the past,
Their actions follow us, and the present holds them fast,
For the days that were first sway the days that are last,
And the on-coming future is built on the past.

- Dr. N. James Brooks, Jr.

*"Enough light exists for those whose only desire is to see, and enough darkness for those with a contrary disposition."*
- Blaise Pascal (Pensees #430)

# CHAPTER ONE:
# How Accurate is Oral History and Legend?

Some of what you are about to read was taken from oral histories and traditions of various ethnic groups around the world. Other things you will read were taken from ancient written documents. For that reason, it is important to ask just how truthful and accurate can we expect such oral and written records to be.

The history of a people is one of their most valuable possessions, for through their history they retain the knowledge of who they are, what they have done, and therefore their sense of self-worth as a people. For that reason, ethnic groups all over the world tend to guard their history and traditions carefully. Even when a people do not have a written history, they will have an oral history that is often highly accurate.

Regarding oral history, we grossly underestimate the ability of humans to memorize and recite from memory without error. Mnemotechnics, or memory enhancing techniques, were a part of the training of the most highly educated people in antiquity (Small, p.83). Further, the official oral history of a nation was usually entrusted to a select few, whose task it was to memorize and to transmit orally that history, without changing or omitting a word.

As the first of several examples of this accuracy, sometime in the early 1900's, a Hungarian cultural anthropologist, Emil Torday, was traveling through central Africa, collecting material for a book he was writing. The Bushongo, a tribe who had never seen a white man before, began reciting the history of their tribe to Torday. They started with their first chief, five centuries before, and began tracing the tribe down through one hundred and twenty chiefs to the present. As the tribal elders recited their people's history, they came to their 98th chief, who had reigned nearly 300 years before. In describing this chief's reign, the elders said nothing eventful happened, except that one day at noon the sun went completely out, leaving the land in total darkness for a short time.

Realizing that the elders were describing a total eclipse of the sun, Torday was eager to know if this part of their oral history was accurate. Upon his return to Europe, Torday began to research the matter. After much searching in the astronomical records of Europe, the anthropologist learned that there had indeed been a total eclipse of the sun directly over that part of central Africa. The total eclipse occurred only over a small portion of the globe, and was not visible in Europe. The eclipse had occurred in 1680. "There was no possibility of confusion with another eclipse, because this was the only one visible in the region during the seventeenth and eighteenth centuries. The tradition of this tribe was that ninety-eight chiefs into the past, the sun had briefly gone out one day. Their tradition, when tested, proved to be correct. (Davidson, p.4)

The Chambers Encyclopedia, 1956 edition, under the topic "Genealogy," informs us of a Maori chief, who, in order to prove his right to certain lands, recited his ancestry to a land commission of the government of New Zealand. Over the course of three days he recited hundreds of names in his family tree, including collateral ancestors and relatives by marriage. Some Somalis, visiting England around 1900, were interviewed and were found able to repeat their genealogy for twenty-two generations, roughly 660 years. (Journal of Transactions of the Victoria Institute, vol. XXXVIII, published by the Institute, 1906. p.66).

What of other peoples? The Irish had a written language of their own that dated back, at the very least, to the 4th century A.D. However, epic sagas, important laws, much of Irish history, and the genealogies of the kings of Ireland were entrusted to the memory of certain high-ranking bards, known as Ollam Fili. Existing Irish records state that certification as Ollam, the highest level of Irish bard, required memorization and verbatim recitation of several hundred epic poems.

Such training typically took twenty-five years. This was of course, extremely difficult, but less difficult than it sounds, because the sagas and history were all in rhyme, which is much easier to remember than simple prose (MacManus, p.56). Rhyming poetry, by the way, comes from Ireland, and though the English adopted rhyming poetry from the Irish, even to this present time rhyming poetry is found only among the English-speaking people.

The Ollam Fili had to be able to recite important histories and genealogies perfectly. Every three years at a gathering at the hill of Tara, the Chief Ollam Fili chanted the national history and royal genealogy. A single important error would cost him his position, so his competitors listened carefully. Everywhere in the ancient world genealogy mattered, because it was the basis of inheritance and legal privileges.

The shift from oral records to written ones did not necessarily affect the accuracy of ancient accounts either positively or negatively. Ancient written accounts seem to have been meticulously kept, at least when they were official histories. In ancient Assyria and Babylonia, the writing and copying of literature was "entrusted to the hands of professional scribes. And the minute care which was bestowed upon the accurate transcription of the texts was extraordinary.

Where we can compare a text compiled, let us say, for one of the Babylonian libraries of Amraphel with a copy of it made for the library of Nineveh fifteen hundred years later the differences are slight and unimportant" (Sayce, p.65). The tablets are full of examples of the scrupulous honesty with which the copyists set about their work. If the copy before them was defective, they state the fact and make no attempt to fill in the missing characters . . . ." (Sayce, p.65).

As yet another example, Jaroslav Cerny tells of an Egyptian papyrus of about 1400 B.C. which bears the following colophon (or note), left by the scribe. The scribe wrote, "The book is completed from its beginning to its end, having been copied, revised, compared, and certified sign by sign" (Černý, p.25).

Other examples of carefully and meticulously copied official histories and such like documents are the Hebrew books that comprise the Old Testament. In those books, "certain letters have come down with the text, from the most ancient times, having a small ornament or flourish on the top. These ornamented letters were quite exceptional, and implied no added meaning of any kind; but so jealously was the sacred text safeguarded, that the scribe was informed how many of each of the letters had these little ornaments" (Bullinger, Appendix 93).

It was to these ornaments that Jesus referred in Mathew 5:18 and Luke 16:17, when He said that not even the merest mark or ornament should pass away from the law until all things should come to pass. (Bullinger, Appendix 93).

A very large body of historical evidence is passed over in silence by most of today's scholars. That body of evidence consists of oral traditions, legends, and yes even written records, left by nations all over the earth, concerning the origins and earliest history of themselves and of all mankind. It is commonly thought

**14**

in this present age that nothing is worthy of our belief unless experience and observation prove it to be true. This idea, part of the now largely discredited philosophy known as "empiricism," says basically that anything which lacks direct corroboration by experience and observation must be discarded as simply not provable. (Merriam Webster's Collegiate Dictionary, tenth edition.)

There is a great many today who apply that idea to the stories in the book of Genesis in Bible. Because they believe the stories in Genesis cannot be proven true, many people do not give them a second thought. They dismiss Genesis and sometimes the entire Bible as of no more value than a fairy tale. But that was not always the case.

Tradition and legends, even if not certified not by an Ollam Fili, should not be rejected out of hand. Mary Francis Cusack, author of a history of Ireland, wrote." . . . tradition is not necessarily either a pure myth or a falsified account of facts." She added that by carefully sifting through legends, we will find much that is true. (Cusack, p.38).

At one time, most people took for granted that all humanity descended from one created couple named Adam and Eve. They also accepted as a fact that a great flood occurred, which wiped out all of mankind except one family, whose patriarch was Noah. It was an accepted belief that everyone descended from one of Noah's three sons.

In fact, at one time many ethnic groups could have told you which of Noah's sons was their direct ancestor. As a point of fact, many still can. They are not basing their belief on faith. They are basing their belief on the writings and oral history handed down from their ancestors.

15

Their knowledge as to where they came from preceded Christianity and even the writing of the Old Testament. Through carefully preserved records, their lineage and origin could and can be traced back to the time of Babel and the dispersal of the nations from the plain of Shinar. From that place and point in time, some records and oral traditions go still further back, to the flood, and preceding that, on back to the first man and woman who walked the earth. As Mary Francis Cusack said of the early writers of history and genealogy, they usually commenced their world histories and their genealogies with the sons of Noah, if not with the first man of the human race.

What is remarkable about these histories and genealogies is that they come mostly from ancient historians and writers, of various nations, who had never heard of the Bible, and who had not the least intention of lending support to any record or statement in it. Their verification of Creation, the flood, the dispersal of mankind from the Tower of Babel, and the rest of the account in Genesis is therefore all the more valuable. It was not until relatively modern times that this evidence began to be ignored.

It began to be ignored because people accepted the theory of evolution. However, there were attempts prior to the spread of the idea of evolution to ignore or deny the evidence presented by these ancient accounts. One of the first scholarly works that denied the received view of the time was Josiah Priest's book on ancient America. Though Priest began his story on Mount Ararat after the flood, he tried to explain the flood in natural terms rather than as an event caused by God (Priest, p.127), and as only a localized flood, not a worldwide one (Priest, p.9).

Once the theory of evolution came upon the scene, it immediately provided a means whereby the ideas of creation, the flood, and the origin and responsibility of mankind could be

16

avoided. As this theory spread, and became coupled with the philosophy of empiricism, many authors of science and history texts either no longer believed that mankind was created or they were afraid of being ridiculed by their peers. As a result, they stopped putting ideas contrary to evolution in their books. Until that point, it was not uncommon for science and history books to mention stories handed down from much earlier times concerning the origin of mankind.

This author once owned a history of England that began by tracing the lineage of the first settlers of that country back to Japheth and his father, Noah. As two further examples, see "Lee's New School History of the United States," p.22, by Susan P. Lee; and "The Illustrated History of Ireland," by Mary Francis Cusack, p.38.

Both of these books were written after Darwin published his theory of evolution, but at a time when science had not yet fully accepted that theory, and before the advent and acceptance of the philosophy of empiricism. Even for a long time after the publication of Darwin's theory of evolution, many science and geology books freely ascribed evidence of extreme cataclysmic occurrences in the earth to the flood.

Evolution became a weapon with which to attack the validity of the Bible, while empiricism became the vehicle with which that attack was launched. Darwin's "Origin of the Species" was first published in 1859. Before its publication, some geologists had begun unknowingly preparing the groundwork for Darwin by claiming that the earth was much older than the Bible said.

As people accepted that idea, it made it easier for them to accept evolution, since the theory of evolution teaches that hundreds of millions of years were needed for modern man to evolve from the original protoplasmic slime from which we allegedly came. Even evolution from apes, which Darwin taught, requires, according to Darwin, many millions of years.

One problem with this is that there is no evidence that the earth has existed that long. The methods used to date fossils are questionable, with multiple dates sometimes being given for the same creature. Even living animals may appear to be thousands of years old if carbon dated, for there are flaws in carbon dating.

If one wishes to believe in Darwin's theory of evolution, one must accept it on faith alone, without any facts to substantiate it, for the facts are simply not there. Evolution is at best an unproven theory that contains many scientific flaws. It is only an interpretation of various facts. It is an interpretation that may be wrong. Evolution certainly has no historical validation.

On the other hand, while we have no scientific proof of a supernatural creation of the world, there are accounts of creation and of early mankind that come from many sources, and which in many instances agree in all the important aspects. In looking at some of those accounts, you will notice that quite a number of accounts of Creation speak of a beautiful garden or sometimes an island as the place where the Creation of the first human couple occurred.

You will also note that in a number of cases the man and woman have names that are very similar to the names they are given in the Bible, Adam and Eve. There are also cases where the name has changed, but the meaning has remained the same, such as Adam, which means "dirt", called by another name, but that new name when translated into English still means "dirt".

The same is true of Eve. Some of these accounts, which occur all over the globe, also involve a serpent that can stand upright, just as the serpent in Genesis could. Additionally, they repeat other things that are found in the Genesis account of Creation, the Temptation, and the Fall of man. Before we look at some of those accounts, let us review the account of creation that the Bible gives us.

## When Radiant The Morn Of Creation Broke

When radiant the morn of creation broke,
And the cosmos alive to God awoke,
When empty was the realm of death,
And man came alive in God's mighty breath,

When the angels with one voice did sing,
In praise of God let their anthems ring,
When each sun was ablaze in a glory of light,
There was no rebellion and all was right.

The stars, each suns, that around Him did roll,
Myriads of planets, turning like on a turning pole,
God's face was not hid from His creation,
In love all gazed on Him in admiration.

Yes, there was a time, far back in the ages,
When o'er the voice of priests and sages,
And words writ in burnished gold on silver pages,
There arose a voice like a torrent that rages,

It caused the wise to be silent and the mighty to tremble,
And stopped the worst fool ere he began to dissemble,
That voice will be heard again in this very day,
Listen, you can hear it now like an ancient lay,
Yes, even today, in these twilight hours,
God has not forgotten this earth of ours,
His love is brooding, and new life is born,
The veil that hides His face will soon be shorn,

And all around there will be,
Myriads and myriads breaking free,
People turning from the Tree that kills,
Listening to the voice that all else stills,

And all across the universe pent,
In waves of glory and gladness sent,
As has not been for six thousand years,
We'll hear the music of the spheres,

The Spirit is brooding, and love will born,
In the hearts of many who are now forlorn,
The spherical orb of this earth shines anew,
God wants to begin earth's conquest with you,

-   **Dr. N. James Brooks, Jr. (2006)**


### Just As It Was Meant To Be

The world in its sleep lies slumbering on,
No signs of awakening they see,
But we're gathered together to greet the dawn,
Just as it was meant to be,

We know that the fig tree is leafy and green
All the signs of Your coming we see,
And soon Your great glory will dawn and be seen,
Just as it was meant to be,

Like a new born babe just opening its eyes,
Like the first glimmer of light on the sea,
We hear a voice saying arise, arise,
Just as it was meant to be,

The red dragon is falling from the skies,
The beast will soon rise from the sea,
But God's on the throne, so open your eyes
Just as it was meant to be,

Now Father, oh Father, show us the sign
Which for ages we've waited to see
A new day will dawn and Your glory will shine,
Just as it was meant to be,

And forever and ever Your word will be law,
Forever and ever Your reign we will see,
Yes all the world over Your word shall be law,
Just as it was meant to be,

The future belongs to Thee,
The future belongs to Thee,
A new day is dawning and we will be free,
Just as it was meant to be.

-   Dr. N. James Brooks, Jr. **(2012)**

*The God of Christians is not a God who is simply the author of mathematical truths, or of the order of the elements; that is the view of heathens and Epicureans. He is not merely a God who exercises His providence over the life and fortunes of men, to bestow on those who worship Him a long and happy life. That was the portion of the Jews. But the God of Abraham, the God of Isaac, the God of Jacob, the God of Christians, is a God of love and of comfort, a God who fills the soul and heart of those whom He possesses, a God who makes them conscious of their inward wretchedness, who fills it with humility and joy, with confidence and love, who renders them incapable of any other end than Himself.*

- Blaise Paschal, Pensees

# CHAPTER TWO:
# Adam and Eve Were Real

If the story of Adam and Eve as told in the Bible is true, then it is reasonable to believe that ethnic groups all over the earth would have some knowledge of them and of the story of Creation as revealed in the Bible. That would be so, because they would all have had some knowledge of our first parents and of the true events of Creation handed down to them from their ancestors.

Some of that knowledge would have been lost over the passage of thousands of years. Some of it might have been distorted by people who did not wish to acknowledge the sin of their first parents. Some people also would have preferred to forget about the one true God, as forgetting about Him would mean they would have an excuse for not serving Him. Nevertheless, the knowledge of what happened in Creation and how it occurred would be remembered in whole or in part by many if not most of the earth's people.

Let us take the first chapter of Genesis a verse or two at a time and see how it compares with accounts of Creation as told by a number of the non-Christian religions.

The first two verses of Genesis relate the following:

*In the beginning, God created the heaven and the earth. And the earth was without form, and void; and darkness was upon the face of the deep. And the Spirit of God moved upon the face of the waters. (Genesis 1:1-2)*

By reading this, we can gain the following ideas of Biblical Creation. Everything was created by one God. After stating that God created heaven and earth, the Biblical account continues by telling that the earth was without form and void (in other words in a chaotic state) that the earth was covered with water and darkness covered the earth.

There are a number of similar accounts by various ethnic groups around the world. The Babylonian account of Creation also tells that in the beginning the earth was a watery chaos, above which darkness brooded, while the earth was without form and void. (Sayce, p.103).

The earliest Chinese account of Creation tells us that "of old in the beginning, there was the great chaos, without form and dark" (Legge, p.28). The Chinese account continues by talking of a single all-powerful God, who created everything.

The Miztecs, a tribe or nation who lived in Mexico when the Spanish came, described Creation as a time when the earth was covered with water and there was nothing but mud and slime on the earth. (Bancroft, vol. III, p.70).

The earliest written account of Creation that we have is an account of Creation as believed by the Phoenicians. Though it is poorly translated into Greek, it has a great similarity to the Genesis account of Creation. This account also speaks of darkness and of the earth being covered with a watery mud. (Lenormant, pp.300-303).

Among the first events recorded in the book of Genesis, after the account of Creation, is the story of the first couple, Adam and Eve, being tempted and doing the one thing that God had commanded them not to do. For doing that one forbidden thing,

Adam and Eve were expelled from the Garden where God had placed them.

In describing all of this, the book of Genesis says the following:

*The Lord God formed man of the dust of the ground, and breathed into his nostrils the breath of life; and man became a living soul. And the Lord God planted a garden eastward in Eden; and there he put the man whom he had formed. And out of the ground made the Lord God to grow every tree that is pleasant to the sight, and good for food; the tree of life also in the midst of the garden, and the tree of knowledge of good and evil. And a river went out of Eden to water the garden; and from thence it was parted, and became into four heads. The name of the first is Pison: that is it which compasseth the whole land of Havilah, where there is gold; and the gold of that land is good: there is bdellium and the onyx stone. And the name of the second river is Gihon: the same is it that compasseth the whole land of Ethiopia. And the name of the third river is Hiddekel: that is it which goeth toward the east of Assyria. And the fourth river is Euphrates. And the Lord God took the man, and put him into the garden of Eden to dress it and to keep it. And the Lord God commanded the man, saying, Of every tree of the garden thou mayest freely eat: but of the tree of the knowledge of good and evil, thou shalt not eat of it: for in the day that thou eatest thereof thou shalt surely die. And the Lord God said, It is not good that the man should be alone; I will make him an help meet for him. . . . . And the Lord God caused a deep sleep to fall upon Adam, and he slept: and he took one of his ribs, and closed up the flesh instead thereof; and the rib, which the Lord God had taken from man, made he a woman, and brought her unto the man. And Adam said, This is now bone of my bones, and flesh of my flesh: she shall be called Woman, because she was taken out of Man. Therefore shall a man leave his father and his mother, and shall*

**25**

*cleave unto his wife: and they shall be one flesh. And they were*
*both naked, the man and his wife, and were not ashamed.*
(Genesis 2:7-25)

*Now the serpent was more subtle than any beast of the field*
*which the Lord God had made. And he said unto the woman,*
*Yea, hath God said, Ye shall not eat of every tree of the garden?*
*And the woman said unto the serpent, We may eat of the fruit of*
*the trees of the garden: but of the fruit of the tree which is in the*
*midst of the garden, God hath said, Ye shall not eat of it, neither*
*shall ye touch it, lest ye die. And the serpent said unto the*
*woman, Ye shall not surely die: for God doth know that in the*
*day ye eat thereof, then your eyes shall be opened, and ye shall be*
*as gods, knowing good and evil. And when the woman saw that*
*the tree was good for food, and that it was pleasant to the eyes,*
*and a tree to be desired to make one wise, she took of the fruit*
*thereof, and did eat, and gave also unto her husband with her;*
*and he did eat. And the eyes of them both were opened, and they*
*knew that they were naked; and they sewed fig leaves together,*
*and made themselves aprons. And they heard the voice of the*
*Lord God walking in the garden in the cool of the day: and Adam*
*and his wife hid themselves from the presence of the Lord God*
*amongst the trees of the garden. And the Lord God called unto*
*Adam, and said unto him, Where art thou? And he said, I heard*
*thy voice in the garden, and I was afraid, because I was naked;*
*and I hid myself. And he said, Who told thee that thou wast*
*naked? Hast thou eaten of the tree, whereof I commanded thee*
*that thou shouldest not eat? And the man said, The woman*
*whom thou gavest to be with me, she gave me of the tree, and I*
*did eat. And the Lord God said unto the woman, What is this*
*that thou hast done? And the woman said, The serpent beguiled*
*me, and I did eat. And the Lord God said unto the serpent,*
*Because thou hast done this, thou art cursed above all cattle, and*
*above every beast of the field; upon thy belly shalt thou go, and*
*dust shalt thou eat all the days of thy life: and I will put enmity*

between thee and the woman, and between thy seed and her seed; it shall bruise thy head, and thou shalt bruise his heel. Unto the woman he said, I will greatly multiply thy sorrow and thy conception; in sorrow thou shalt bring forth children; and thy desire shall be to thy husband, and he shall rule over thee. And unto Adam he said, Because thou hast hearkened unto the voice of thy wife, and hast eaten of the tree, of which I commanded thee, saying, Thou shalt not eat of it: cursed is the ground for thy sake; in sorrow shalt thou eat of it all the days of thy life; thorns also and thistles shall it bring forth to thee; and thou shalt eat the herb of the field; in the sweat of thy face shalt thou eat bread, till thou return unto the ground; for out of it wast thou taken: for dust thou art, and unto dust shalt thou return. (Genesis 3:1-19)

The Bible states that God made the first man out of the dust of the ground and breathed into his nostrils the breath of life, making this first man a living being. God named the man and all of mankind, Adam, which means "dirt." That was to remind us that we are made of dirt and that one day our bodies will return to dirt or dust, while our spirits will return to God who gave us life. The name Eve means life or living. She was named this because after God created the first couple, all further human life came from Eve, the ancestral mother of us all.

It says further that God planted a garden in a place called Eden, and there He put the man He had created. God then made every tree that is pleasing to look at and/or that bears good fruit to grow in the garden. Eden means "delight," so the "Garden of Eden," in English means the "Garden of Delight."

Of the many other similar accounts of Creation, the Temptation and the expulsion of man from the Garden, the lengthiest and the most similar to that in the Bible is that of

Josephus. He was a Jewish priest who was born during the lifetime of Jesus.

As a priest, Josephus served at the temple in Jerusalem. In the temple, the Israelites had stored all the records of their people, along with many ancient books. When the Romans destroyed the temple in 70 A.D., Josephus wrote a book in which he recorded all the history of the world, as relating to the Jewish people, that he could recall from the records that had been stored in the temple.

Here is Josephus' account of Creation, the Temptation of Adam and Eve, and what followed, based on the information that he had read in the temple archives. Though there are other and similar accounts of Creation, the Temptation, and the Fall, the account by Josephus is the longest such account. It is in a number of places different from the account in the Bible, but nevertheless, it follows it closely.

The following paragraphs give that account as Josephus wrote it:

> *In the beginning God created the heaven and the earth. But when the earth did not come into sight, but was covered with thick darkness, and a wind moved upon its surface, God commanded that there should be light: and when that was made, he considered the whole mass, and separated the light and the darkness; and the name he gave to one was Night, and the other he called Day: and he named the beginning of light, and the time of rest, The Evening and The Morning, and this was indeed the first day. But Moses said it was one day; the cause of which I am able to give even now; but because I have promised to give such reasons for all things in a treatise by itself, I shall put off its exposition till that time. After this, on the second day, he placed the heaven over the whole world, and separated it from the other parts, and he determined it should stand by itself. He also placed*

*a crystalline [firmament] round it, and put it together in a manner agreeable to the earth, and fitted it for giving moisture and rain, and for affording the advantage of dews. On the third day he appointed the dry land to appear, with the sea itself round about it; and on the very same day he made the plants and the seeds to spring out of the earth. On the fourth day he adorned the heaven with the sun, the moon, and the other stars, and appointed them their motions and courses, that the vicissitudes of the seasons might be clearly signified. And on the fifth day he produced the living creatures, both those that swim, and those that fly; the former in the sea, the latter in the air: he also sorted them as to society and mixture, for procreation, and that their kinds might increase and multiply. On the sixth day he created the four-footed beasts, and made them male and female: on the same day he also formed man. Accordingly Moses says, That in just six days the world, and all that is therein, was made. And that the seventh day was a rest, and a release from the labor of such operations; whence it is that we celebrate a rest from our labors on that day, and call it the Sabbath, which word denotes rest in the Hebrew tongue.*

*Moreover, Moses, after the seventh day was over begins to talk philosophically; and concerning the formation of man, says thus: That God took dust from the ground, and formed man, and inserted in him a spirit and a soul.(2) This man was called Adam, which in the Hebrew tongue signifies one that is red, because he was formed out of red earth, compounded together; for of that kind is virgin and true earth. God also presented the living creatures, when he had made them, according to their kinds, both male and female, to Adam, who gave them those names by which they are still called. But when he saw that Adam had no female companion, no society, for there was no such created, and that he wondered at the other animals which were male and female, he laid him asleep, and took away one of his ribs, and out of it formed the woman; whereupon Adam knew her* when she was brought to him, and acknowledged that she was made out of himself. Now a woman is called in the Hebrew tongue Issa; but the name of this woman was Eve, which signifies the mother of all living.

Moses says further, that God planted a paradise in the east, flourishing with all sorts of trees; and that among them was the tree of life, and another of knowledge, whereby was to be known what was good and evil; and that when he brought Adam and his wife into this garden, he commanded them to take care of the plants. Now the garden was watered by one river, which ran round about the whole earth, and was parted into four parts. And Phison, which denotes a multitude, running into India, makes its exit into the sea, and is by the Greeks called Ganges. Euphrates also, as well as Tigris, goes down into the Red Sea. Now the name Euphrates, or Phrath, denotes either a dispersion, or a flower: by Tiris, or Diglath, is signified what is swift, with narrowness; and Geon runs through Egypt, and denotes what arises from the east, which the Greeks call Nile. God therefore commanded that Adam and his wife should eat of all the rest of the plants, but to abstain from the tree of knowledge; and foretold to them, that if they touched it, it would prove their destruction. But while all the living creatures had one language, at that time the serpent, which then lived together with Adam and his wife, shewed an envious disposition, at his supposal of their living happily, and in obedience to the commands of God; and imagining, that when they disobeyed them, they would fall into calamities, he persuaded the woman, out of a malicious intention, to taste of the tree of knowledge, telling them, that in that tree was the knowledge of good and evil; which knowledge, when they should obtain, they would lead a happy life; nay, a life not inferior to that of a god: by which means he overcame the woman, and persuaded her to despise the command of God. Now when she had tasted of that tree, and was pleased with its fruit, she persuaded Adam to make use of it also. Upon this they perceived that they were become naked to one another; and being ashamed thus to appear abroad, they invented somewhat to cover them; for the tree sharpened their understanding; and they covered themselves with fig-leaves; and tying these before them, out of modesty, they thought they were happier than they were before, as they had discovered what they were in want of. But when God came into the garden, Adam, who was wont before to come and converse with him, being conscious of his wicked behavior, went out of the way. This behavior surprised God; and he asked what was the cause of this his procedure; and why he, that before delighted in that conversation, did now fly from it, and avoid it. When he made no reply, as conscious to himself that he had transgressed the command of God, God said, "I had before determined about you both, how you might lead a happy life, without any affliction, and care, and vexation of soul; and that all things which might contribute to your enjoyment and pleasure should grow up by my providence, of their own accord, without your own labor and pains-taking; which state of labor and pains-taking would soon bring on old age, and death would not be at any remote distance: but now thou hast abused this my good-will, and hast disobeyed my commands; for thy silence is not the sign of thy virtue, but of thy evil conscience." However, Adam excused his sin, and entreated God not to be angry at him, and laid the blame of what was done upon his wife; and said that he was deceived by her, and thence became an offender; while she again accused the serpent. But God allotted him punishment, because he weakly submitted to the counsel of his wife; and said the ground should not henceforth yield its fruits of its own accord, but that when it should be harassed by their labor, it should bring forth some of its fruits, and refuse to bring forth others. He also made Eve liable to the inconveniency of breeding, and the sharp pains of bringing forth children; and this because she persuaded Adam with the same arguments wherewith the serpent had persuaded her, and had thereby brought him into a calamitous condition. He also deprived the serpent of speech, out *of indignation at his malicious disposition towards Adam. Besides this, he inserted poison under his tongue, and made him an enemy to men; and suggested to them, that they should direct their strokes against his head, that being the place wherein lay his mischievous designs towards men, and it being easiest to take vengeance on him, that way. And when he had deprived him of the use of his feet, he made him to go rolling all along, and dragging himself upon the ground. And when God had appointed these penalties for them, he removed Adam and Eve out of the garden into another place* (Josephus, pp.40-42).

As previously mentioned the Bible states that God made the first man out of the dust of the ground and breathed into his nostrils the breath of life, making this first man a living being. God named the man and all of mankind, Adam. Adam, you will recall, means dirt. That was to remind us that we are made of dirt and that one day our bodies will return to dirt or dust, while our spirits will return to God who gave us life. The name Eve means life or living.

She was named this because after God created the first couple, all further human life came from Eve, the ancestral mother of us all. It says further that God planted a garden in a place called Eden, and there He put the man He had created. God then made every tree that is pleasing to look at and/or that bears good fruit to grow in the garden. Eden means "delight," so the "Garden of Eden," in English means the "Garden of Delight."

As far as one man being the father of all mankind, science itself agrees with that. Consider the following information, in 1995, the journal "Science" published the results of a study in which a segment of the human Y-chromosome from 38 men from around the world was studied. The research determined that every man alive today is descended from a single male ancestor. (Dorit, Akashi, and Gilbert, pp.1183–1185).

Eden was a place, and within that place was the Garden of Eden. God also planted two unique trees in the garden. One was the Tree of Life. If you kept eating of its fruit, you would never grow old and would never die. The other tree was called the Tree of the Knowledge of Good and Evil. God commanded Adam not to eat of the Tree of the Knowledge of Good and Evil, telling him that if he ate of its fruit, he would die.

> *"And the Lord God took the man, and put him into the Garden of Eden to dress it and to keep it. And the Lord God commanded the man, saying, of every tree of the garden thou mayest freely eat: but of the Tree of the Knowledge of Good and Evil, thou shalt not eat of it: for in the day that thou eat thereof thou shalt surely die."* (Genesis 2:15-17).

God later put Adam to sleep, took a rib from his side, and created the first woman from Adam's rib. Adam named her Eve and she became his wife (Genesis, chapter 2, verses 7–10, and 15-23, KJV).

Just as science agrees with the Bible that all people are descended from one man, so science likewise agrees with the Bible that all people are descended from one woman. Studies show that all humans are descended from one woman, whom scientists have named 'Mitochondrial Eve.' Some of this research is mentioned in the August 17, 2010 issue of Science Daily. The article there is drawn from material provided by Rice University. (Science Daily, June 10, 2014).

Besides the Bible and the writings of Josephus, ancient writings and legends of a number of other ethnic groups have similar stories of Creation and of the first man and woman. For example, some of the more ancient writings of the Hindus say that the first man was named Adima, which means "the first" (Dods, p.14), while the name of the first woman was pronounced as Eve

(Titcomb, p.251). In the ancient Assyrian records, the name of the first man is Admu or Adamu. (Dods, p.14).

In relation to the Assyrians and the Hindus calling the first man by a name very similar to Adam, let us look at the Miao story of creation, and the name they use for the first man. The Miao are a people who live in southern China near the border with Thailand. They are not ethnic Chinese, but are a separate people. The name used for the first man by the Miao is not Adam, but rather a name in their own language. The meanings of the two names however, are almost identical. Both the Hebrew name, Adam, and the Miao name for Adam mean "Dirt" (Traux, September 24, 2005).

Some of the more ancient accounts of the flood state that Noah and his wife were brother and sister. Indeed, many of the men born before the flood were said to have married their sisters.

Adam and Eve, the first man and woman according to the Bible, and therefore the parents of us all, are called in Greek mythology, Zeus and Hera. The Greeks called them the parents of both the gods and of mankind.  Adam and Eve, in Genesis, lived in a beautiful garden. Likewise, in Greek mythology, the first couple, the parents of gods and men, Zeus and Hera, once lived in a beautiful and wonderful place that was "untouched by sorrow" (Johnson, p.41; see also Hesiod, "Works And Days," p.7). Here a tree grew that bore golden apples. (Johnson, p.40). This is undoubtedly where the story comes from that the fruit that Adam and Eve ate was an apple.

Another story about mankind at the beginning of Creation was told by the Greek writer, Ovid. In what he called the "Golden Age," Ovid said that mankind did not have to work for their food, but had all they needed free from nature, just as the Bible described life in the Garden of Eden. He said there was no need to plow the earth, as the earth brought forth all things necessary for man, without the labor of plowing or sowing. It was always spring, wrote Ovid. Flowers sprang up without being sown, and there was a great abundance of food. (Ovid, pp.6, 7). The Greeks said that when the people of the Golden Age died a normal death, there was no pain involved, that dying for them was like falling asleep (Rawlinson, "The Testimony of The Truth of Scripture," p.9).

Likewise, early Persian literature relates that the first Iranic king and his people enjoyed uninterrupted happiness. There was no sin, violence, poverty or deformity where they lived. They lived on a special food that never failed. (Rawlinson, "The Testimony of The Truth of Scripture," p.9).

Early Hindu literature tells of a "first age of the world," when justice and virtue reigned, when nothing base was found in mankind, and mortals were free of all disease. (Rawlinson, "The Testimony of the Truth of Scripture," p.10).

The beliefs of the ancient Chinese about the early days of mankind, as found in some of their ancient writings, say that during the early days of the earth, which they called the "period of the first heaven," all of creation "enjoyed a state of happiness: everything was "beautiful: everything was good: all beings were perfect in their kind. In this happy age . . . there was no jarring in the elements, no inclemency in the air: all things grew without labor, and universal fertility prevailed" (Rawlinson, "The Testimony of the Truth of Scripture," pp.9-10).

The ancient Chinese taught that mankind once lived in "pure pleasure" while "perfect tranquility reigned everywhere. There was neither labor, nor pain, nor sorrow. The heart rejoiced in truth; and there was no mixture of falsehood' " (Titcomb, October 5, 2005). An ancient Chinese nursery rhyme says, "In the

35

beginning, man's original character was virtuous." (Kang & Nelson, p. 67).

Remembering that Eden means "pleasure or delight," it becomes very interesting to discover that the ancient Chinese wrote about a "realm of delight," which was lost because the inhabitants of the earth would not live by "laws of virtue" (Campbell, p.228). They spoke also of an age of innocence, when the "whole creation enjoyed everything that was good, all beings were perfect in their kind." (Rawlinson, "Origin of the Nations," pp.10-11).

The Chinese ideogram for happiness is composed of the symbols for: "God, first, person, garden." (Kang & Nelson, p. 44.) This appears to refer to Adam, the first man, and his emotional state when first created and placed in the Garden of Eden, just as the previously given nursery rhyme describes the original character of mankind.

The Apaches have a legend that "the first days of the world were happy and peaceful days." (Bancroft, p.76).

In Genesis, Adam and Eve are described as being naked while they lived in the Garden. An Aztec legend says, "The sun was much nearer the earth then than now, and his grateful warmth rendered clothing unnecessary" (Donnelly, p.199). A Papago legend says the same thing. (Frazer, p.110).

Plato, discoursing on the early life of mankind, informs us that at that time "they lived naked (as the Bible says), in a state of happiness, and had an abundance of fruits, which were produced without the labor of agriculture; and that men and beasts could then converse together" (Deane, p.335).

All accounts describing the early life of mankind as a happy one also has a tradition of a fall of mankind (Rawlinson, "The Testimony of The Truth of Scripture," p.11). Sometimes this was caused by a snake but sometimes by other means.

We do not know how long after the creation of Eve this happened, but the Bible tells us in the third chapter of Genesis that "the serpent" persuaded Eve to eat of the fruit of the Tree of the Knowledge of Good and Evil. Eve then persuaded Adam to eat it. The result was that they were both thrown out of the garden.

Cut off from the Tree of Life, they both knew that in time they would grow old and die. As a further punishment, Adam was told that in the future he would have to till the ground for his food. Eve's additional punishment was that she would suffer pain in childbirth.

The Bible says of Adam after he and Eve ate the forbidden fruit, "therefore the Lord God sent him out of the Garden of Eden to till the ground from which he was taken." (Genesis Ch. 3, verse 23). Note it does not say Adam and Eve were driven out of Eden, but only out of the Garden of Eden. Josephus said that God "removed Adam and Eve out of the garden into another place."

The oldest recorded history of Creation is that written by a Phoenician, Sanchoniatho. He took his information from the inscriptions in the temples of Phoenicia. His history was written around the time of the Trojan War, which is believed to have occurred between 1184 and 1194 B.C.

His information was later translated into Greek. Part of the translation was preserved by the famous leader of the Early Church, Eusebius, in a book of his own. An English translation was published in 1720. In the Phoenician account, the first couple on the earth were a man and a woman, and the woman was the first to eat fruit from trees. (Cumberland, p.xxix).

Pertinent to the Biblical story is the serpent, which is commonly held to have been the evil angel known as Satan. Elsewhere in the Bible, Satan is referred to as a serpent, or dragon. (Satan is referred to both as an ophis, that is a snake, and also as a drakon, or dragon.) It is an ancient tradition among Jews, a tradition which the early Christians adopted, that the serpent was actually Satan, God's main adversary.

This belief is shown in two verses, both in Revelation, the last book of the Bible. Revelation 12:9 says, "And the great dragon (Greek "drakon") was cast out, that old serpent (Greek "ophis"), called the Devil, and Satan, which deceives the whole world: he was cast out into the earth, and his angels were cast out with him," and Revelation 20:2 says, "And he laid hold on the dragon, that old serpent, which is the Devil and Satan, and bound him for a thousand years."

After eating the fruit, they had been forbidden to eat, Adam and Eve were driven from the garden and forced to work for their food. Being driven from the garden, they could therefore never eat of the fruit of the Tree of Life and would therefore begin to grow old and would one-day die. Even so, the life spans of Adam and Eve, and those of their descendants for many generations, remained far greater in length than our life spans today.

We find other literature besides the Bible which refers to this much longer life span in ancient times. In the sacred Hindu books, for example, it is taught that in the first ages people lived for centuries. There is also a record of a Chinese emperor who proposed an inquiry to learn why the ancients lived so much longer than people in his own time. (Rawlinson, "The Testimony Of The Truth of Scripture," p.14).

Interestingly enough, Australian tribes regard the snake as bringing death into the world, (The New Schaff-Herzog Encyclopedia of Religious Knowledge, Volume 10. p.370).

Just as Adam and Eve were punished, so was the serpent. The serpent was told that it would no longer be able to go upright, but would have to crawl on its belly. (Genesis 1:14. "And the Lord God said unto the serpent, because thou hast done this, thou art cursed above all cattle, and above every beast of the field; upon thy belly shalt thou go, and dust shalt thou eat all the days of thy life.") Just as we are not told how long it was after their creation before Adam and Eve sinned, so we are not told anything further about the "serpent," at least not in Genesis.

Since God said the snake would go upon its belly because it tempted Eve to sin, we must assume that snakes at one time had legs. There is a depiction of a snake in an Egyptian temple at Dendera, Egypt. Here the serpent has legs. (Banks, p.54). The Bürgermeister Müller Museum in Solnhofen, Germany has a snake fossil from South America that they have dated to the early Cretaceous period. It has two small front legs and two small rear legs. David Martill from the University of Portsmouth, England, who first brought attention to these legs, named the snake Tetrapodophis, meaning four-legged snake. (Martill). Likewise, there was a fossilized snake found in Lebanon (Science Daily, March 2, 2011) that also has small legs.

The ancient Chinese had their own version of the Temptation and the Fall. The written language of China, which was invented around 2500 B.C. (Kang and Nelson, pp.xiii & 12), is still in use today, though slightly revised by the Communists in the 1950s. In that system, most words are composed of several smaller "words" or by several symbols, sometimes by stylized or abbreviated pictures, each of which has its own separate meaning. In such a manner, their written word for temptation is a garden with two trees and a woman in it (Kang, & Nelson, p.57-58). Likewise, the Chinese word for devil is shown in writing as a snake and a garden with two trees in it (Kang and Nelson, p.62).

Further the Chinese also believed that mankind once lived many times longer than we do today. So, convinced were they of this, that one Emperor, the author of a medical book, "proposed an inquiry into the reasons why the ancients attained to so much more advanced an age" than more modern people. (Rawlinson, "The Testimony of the Truth of Scripture," p.14).

In 1836, C. S. Rafinesque published in Philadelphia, Pa., a work called "The American Nations," in which he gave the historical songs or chants of the Lenni-Lenapi, or Delaware Indians. After describing a time "when there was nothing but sea-water on top of the land," and the creation of sun, moon, stars, earth, and man, the legend describes the Golden Age and the Fall in these words: "All were willingly pleased, all were easy-thinking, and all were well-happified.

But after a while a snake-priest, Powako, brings on earth secretly the snake-worship (Initako) of the god of the snakes, Wakon. And there came wickedness, crime, and unhappiness. And bad weather was coming, distemper was coming, with death was coming. All this happened very long ago, at the first land, Netamaki, beyond the great ocean Kitahikau". (Rafinesque, p.127)

An account of Creation as told by the Masai, a tribe in East Africa, relates that the Fall was occasioned by a four-headed serpent that tempted and deceived mankind. ("Journal of Transactions of the Victoria Institute,". vol. XXXVIII, p.66)

The true Chinese people are known as Han Chinese. There are also many minority groups within China who speak their own languages and who have different cultures. One of these groups is the Miao, also known as the Miautso. The Miao inhabited most of China south of the Yellow River, according to their account, when the Han entered the country. They were gradually pushed south and into the mountains by the Han, many of them being pushed out of China altogether. Today, they live along the border of Burma. Miao legends mention a "golden age" lost to mankind through disobedience, a great flood, and the subsequent dispersal of the human family throughout the world.

The Miao account of Creation and the flood are very similar to that of the Bible. This is in an oral tradition, as they have no written language. This oral tradition was translated from the Miao language into English by Edgar Traux. (Truax).

The story of creation as recited by the Miao tells of the creation of the earth, of the various animals, and then of the creation of mankind. They say that the first man was created out of the dirt of the ground, and that the first woman, his wife, was formed from the man. (Truax). (Note that the Miao call Adam, "Dirt," and remember that in the Hebrew language Adam does mean dirt or dust.)

The Greek teaching of the fall and the end of what they called the "Golden Age" is contained in the story of Pandora's box, a well-known myth of the ancient Greeks. This legend says that Pandora was the first woman and perfect in every way. She was created in heaven to be the wife of the first man, and was given every great and good gift by the gods.

One such gift was a box that she was told never to open, but she yielded to temptation and opened it. Inside the box was every kind of trouble and sickness, which was let loose upon the earth when Pandora opened the box. According to the Greek legend, if she had not opened the box, mankind would have lived forever and never aged, all in a world without sickness or hardship. (Gascoigne, p. 39.)

The Tibetans speak of a fruit that they call Amrita, or Immortal; and in their mythology, they say this was the fruit of a tree, growing in an unknown place from which four sacred rivers flow, deriving their several streams from a common source. (Jones, p.31).

The comment about the four sacred rivers flowing from a common source is especially interesting, since the Bible speaks in Genesis of four rivers flowing out of the Garden of Eden. The Tibetan account mentions the "immortal" fruit, just as the Garden in Eden had a tree that bore fruit that caused those who ate it to live forever.

We shall soon see that not only are many of the elements of the story of Creation and the Fall seen in other legends and historical accounts, but that in general, "This recollection of the fall of man seems to have been universally stamped upon the human mind. It meets us everywhere." (Titcomb, p.235).

Sumeria is the first known civilization after the flood. The Sumerian legend of the Garden of Eden refers to it as a garden called Dilmun. Dilmun is described as a land that is "pure," "clean," and "bright," where sickness and death are unknown (Kramer, p.142), and where the animals do not harm one another. (Hooke, pp.33, 114.)

The legend further tells of a plant in Dilmun that kept one young as long as the person ate it. (Hooke, pp.33, 54-55.) This plant is comparable to the Tree of Life, of which God said that if Adam and Eve ate of it, they would live forever.

There are too many similarities in the Sumerian and Genesis accounts to be coincidental. In the Sumerian account, the plant that kept those who ate it forever young was stolen by a serpent (Hooke, p.54-55) and lost to mankind forever. The correlation between a serpent stealing the plant that kept one forever young, and a serpent 'stealing' from Adam and Eve the Tree of Life, that would have allowed them to live forever, is too similar not to have had the same origin.

Also, according to Sumerian myth, the only thing Dilmun lacked was fresh water. The sun-god brought up fresh water from the ground to water the garden (Hooke, p.33, 114). In the account in Genesis of the Garden of Eden, it never rained. The garden was watered by a mist which rose from the ground each morning.

The Sumerians also believed in a goddess named Niniti, which means "Lady of the Rib," which can also be translated as "Lady of Life" (Hooke, p.115). The Bible says that Eve was taken from Adam's rib, and that her name means "living" because she became the mother of all living people.

The Babylonians appear to have at one time known the story of the Fall, along with the involvement of a fruit tree and a snake. There is a Babylonian cylinder seal showing a man and woman seated on each side of a fruit-tree, both in the act of plucking the fruit. Behind the one that appears to be the woman, and with its head close to her ear, stands a serpent erect upon its tail. (Fergusson, p.12).

The Egyptians too must have at one time known the story of the Fall of Mankind, for a painting in the temple of Osiris at Philae, in Egypt, shows a man and woman standing by a tree, from which one of them has plucked some fruit and shared it with the other. A serpent stands erect by their side. (Titcomb, p.242).

The Polynesian people inhabit numerous islands in the South Pacific. The Hawaiian Islands, Samoa, New Zealand, and Tahiti are among the islands of Polynesia. In Polynesia, there is a legend about an island paradise, creation, and the fall of mankind.

The legend was old before the first missionaries came. Different parts of Polynesia have slightly different accounts of the story. The version in Tahiti says that the first human pair were made by Taaroa, the principal deity formerly worshipped by the Tahitians. After Taaroa had formed the world, he created man out of araea, red earth.

In connection with this, some relate that Taaroa one day called for the man by name. When he came, he caused him to fall asleep, and while he slept, he took out one of his ivi, or bones, and with it made a woman, whom he gave to the man as his wife, and that they became the progenitors of mankind. The Tahitians, relating this story in the 1850's, repeatedly said that it was a tradition among them before any foreigner arrived. Some also stated that the woman's name was Ivi, which is pronounced as if written Eve. Ivi is a Tahitian word, and is not only the name of the first woman, but also signifies a bone. (Ellis, p.111).

Eve in Tahiti being called Ivi, is, as you will recall, similar to Eve's name in the Institutes of Manu, one of the ancient written records of India. The Institutes of Manu were originally written in Sanskrit, being translated only in the last 200 years. In the Institutes of Manu, the first man was named Adim, and the name of his wife was spelled in English as Iva. Her name, however, was pronounced as "Eve." (Wilford, p.231-232).

Just as the Tahitians called the first woman Eve, so the ancient Assyrians called mankind Admi or Adami (Smith, George, p.86). This is similar to the book of Genesis using Adam as both the name of the first man, and the name of the human race.

(Genesis 5:2, "Male and female created he them; and blessed them, and called their name Adam, in the day when they were created.")

The Hawaiian version says that the first man and woman were created by the gods and placed on a beautiful island. This legend also says that the body of the first man was made out of red earth, just as Josephus, a first century Jewish historian, says that Adam was made of red earth. Adam means dirt, but it specifically means red tinted dirt. Adam is a word that "in the Hebrew tongue signifies one that is red because he was formed out of red earth" (Josephus, p.40). This does not mean that contrary to everyone alive today, and contrary to everyone whom we know has ever lived, that Adam was red colored. It rather means that Adam had a ruddy or reddish complexion.
Adam, "the Hebrew word for man, could be ultimately derived from the Hebrew אדם ('adam) meaning "to be red," referring to the ruddy color of human skin, or from the Akkadian adamu meaning "to make" (http://www.behindthename.com/name/adam, February 25, 2016). As a youth, King David was "ruddy and of a fair countenance" (1 Sam. 17:42 KJV). "Ruddy: red; reddish; of the colour of healthy skin in white-skinned peoples" (Chambers Concise Dictionary, 1988, p.932).

According to the Hawaiian legend, Atea, or Kumuhonua, was the name of the first man. He was sometimes called Honua-ula, meaning "made of red earth." The gods fashioned a wife for him out of his right side (editor's note – just as it happened to Adam), and they called her Iwi, Ke-ola-Ku-honua, or Lalo-honua, depending on the variation of the legend and in which part of Polynesia you hear it. On this island, they never grew sick or old. The food was plentiful and delicious, but one day the woman ate the fruit of a tree that the supreme god, Kane (called Tane in some parts of Polynesia, and sometimes called Io, in Hawaii), had forbidden them to eat. This was the only commandment Kane, or Io, had given them. Because she broke this commandment, they were forced to leave the island and could never return. People would sometimes see the island, but no one could ever go there again. (Beckwith, p.42-45; see also, Kikawa, p.39-40).

Another Polynesian version of creation and the fall says that all things except man were created during a five-day period of creation. Lastly, during the sixth period of creation, man was created (See also Genesis, chapter one, verses 27-31, where God created man on the sixth day). The gods made the first man a chief to rule over the whole world, and placed him and his wife in a garden, which in some versions of the legend is known as "The Great Land of Kane." Here they live happily until Lalo-honua met a seabird that persuaded her to eat some sacred apples. Because of this sin, the couple was banished from the garden and could never find their way back. They were also told that instead of living forever, they would eventually grow old and die, because they had eaten the forbidden fruit (Beckwith, p.45.)

Considering that most accounts involve a snake in the temptation, and knowing that there are no snakes in Polynesia, it becomes very interesting that in some parts of Polynesia, it is not a seabird that tempts the first woman to eat the sacred apples, but a snake. In a land that does not have snakes, where did the Polynesians get a snake from? There are sea-snakes in the ocean around the islands, and it is sometimes a sea-snake that tempts the woman in the Polynesian account. A further question is, in a land that does not have snakes, why would an ancient legend have a sea snake coming upon the land (which they never do) to tempt the first man and first woman. One logical explanation would be that their story of the Temptation of Adam and Eve came from fact. When they had no land snakes, they used a sea snake in their Temptation Story, simply because they had no way to identify with any other type of snake.

Adam and Eve, in Genesis, lived in a beautiful garden, and are said to have eaten the fruit of the Tree of the Knowledge of Good and Evil, after being urged to do so by a serpent. Likewise, in Greek mythology, the first couple, the parents of gods and men, Zeus and Hera, once lived in a beautiful and wonderful place that was "untouched by sorrow" (Johnson, p.41; see also Hesiod, "Works And Days," p.7). Here a tree grew that bore golden apples. (Johnson, p.40). This is undoubtedly where the story comes from that the fruit that Adam and Eve ate was an apple.

In the Bible, the serpent told Eve that if they ate of the fruit of the forbidden tree, the Tree of the Knowledge of Good and Evil, they would become as wise as God. Continuing to eat of the Tree of Life would of course have kept them forever young and with eternal life.

In the Greek legend, there was no forbidden tree. The tree belonged to Hera. The tree that bore the golden apples was in a far off distant isle in the Atlantic, where Zeus and Hera once lived. The island was called "The Isle of the Blessed" (Hesiod, "Works and Days," p.7), also called the "Fortunate Isle." On this island was a garden in which the tree grew. This garden was called the "Garden of the Hesperides." (Hesiod, "The Theogony," II.211-225).

The golden apples on the tree made you wise and kept you forever young, as long as you continued eating them. The tree was guarded for Hera by a serpent. In the Biblical account wisdom was promised as a trick to get Adam and Eve to eat of the fruit. Eating of it also cost them their immortality, while in the Greek story it gave them immortality. The serpent also changed from being their deceitful enemy in the Bible to being the one who guarded the golden apples. (Bulfinch, p.4). This is a twist on the actual story of the Fall, since in the Greek account the Forbidden Fruit did actually make those who ate it wise and also kept them young. In the account in Genesis, it was a bad thing and brought punishment on those who ate the fruit. In the Greek legend, eating the fruit of the tree was a good thing to do.

The Greeks had two stories about the Temptation and Fall of man. The story that is most like that in the Bible is where we get the idea that the Forbidden Fruit was an apple. In that story, there was no temptation and the first parents of mankind did not fall, rather they did go from being mere mortals to being gods, just as the serpent promised.

Far away in the New World, the Aztecs of Mexico worshipped a goddess whom they also spoke of as the first woman. They said that because of her, sin came into the world and women were caused to suffer pain in childbirth. She was usually represented with a serpent near her. Her name was Cioactl, meaning "serpent woman" symbolizing a close relationship of some kind between her and the serpent, as was true with Eve and the serpent of the Bible, Eve's wily nemesis". (Titcomb, p.235). There was an Aztec painting of this goddess/woman that was sent to the Vatican. It shows her in actual conversation with a serpent. (Titcomb, p.235). Furthermore, the serpent is drawn erect, as it undoubtedly was before it was cursed and forced by God to crawl on its stomach.

Cioacoatl is described as "the first goddess who brought forth." (Titcomb, p.235). Though the Aztecs worshipped her as a goddess, her identity with Eve seems beyond dispute. The Aztecs called her, "woman of our flesh," and considered her the mother of all mankind. (Titcomb, p.235). Whenever the Aztecs portrayed her, it was always with a large serpent. (Deane, p.351). The Aztecs believed that she "bequeathed the sufferings of childbirth to women," and that by her "sin came into the world." Another term used for her was "our lady and mother." (Prescott, p.583). In all the above we see much to remind us of Eve, the mother of the human race as described in the book of Genesis.

It is especially interesting that in the Aztec painting, the serpent was drawn erect, as if it had legs. Since God cursed the serpent and said that it would have to crawl upon its belly in the future, the implication is that when it tempted Eve to sin, the serpent could walk upright. In many ancient depictions of the serpent and Eve the serpent is raised in an upright position. These depictions are all non-Jewish and predate Christianity. (Titcomb, p.235). Likewise, as already mentioned, a fossil of a prehistoric snake has been found and the fossilized snake had front and rear legs (see page 30).

The Toltecs of Mexico "had paintings of a garden, with a single tree standing in the midst; round the root of the tree is entwined a serpent, whose head appearing above the foliage displays the face of a woman. The Toltec historians stated that this was "the first woman in the world, who bore children, and from whom all mankind are descended." (Donnelly, p.199. citing Kingsborough, "Mexican Antiquities").

An ancient Chinese legend said that humans were the creation of the primeval goddess Nu Wa, who had a human head and a snake's body. In later years the account changed somewhat. In the later account, Nu Wa was considered mortal, rather than a goddess, and was said to be the first woman and the mother of all mankind. In this account, Nu Wa and her brother Fu Xi were the first mortals and the progenitors of humankind. (Chang, Maria Hsia, p.37). If you find it too much of a coincidence to be accidental that the Toltec and the Han Chinese accounts of the mother of mankind both said she had a snake's body, you are not alone. It gives the impression that the Toltecs may have migrated to Mexico from China.

Something that must logically be considered is that if the Biblical story of Creation and the Fall of Mankind are true, then ethnic groups all over the world would know of those events, or would have known them at one time. This is even true of the idea of a snake talking. If it really happened then stories of it would predate the Old Testament and would be found in many cultures. Josephus tells of a Jewish tradition that many of the animals could talk before the flood. (Josephus, p.41 fn.). The Papago Indians of Arizona also believe that animals could talk before the flood. (Frazer, p.110). A number of other tribes of North America have similar legends (Lenormant, p264). Additionally, the conversation of Eve with the serpent is "remembered in the mythologies of Egypt, Greece, Syria, Hindûstan, Northern Europe, and North and South America," while the Maori of New Zealand have a tradition that the serpent was once able to speak with a human voice. (Deane, p.355).

There are some ethnic groups that even today recall in their legends much more than the idea that snakes could once talk.

The Santal, a tribe who live in northeastern India, were visited in 1867 by two Norwegian missionaries. One of the missionaries quickly became fluent in the Santal language. He was astonished one day, to hear a Santal sage telling the Santal people that the missionaries arrival and the message they brought meant that the "Genuine God" had not forgotten the Santal people. The sage then explained to the startled missionary that the Santal had once known God, but had turned away from Him. The sage proceeded to tell the missionary of the creation of mankind by God, who placed the first man and woman in a place far to the west of India. These two were tempted, the Santal believed, by an evil being and yielded to the temptation. This was the first sin. After committing this sin, the couple realized that they were naked, and were ashamed. (Richardson, p.43).

The sage then told of a great flood which drowned all of mankind, except for one couple, who were preserved in a cave on a mountain named Harata. (Notice the resemblance to the Mountain of Ararat, where the ark landed.) In just a few brief years after being exposed to Christianity, over 100,000 Santal became Christians. How did this happen? It happened because the Santal already knew about God and were eager to know more. They had been praying for generations for the "Genuine God" to send someone to teach them more about Him (Richardson, p.41-47). Stories similar to the one just given are told by other ethnic groups, including several in Burma. (Richardson, pp.73-98.)

One such people, the Karen, who live in Burma, have no written language of their own. They do have a history that is memorized by individuals who dedicate their lives to learning and keeping alive the history of the Karen. Their account of the creation of the first man and the first woman, their temptation and their fall into sin is very similar to the account in the Bible. Here is their account.

"God created man; and of what did he form him? He created man at first from the earth. He created woman; and of what did He form her? He took a rib from the man and created the woman . . . . . Our Father God spoke and said, 'My son and My Daughter, I shall make for you a garden; and in the garden will be seven different kinds of trees, bearing seven different kinds of fruits. But among the seven different kinds of fruits, there will be one not good for you to eat. If you eat of it, sickness, old age, and death will come upon you. Eat not of it.' . . . . "(Titcomb, "British-Israel; How I Came To Believe It," p.50).

Among other such ethnic groups there are the Kui, who live in Burma and Thailand. These people built structures where they expected to worship "the Great God Above," once someone came to give them the knowledge of the God that they said their ancestors had had. Most of them today are Christians. (Richardson, p.89).

There are the Mizo, a people living in western India along the Burmese border, numbering about 350,000, they worship a god who lives above the sky, a god who in one of their dialects is called the "Holy Father," a God of goodness who they say created everything. Ninety-five percent of the Mizo are today Christians. (Richardson, p.91).

The original knowledge and understanding of the Creator God which was had by the ethnic groups mentioned above can be called a general understanding of God. They did not claim to know more than the most general things about God, nor did they have specific laws or rituals relating to His worship. They had only a vague and general understanding of God and His requirements for them. When Christianity reached them, with its more complete revelation of God, most of those peoples were quick to convert.

Thus far we have only scratched the surface of the multitude of stories found all over the world that agree with the Biblical story of the Garden of Eden and the Fall of Man. We have reviewed enough of them, however, to see that those stories have been known and told all over the world, by every ethnic group and in every clime.

The Bible and all other accounts that have been found of Creation, seem to describe the world, as God first made it, as a wonderful place in which to live. The people who first lived in it are pictured as enjoying health, vitality, and youthfulness, for many centuries. "It will scarcely be denied that the mythical traditions of almost all nations place at the beginning of human history a time of happiness and perfection, a "golden age" which has no features of savagery or barbarism, but many of civilization and refinement (Rawlinson, "Origin of the Nations," pp.10-11).

What was that world like?

What were some of the people who lived in it like?

Were they like us in temperament and nature, or were they entirely different?

The next several chapters tell something of what we know about those people and their world.

*"Faith is different from proof;*
*the latter is human,*
*the former is a Gift from God."*
\-     Blaise Paschal

# CHAPTER THREE
## The Climate Before The flood

Life did not end after our first ancestors ate of the fruit of the forbidden tree. Before they ate of the forbidden tree, the Tree of the Knowledge of Good and Evil, all the food they needed could be picked from the other trees in the Garden. After they ate of the forbidden tree, Adam had to begin working the ground, in order to grow food. Dating by the Bible, this state of things lasted for roughly 1,500 years before the next major change occurred. We do not know a great deal about those days. A little knowledge of that time has been handed down to us, both through the bible and through a few other scattered legends and stories. A great deal more information has been given to us by scientists studying our present-day world. Together, science and the bits and pieces of knowledge given us by legend and by ancient history, provide an interesting look into that bygone vanished time.

There is much that science can tell us about life on this earth many years ago. Scientists tell us that at one time in the past the earth was uniformly warm, even at the poles. Fossilized plants such as ferns, oaks, magnolias, cinnamons, ginkos and breadfruits have been found on Greenland and on Spitzbergen Island, which is above Norway, near the Arctic Circle. Similar fossils have been reported from Alaska and even Antarctica. (Nelson, p.28-29).

Thousands of well-preserved fossilized leaves have been found in Antarctica, showing that the climate there must once have been much warmer. (Raymond, p. A9). Admiral Richard Byrd, the famous explorer of Antarctica, told about discoveries in a mountain range on that continent. He told of the discovery of "conclusive evidence that the climate of Antarctica was once temperate or even sub-tropical." (Hooker, p.44)

Scientists have mined coal scarcely two hundred miles from the South Pole, eager to learn how it could have formed there. The outlines of fern leaves found in the layers of coal, and whole petrified logs that have also been found there, show that Antarctica was once covered with a flourishing rain forest. Petrified logs have been found near the very center of Antarctica. (Dukert, p.61). Sequoias and even palm and fig trees once grew there. (Dukert, p.56-57).

Obviously, there was a dramatically different and much warmer climate at both poles at one time in the past. Along with other evidence that the North and South Polar areas were once warm, are the remains of extinct animals that have been found in both places in large quantities.

Wooly mammoths have been found by the thousands in Arctic areas, not fossilized, but quick frozen, sometimes encased in ice, and generally buried in the frozen soil beneath the permafrost, along with evidence of them having lived in a temperate climate. (Sanderson, p.82).

"The bones of at least three dinosaur species . . . . and two other reptiles have been recovered from a site in the Alaskan tundra by researchers from the University of California at Berkeley. Researchers say the fossil finds indicate dinosaurs were at the Alaska site in great numbers . . . . This adds further weight to the idea that the earth has had a period of time which was far more uniform in warm tropical-like conditions than it is at the present." (Science News, August 31st, 1985). The fossil record further reveals that the winter weather of Wyoming was once warm enough for crocodiles. (Kerr, p. 682.)

In northern, or upper, Siberia, the remains of frozen extinct animals with the flesh still on them are found, sometimes even entire carcasses. This is because the ground remains frozen year-round in upper Siberia. Some of the mammoths have been found with the remains of buttercups frozen and undigested in their stomachs (McLean, pp.179-180, as cited in Cranfill, p.45).

Writing in 1887, Henry H. Howorth
, a geologist, told of seeing evidence in Siberia and islands of the Arctic to the north of Siberia, showing that a 'very great cataclysm or catastrophe" had once occurred. Though Howorth did not believe in Noah's flood, he stated that the evidence showed there had once been a flood of massive proportions that had suddenly killed large numbers of animals, burying them in beds of loam or gravel. Simultaneously with this, there was a drastic and very sudden change of climate in Siberia, by which the drowned animals were quick frozen while buried underground, and have remained frozen ever since. (Nelson, p.118-119).

Howarth spoke of northern Siberia, where today only ground moss grows, and described the mammoths and other animals lying frozen in the ground, "so well preserved in the frozen soil that bears and wolves can feed upon them" (Nelson, p.120). "Whole herds of animals were apparently killed together, overcome by some common power" (Hibben, p.170).

The first recorded reference to frozen mammoths being found in Siberia comes from the Chinese, who traded for mammoth ivory with the people living in today's northeast Siberia (Stone, p.20). The mammoth is no bigger than the elephant, but its tusks are up to 16 feet long. The woolly mammoth was obviously once abundant in Siberia. (Stone, p.2, 6, 8). It is hard to determine how many wooly mammoths lie frozen in the permafrost. We have no way of knowing even how many mammoth carcasses have been found. Ivory hunters have combed Siberia for centuries, finding thousands of mammoth tusks, but they had no interest in reporting their finds, only in selling the tusks.

Pleistocene geologist William R. Farrand of the Lamont-Doherty Geological Observatory, states: "Sudden death is indicated by the robust condition of the animals and their full stomachs . . . the animals were robust and healthy when they died" (Farrand, p.729 fn). "Asphyxiation is indicated . . . by the blood vessels of the head of a woolly rhinoceros. . . . . The well-preserved specimens, with food in their stomachs and between their teeth, must have died suddenly, probably from asphyxia resulting from drowning," (Farrand, p.734).

"No gradualistic process can result in the preservation of tens of thousands of tusks and whole individuals, even if they died in the winter. They must have been frozen suddenly" (Lippman, p.449). This quick freezing of animal and plant life could only have been caused by a rapid and tremendous drop in temperature. (Digby, pp.51-55). Birds Eye Frozen Foods Company ran an experiment based on heat conduction and the state of preservation of the stomach contents of the mammoths. They concluded that the atmospheric temperature had to quickly fall far below freezing. (Dillow, pp.383-96).

Proving that not only animals but also plants once grew there that no longer can, is the discovery of seeds of various plants and trees, buried in the ground by ground squirrels. An example is a plant growing today in the laboratory of some Russian scientists in Siberia. On the frozen edge of the Kolyma River in northeastern Siberia, in an ancient burrow of a ground squirrel, scientists found the seeds of a flowering plant buried. The seeds had frozen in the cold ground and were preserved in the permafrost. The seed sprouted in 2012 and today grows in a tub in a Russian lab. The plant or flower is a narrow-leafed Campion, though it is somewhat different from the modern-day version of the plant, whose Latin name is Silene Stenophylla. Of further interest is the fact that seeds of the rejuvenated plant had a 100% rate of germination, higher than that of the control plants. (Boyle, June 10, 2014).

Since temperature differentials are the chief cause of wind movements and storms, with a constant temperature world round, we can infer that storms and strong winds were unknown before the flood. (Starr, p.45). Further, meteorologist Brian Farrell, of Harvard University, feels the overall circulation of the earth's atmosphere had to be greatly different from what it is today, in order to distribute the heat needed for those plants and animals known to have once existed there. (Kerr, p.682.)

What could have caused this uniform mild climate all over the earth? Josephus said that on the second day of creation, God placed a crystalline barrier or firmament around the earth. The Hebrew word translated firmament is raqia, which means to press or pound into thin metal sheets. This firmament was apparently composed of hydrogen atoms surrounded by ice. Experiments at Lawrence Livermore National Laboratories have shown that when water is compressed under super cold conditions (which are the conditions in our upper atmosphere), the hydrogen atoms take on metallic characteristics, and become crystalline, transparent, fiber optic, superconductive, and ferromagnetic (Baugh, pp.50-51, 55).

God also created a water vapor canopy on the second day, the "waters above the firmament" (Genesis 1:7) and "put it together in a manner agreeable to the earth, fitting it for giving moisture and rain, and for affording the advantage of dews" (Josephus, p.40). The firmament surrounding the earth apparently kept the heat of the sun inside the earth's atmosphere and distributed it evenly around the globe. Such a blanket of water vapor over the earth, combined with the firmament, would have been "productive of a marvelous greenhouse effect which maintained mild temperatures from pole to pole, thus preventing air-mass circulation and the resultant rainfall (see Genesis 2:5).

But what caused the sudden freezing of the Arctic and Antarctic regions of the earth, with the resultant quick freezing of thousands of mammoths and other animals and the sudden and very great amounts of ice and snow deposited there?

The explanation of some is that the drastic climate change in the Arctic and Antarctic regions was caused by the earth shifting on its axis. There is evidence that the axis (tilt) of the earth has shifted more than once. However, none of those shifts were great enough to move either the Arctic or Antarctic from a subtropical climate to a subzero one, certainly not quickly enough to freeze buttercups in a mammoth's stomach. The mammoths were so quickly frozen that they can be eaten thousands of years later. It is well within the realm of probability that the flood and the resulting convulsions in the earth could have been responsible for both the shifts in the earth's axis and for the quick freezing of the mammoths and other mammals, which would have certainly occurred when the firmament over the earth was destroyed. "Throughout the Alaskan mucks," said scientist Frank C. Hibben, "there is evidence of atmospheric disturbances of unparalleled violence." (Hibben, p.177).

What would have happened when the firmament collapsed? The great mass of water above the firmament would previously have acted as insulation, trapping the heat from the sun and keeping it on the earth, thus keeping the earth's temperature warm and constant, even in areas such as the North and South Poles. With the collapse of the firmament, the water above the firmament fell upon the earth, producing the flood. With the firmament and the thick layer of water above it gone, the earth had nothing to keep its temperature constant and warm. The result was drastic and sudden. The northern and southernmost regions of the earth experienced a severe temperature drop and extreme cold. It was this that caused the resultant quick freezing of the animals around and above the Arctic and Antarctic circles.

In the Arctic and Antarctic regions, the temperature dropped quickly enough that the descending water froze. This caused ice caps to form that are in places miles thick. The farther north one goes, the more bones of prehistoric animals there are. The White Sea is entirely inside the Arctic Circle. The soil of the islands of the White Sea consists largely of the bones of mammoths, mingled with the bones of sabre-tooth tigers, giant elk, cave bears, and musk ox. The trunks and stumps of trees are also found rooted in the soil, even though there are now no trees in that region. The nearest trees are now hundreds of miles away. (McGee, p.45).

When it was in existence, were there any other effects that the firmament would have had on the earth? Storms are caused by temperature differences in the earth's atmosphere. "Temperature differentials are the chief cause of wind movements and storms, so with a fairly constant temperature world round, we can infer that storms and strong winds were unknown before the flood." (Starr, p.45) Likewise, rainfall would have been unknown (Morris, p.211). See also Genesis 2:5, which says, "the Lord God had not caused it to rain upon the earth, and there was not a man to till the ground."

In addition to this, stories from a number of lands say that the stars make music as they move through the heavens. The Bible itself mentions this. In Job chapter 38, verses 1-7, God speaks of the creation of the earth, and describes it as a time when "the morning stars sang together" (Job. 38:7). This music was called in ancient times "the music of the spheres," spheres meaning the heavenly bodies.

Though the unaided human ear cannot hear them, the stars do give off regular vibrations on specific wavelengths. (Baugh, p.63). Scientists today can pick up those vibrations, and even regular bursts of sound, on powerful radio receivers built for the special purpose of listening to the stars. It does sound like music, for NASA says the radio bursts from the stars are harmonious and are in a major key. (Baugh, p. 64).

How could people in ancient times have known this, since no one could hear the music? Before the flood, the radio waves from the stars were enhanced by the firmament and the vapor canopy, to such an extent that the music of the spheres would have been audible to the human ear in the early morning hours. (Baugh, p.64-65.)

What effect might this "music," these vibrations, have had on earth? One man was inspired by Genesis 2:6 to experiment with using mists to water plants. He also used the recorded music of birds because certain oscillating frequencies cause the water absorbing pores of plants to open. While these pores were open, he had the leaves sprayed with a mist enriched with a plant nutrient enzyme. The results were an amazing increase in plant growth, and in the size and amount of fruit and vegetables produced. ("Sonic Bloom," p.24-31.) Without a doubt the music of the spheres, along with the mist that watered the earth, had the same effect on plant life before the flood.

This then was the climate of the world before the flood, that marvelous climate in which our remote ancestors lived, a climate very conducive to long life, good health, and the spread of civilization.

*"This world is but the opening scene."*
    -    Patrick Ronayne Cleburne

# CHAPTER FOUR
## Health Before the flood

The last chapter spoke of the climate that the earth had before the flood. This climate was, based on both scientific evidence and ancient records, one that was conducive to cause the earth and its inhabitants to flourish. A flourishing person is obviously a healthy person and great and good health tends to give one a long life. Our ancestors before the flood were, by all ancient accounts, a very long-lived people. In his book "The Beginnings of History," Francois Lenormant mentions that there was a belief, "common to all nations, in an extreme longevity among the earliest ancestors of the human race." (Lenormant, p.293, 294).

This amazing long life had nothing to do with eating the fruit of the Tree of Life. The children and other descendants of Adams and Eve never ate of that tree. They did however, up until the generation that was born after the flood, have lives that often lasted for over nine hundred years. Adam lived a total of nine hundred thirty years before he died. Seth lived to the age of 912 years. Seth's first-born son, Enosh, lived a total of 905 years. Most of the men mentioned in the Bible, as living before the flood, lived to be more than 900 years old.

Many people have dismissed such long-life spans as impossible. It is important to note, however, that we find other literature besides the Bible which refers to a much longer life span in ancient times. The Greeks and Romans, for instance, believed that mankind had once had a lifespan of between 800 and 1,000 years. (Rawlinson, "The Testimony Of The Truth of Scripture," p.14; see also Josephus, piii, & p.9). There is also a record where a

Chinese emperor proposed an inquiry into why the ancients lived so much longer than people in his day. (Dods, p.29).

Josephus, in "Antiquities of the Jews," speaking of a common belief that our ancient ancestors typically lived for many centuries, wrote:

> *"Now I have for witnesses to what I have said, all those that have written Antiquities, both among the Greeks and barbarians; for even Manetho who wrote the Egyptian History, and Berosus who collected the Chaldean Monuments, and Mochus, and Hestiacus, and besides these, Hieronymus, the Egyptian, and those who composed the Phoenician history, agree to what I here say. Hesiod also, and Hecatacus, Hellanicus, and Acusilaus; and besides Ephorus and Nicolaus relate that the ancients lived a thousand years"* (Josephus, p.46).

Hesiod, one of the historians mentioned in the paragraph above, calls the first age of mankind a Golden Age, in which people lived very long and did not appear to age. (Hesiod, p.6). He describes those people thusly: "miserable age rested not on them; . . . . they died, it was as though they were overcome with sleep, and they had all good things; for the fruitful earth, unforced bare them fruit abundantly and without stint" (Hesiod, p.6).

The earliest known civilization after the flood is that of Sumer, or the Land of Shinar, as it is called in the Bible (Langdon, p.xviii). This civilization was on a flat plain that stretched between the Tigris and Euphrates rivers, in what is now the country of Iraq. Here, over 4,000 years ago, the first known cities after the flood were erected.

The Biblical account lists ten generations from Adam through Noah. That is, ten patriarchs who lived in succession to each other prior to the flood. Because of their extreme longevity, the pagan religions that arose after the flood often spoke of those men as gods. The sacred books of the Iranians, attributed to Zarathustra, and used in their religion prior to their conversion to the Muslim faith, spoke of ten men, ten generations, that existed in the beginning, long before recorded history. The same thing is true of the Hindu religion, where its sacred writings also speak of ten generations and ten men who are known to them as the ten fathers, those who lived in the time that their most ancient legends or myths speak of as coming at the beginning of the earth. The Egyptians also believed in ten kings who ruled at the beginning of things. (Lenormant, p.132). Other peoples also told of ten kings ruling before the flood. This would agree with the lineage of Noah, which includes ten men, counting from Adam to Noah. Berosus, who has already been mentioned as a Babylonian priest who wrote a history of Babylon beginning with Creation, and who lived during the time of Alexander the Great, ended his history of the pre-flood world with the words, "so the sum total of all the kings (before the flood) is ten. (Dods, p.28). Indeed, the tenth king is, according to both the Sumerian and the Babylonian accounts, the man who built the ark. This, of course, would make him Noah. There is also a second list of kings left by the Sumerians. These kings appear to have been contemporaneous with the ten kings of the first list. The kings in this list would agree with the eight men in Cain's line, beginning with Adam and ending with the generation of the flood. (Jacobsen, pp.71, 77). Other historical accounts, such as that of Josephus, also call Noah a king or ruler.

The King Lists, as they are called, give a few details of the lives of each of those in the lists. Some of the details are such that many scholars are persuaded that the pre-flood rulers are the same men as those mentioned in the Bible, as living before the flood. This is true even though their names are not the same as those in the Bible.

One evidence that these histories are consistent, that the King Lists are an accurate list of the men mentioned in the Bible as living before the flood, is seen in the fact that the kings in these lists have Sumerian names (Soden, p.47), while the names of the pre-flood people in the book of Genesis are Semitic names. This is a confirmation of the truth of the two accounts, as well as proof that both accounts have a common source, but that each account evolved independently of the other.

When a story found in one culture or nation is retold or rewritten in the language of another people, personal names are rarely changed. They tend to remain the same. That helps in tracing the origin of legends and myths. Since the personal names in the book of Genesis are Semitic, rather than Sumerian, it is logical to assume that the stories of Creation and the flood given in the book of Genesis were not copied from the Sumerian stories. It makes it appear, instead, that the two stories, along with many other similar ones, provide independent verification and support for the truthfulness of each other. We thus have evidence that though the Sumerians and the ancient Hebrews had highly similar stories about Creation and life before the flood, neither is likely to have borrowed their stories from the other culture. This makes it seem more likely that the stories of the two cultures have a common source in a common event.

A major problem has been the life spans often believed to be involved in the King Lists. Some of the individual men listed in the King Lists supposedly ruled for fifty to sixty thousand years, according to most translations of those writings. One example of the longer King List names eight kings who reigned for a total of 241,200 years. This list does not include either the first or the last king before the flood. (Jacobsen, pp.71, 77). The Sumerian King Lists also name their own kings who reigned for a time after the flood. The reigns of these kings are shorter, but each is still many hundreds of years in length. (Pritchard, p.265). These reigns are too incredibly long to be realistic.

However, there are two ways to interpret the unit of time upon which these long reign spans are based. The unit of time in question is the Saros. It is commonly taken to signify a period of 3,600 years. (Cory & Hodges, p.53). However, Suidas, a Greek writing in the later part of the 10th century, stated that there were two values for the Saros, with the shorter value being equivalent to 18 years and 6 months. (Jones, p.114). Using this lesser value of the Saros (the plural is Sari), causes the reign spans of the Sumerian King Lists to shrink enough that they more nearly approximate the record of the Bible. (Custance, p.23).

### Table of Length of Reigns of Kings Before The flood, Given in Sari and in Years.

| Name | Sari | Shorter Value Converted to Years |
|---|---|---|
| 1. ALORUS | 10 | 185 |
| 2. ALAPAROS | 3 | 55.5 |
| 3. AMELON | 13 | 240.5 |
| 4. AMMENON | 12 | 222 |
| 5. AMEGALAROS | 18 | 333 |
| 6. DAONOS | 10 | 183 |
| 7. EDPRANCHOS | 18 | 333 |
| 8. AMEMPSINOS | 10 | 185 |
| 9. OTIARTES | 8 | 148 |
| 10. XISUTHROS | 18 | 333 |
| TOTALS | 120 | 220 |

Thus, in the example above, we see that one of the two longest reigns of the pre-flood kings listed by the Sumerians was that of Xisuthros. Xisuthros was the name by which the Sumerians

68

called Noah. It means, "He of Long Life," probably referring to the fact that Noah lived to be 950 years old (Josephus, p.44). In ancient and even in not so ancient times, a person's name was often changed to denote some event or occasion in their life that was especially worthy of note. Living to be past 900 years old, at a time (after the flood), when his own grandchildren had lifespans half that of his, would certainly have been an event to be noted, and could easily have been responsible for Noah's name to be changed to denote his extraordinary long life, compared to those born after the flood.

Since Noah was 600 years old when the flood came upon the earth, and considering that if he were indeed a king he would not have reigned until the death of the king before him, three hundred and thirty-three years would not be to long for him to reign. It would mean that he was roughly 267 years old when he became king. If we reduce Noah's life span before the flood to a life span relative to our own, he was 27 when he became king and he reigned until he was 60, at which time the flood came.

Another effect that living before the flood had on people, was that they aged slower. The Lagash Kinglist, from the city of Lagash in Sumer, not only gives long lifespans, but also adds that life was much 'slower,' that is, people were children for much longer periods of time (100 years) and men had their first children when much older in life that today, even comparatively speaking (Hess, Richard, and Tsumura, David, (eds.), p.135). It is interesting how this 100-year childhood is the same time frame as the bible uses in describing the length of childhood during the millennial rule of Jesus. Isaiah 65:20 says in that regard, "There shall be no more thence an infant of days, nor an old man that hath not filled his days: for the child shall die an hundred years old; but the sinner being an hundred years old shall be accursed."

Since Adam and Eve's descendants did not eat of the fruit of the Tree of Life, not even once, what could have given them such long and apparently healthy lives? The water vapor canopy, mentioned in the previous article, would have had the "effect of filtering out harmful radiation from space, which would have drastically decreased the rate of aging and death (Morris, p.211)." There is also evidence that the earth's magnetic field was far stronger then than it is today. This would have acted as an additional shield against cosmic radiation and further helped to produce the healthy environment of the pre-flood world. (Humphreys, p.63).

A modern-day experiment has proven that the filtering out of harmful radiation, such as ultraviolet rays, is beneficial in many ways. A professor at Kao University in Tokyo began raising plants under light from which both Infrared Radiation and Ultraviolet Radiation had been filtered, using coaxial cable. After extensive experiments, he stated that it promoted healing and "because the ultraviolet is blocked, this sunlight does not fade fabrics or damage skin." (Gilmore, p.75).

Although no further experiments have been done (to this writer's knowledge), the blockage of the ultraviolet rays would have benefited all life under the firmament. The rays of both UVA (Ultraviolet A) and UVB (Ultraviolet B), cause cancer because they penetrate the DNA of exposed skin cells. UVA rays also activate a gene that causes the skin to wrinkle, yellow and sag. This is not considering additional harm, such as permanent damage to other genes, also done by ultraviolet rays.

The energy contained in infrared rays causes the molecules of the substances they hit to vibrate back and forth. However, the energy contained in ultraviolet rays is higher, so instead of just causing the molecules to shake, it can knock electrons away from the atoms, or causes molecules to split. This results in a change in the chemical structure of the molecule. In addition to cell damage, the ultraviolet rays can cause deformities, by mutating the genetic code of a cell. The fact that the pre-flood population of the earth was protected from harmful radiation would help explain why our ancestors could have lived much longer than we do today.

There is a legend that the sun was brighter before the flood. This would have been true, as scientists have determined that the stars as seen by man would have been about three times brighter than we see them today. (Baugh, p.61). The stars would have been plainer and easier to see, as the water canopy and the firmament, or thin metallic base to the water canopy, would have caused the stars to stand out more plainly than otherwise. Baugh, p. 61. This could in part have been the reason the pre-flood people were said to have become great star-gazers, studying the heavens and watching the orderly movement of the stars as they slowly moved across the night sky. (Baugh, p.61).

An additional effect of the firmament and the water canopy would have been to increase the atmospheric pressure. The atmospheric pressure today at sea level is 14.7 pounds per square inch. Before the flood, the atmospheric pressure would have been about twice that. This would also have greatly increased the amount of oxygen in the air, (Baugh, p.56-57). The increased amount of oxygen in the air, plus the increased atmospheric pressure, would have put more oxygen into the blood. This would have caused people to be possibly 20% larger than they are today. (Baugh, p. 58). Likewise, the greater oxygen content of the water would have produced the larger marine life, sometimes reaching huge size, that fossil remains show existed before the flood. (Baugh, p.58).

Due to the extra oxygen in the atmosphere, and with the greater amount of oxygen in the blood that that would have caused, people were possibly twenty percent larger than they are today. (Baugh, p.58), and would have been able to run up to two hundred miles without fatigue (Baugh, p.57). Scientists have also puzzled over how the pterosaur, a flying reptile (dinosaur) with a stubby body and a wingspan of up to 36 feet, could possibly have stayed airborne in the earth's present atmosphere. In the denser atmosphere before the flood it would have had no problem flying. (Anderson, p.25).

The idea that the earth's atmosphere once had far more oxygen in it is backed by science. Robert Berner of Yale and Gary Landis of the U.S. Geological Survey ran an analysis of microscopic air bubbles trapped in fossilized tree resin, trapped, they believed, since the earth's early days. Using a quadrupole mass spectrometer, a device that identifies the chemical composition of a substance, they slowly crushed the amber, releasing tiny bubbles of air. Surprise! Their research disclosed evidence that the "ancient air contained 50 percent more oxygen than the air today" (Discover, February, 1988, p.12). The spectrometer also disclosed that the atmospheric pressure was much higher at the time the bubbles formed in the amber.

After the flood, the lower atmospheric pressure and less oxygen in the blood would have had an adverse effect on people and animals whose bodies were designed for pre-flood conditions. There are those who believe that due to the relatively small lung capacity of many of the dinosaurs, the drastic reduction in air pressure and oxygen could have led to the dinosaurs' extinction. (Anderson, p.25.) The sudden drop in air pressure and oxygen would have been another factor in the tremendous decrease of longevity in humans after the flood.

Another thing scientists can tell us about the antediluvian world is that people would have healed of injuries much faster. This has been proven by the use of hyperbaric atmosphere chambers. Designed originally to treat the bends, a sometimes-fatal condition that deep sea divers face, hyperbaric chambers simulate the pre-flood atmosphere, in that they artificially increase both air pressure and oxygen intake. Experiments have shown that under these conditions, in pre-flood days an open wound would have healed overnight. (Baugh, p.57). Getting oxygen throughout the body at a higher pressure has become a modern medical treatment called Hyperbaric Oxygen Therapy.

Hyperbaric Oxygen Therapy (HO2) was first used to assist wound healing when it was noted in 1965 that the burns of victims of a coal mine explosion, treated with HBO2 for their carbon dioxide poisoning, healed faster. In hyperbaric oxygen therapy, the patient breathes pure oxygen at increased atmospheric pressure, thus increasing the oxygen level in the body, speeding healing and promoting the fighting of infection. When patients are placed in a container of pure oxygen pressurized at 1.5 to 1.75 times normal air pressure, the amount of oxygen reaching the brain is about six times the normal amount. (Catalano, p.32).

Nick Nolte, famous actor and film producer, spent ten hours in a hyperbaric chamber to repair brain damage and showed miraculous improvement. This was the same treatment that Edward Teller, the father of the H-bomb, used to repair damage to his own brain after he had a stroke. (Felker, p.11).

An article in "Insight on the News," titled "New Treatment May Awaken Patients from Severe Comas," states that comatose patients not only have been revived but have been returned to nearly normal functioning through multiple treatments of hyperbaric oxygen. The article also quotes Dr. Richard Neubauer, medical director of the Ocean Hyperbaric Center of Lauderdale-by-the-Sea, in Florida, who, in a report published in 1985, stated that 12 of 14 severe coma patients he had treated showed moderate or good recovery. In a later control study of 30 vegetative patients who had been in comas from two and a half to twenty-two months, Neubauer reported a 50 percent recovery rate, which is dazzling compared with standard outcomes. Other benefits of HBO are wide-ranging.

A study reported in 1992 by physician Gaylan Rockswold and associates at the Hennepin County Medical Center in Minnesota showed that HBO treatment soon after acute head injury reduces mortality by more than 40 percent. HBO can be used to speed healing in burn victims, and has been proved effective for treating patients bitten by the brown recluse spider. (Catalano, p.32). Comatose patients not only have been revived, but returned to nearly normal functioning through multiple treatments of hyperbaric oxygen. (Catalano, p.32).

A report online by the Canadian government states that "A brain injury is like any other wound and can be healed like any other wound with oxygen." It continues by saying that hyperbaric oxygen therapy is recognized as an effective treatment for 13 specific conditions, adding that "the operators of some private and overseas clinics claim it can also be used to treat such conditions as multiple sclerosis, cerebral palsy, cancer, AIDS, stroke and migraine headaches." (Health Canada, December 30, 2005. "The therapy promotes healing by delivering a high concentration of oxygen quickly and deeply into the affected areas of the body." (Health Canada, December 30, 2005).

Raising oxygen levels fights infection by killing bacteria. It creates "free radicals," unstable oxygen molecules that are lethal to germs, and it stimulates immune cells called phagocytes, which destroy infectious microbes. Oxygen also increases the production of collagen, the main wound-repairing connective tissue in the body. By speeding up the healing process, oxygen may also increase the regeneration of nerve cells." (Whole Health, December 30, 2005).

The modern medical world has proven to its own satisfaction that increased atmospheric pressure speeds up the body's natural healing process until healing becomes incredibly fast. For this reason, hyperbaric atmosphere chambers are used today by every hospital that can afford one.

Though the Bible does not say that there was no sickness, either in the Garden or in the period from creation to the flood, a world with little or no sickness would seem to be in keeping with the biblical picture of the early world. The people of India, in their oldest writings, say that there was no sickness in the "first age of the world" (Rawlinson, "The Testimony Of The Truth of Scripture," p.14). You will recall that the Greeks also, in some of their writings, say that if Pandora had not opened the box she was forbidden to open, mankind would have lived forever and never aged, all in a world without sickness or hardship. (Gascoigne, p.39.)

If there was little or no sickness in the pre-flood world, it is logical to assume that there was also no mental retardation and no physical abnormalities. Certainly, there is no mention of deformed, retarded, or abnormal children in literature or legends referring to the time before the flood. Such things could not occur unless there were genetic abnormalities present in the parents. Therefore, we have long had laws against the marriage of close relatives. It was from a desire to reduce the likelihood of children being born with deformities and mental retardation. Where there are no damaged genes, there is very little likelihood of deformed or retarded offspring. This could explain why God allowed marriage between close kin, even between brothers and sisters, both before the flood and for a short time after it.

Since the human race began with a single couple, the second and third generations would have been forced to marry close relatives. The same situation arose after the flood; the children of Shem, Ham and Japheth had only brothers, sisters, and first cousins as a choice of marriage partners. Josephus and other Jewish writers state that the wives of Cain and Abel were their sisters (Josephus, p.42). The Book of Jubilees, written in the second century B.C. and believed to have been composed by a Jewish writer from earlier material, says that Cain married his sister Awan, who bore him Enoch about 200 years after creation. Likewise, Abraham's wife Sarah was his half-sister, yet they had a healthy son (Genesis 20:12). Not until the time of Moses do we see marriage between close relatives outlawed by God (Leviticus 18).

In speaking of the greater health before the flood, mental health must not be forgotten. The firmament would have filtered out some colors, leaving sunlight pink in color, rather than yellow. (Baugh, p.52). Scientists and researchers are finding that the most important color in the entire spectrum is pink. This is the color that is produced by energized hydrogen. Pink, we are told, is the most relaxing of all colors and the most restful to the eyes. (Baugh, p.51-52). It has likewise been discovered that individuals find themselves in a more positive mood under pink light. When a person is affected by the right spectrum of pink light, the brain secretes norepinephrine, which is a natural tranquilizer and neurotransmitter.

Biologists have also found that the greatest plant growth is under pink light. Investigation has revealed that it is pink light which optimally triggers the growth of cells within plants. We can therefore assume that a contributing factor to the enormous size of plant life before the flood was the energized hydrogen in the firmament giving off a pinkish glow. (Baugh, p.56-64).

A good question, and one that is often heard when a discussion of the pre-flood world arises, is how many people were there before the flood?  We do not know the answer to that question, but we know that people lived roughly 10 times longer than the average lifespan today. Consider also that according to the ancient legends, sickness was unheard of before the flood. Barring accident or murder, people lived a very long time in a state of perfect health.

The childbearing age was much longer than it is today. It would have been quite possible for the average couple to have had 15 or 20 or more children. Indeed, if ancient accounts are to be believed, couples had far more children than a mere 15 or 20! Imagine the population explosion that would have resulted under these conditions! We don't know for sure how many children Adam & Eve had, since only three of them are mentioned by name. The bible does tell us there were others. Josephus says they had a total of 33 sons and 23 daughters (Josephus, fn. p.43). He further says that Lamech had 77 children by his two wives, Zillah (whom Josephus calls Silla) and Adah (Josephus, p.42). If the average family in the pre-flood age had only 10 children, which looks like a far less number than they had, then even by that extremely conservative estimate, barring massive deaths due to war, by the tenth generation before the flood the population would have numbered many millions.

We have discussed some of the benefits of living in that world before the flood, the world our ancestors threw away in their rebellion. The Sumerian account of the world before the flood ended with the comment "the flood swept over the land." (Jacobsen, pp.71, 77).  As we will see, that is what happened. The flood came and swept it all away.

---

**Day is Dying**

Day is dying in the West, darkness spreads its raven crest
Night comes, but brings no rest, it floods upon the land
I herald the coming of the night, I herald the fall of man
When might makes right, with houses built on sand

When Truth is ignored, and none take it to mind
Darkness spreads apace, and evil enthroned you find
Ignorance reigns, minds are polluted, not pristine and clean
And like tiny banners, waving green,
Blades of grass in the streets of our cities will be seen

"The night is almost here," the trumpets blast
Their warning shrills against the light's last glow
But men's ears are attuned to a sound from the past
The voice of a serpent, from a garden long ago

I herald the dying of the day, the coming of the night
Thralldom to the dark, that rages against the light
I herald the advance of doom, of darkness and of evil's might

But wait, take of the book and read,
The night is not triumphant, tho across the land it speed
Righteousness and peace will meet together
And Truth from the earth will spring

As the phoenix, newborn, rises from the ashes of the old
So all that is Good shall triumph, as prophets have foretold
So I herald the advent of the dawn, I herald the fall of night!
I herald the reign of Absolute Truth, Behold the Light!

- Dr. N. James Brooks, Jr.

*"Afflictions, bitter as they seem at the moment,
are often of inestimable value; they soften our hearts,
they humble our pride, they cause us to look more
impartially on ourselves, and more charitably on others."*

- Patrick Ronayne Cleburne

# CHAPTER FIVE
# The Degree of Civilization Before
# The flood

A world existed before Noah, but we know very little about it. The flood wiped virtually every trace of it away. Fortunately, a little knowledge of those pre-flood days has been handed down to us through the Bible and through scattered legends and stories. The pre-flood world is often called the antediluvian world, which is Latin for "before the flood."

The bits and pieces of knowledge that we have of that time give an interesting look into that bygone vanished world. By closely examining this somewhat limited information, we will discover that much of the available information is consistent from source to source. The most readily available accounts are those in the book of Genesis and the information left us by Josephus, a Jewish priest. The Jews, Josephus tells us, had many volumes of information stored in the temple, which included a huge complex of rooms and passageways, many of which were underground. After the destruction of the temple by the Romans, Josephus recorded as much of that information as he could from memory. This is where much of our information on the pre-flood world comes from, outside of the Bible. Some of our knowledge of that by-gone world also comes from discoveries of artifacts that were not made by modern man, but which appear far too advanced for people of any time before this modern age. We are left feeling that if some advanced civilization produced those artifacts, then it was either that of the pre-flood world, people living later than the flood but with knowledge saved from that prior time, or, as some believe, knowledge left with us by aliens from outer space. If that knowledge and those artifacts came from the pre-flood time, what was that time and that early age of mankind like?

"It will scarcely be denied that the mythical traditions of almost all nations place at the beginning of human history a time of happiness and perfection, a 'golden age,' which has no features of savagery or barbarism, but many of civilization and refinement, (Rawlinson, pp.10-11).

Genesis tells us that the first two sons of Adam and Eve were Cain and Abel. God approved of Abel's actions, but disapproved of Cain's actions. Cain's response was to kill his brother. Cain showed no remorse for his deed, and God then cursed Cain and further told him that he would become a fugitive and a wanderer on the earth. We are next told that Cain "went out from the presence of the Lord and dwelt in the land of Nod, on the east of Eden." (Gen. 4:16) Nod means wandering.

In addition to the small amount of information that the bible and other sources give, the names of the above individuals can tell us a little about them. You will recall that Adam means dirt. He was named this by God, for he was made from dirt. Abel means breath, a vapor, or vanity. The idea seems to be that Abel's name was to remind both him and others that our natural life on this earth is just a breath, a vapor and vanity. What really counts is whether or not we live our lives in a manner pleasing to God, which prepares us for our eternal life to come. This was true even when people ordinarily lived for many hundreds of years, as they did in the pre-flood world. Cain means both possession and possessed. Names in the pre-flood world commonly had more than one meaning. Indeed, throughout the time of the Old Testament, Semitic names in general had more than one meaning. At any rate, Cain certainly does appear to have been possessed by evil to kill his own brother out of jealousy.

In the British Museum, there is a clay tablet, No. 74329 that contains what may be a 4,000-year-old version of the story of Cain. This tablet speaks of a group of people who were tillers of the soil, which Cain had been. The leader of these people is called Cain. They are referred to on the tablet as the "People Who in Sorrow Roam," which Cain was forced to do for a long time. The tablet tells that this man eventually built a city for himself. We cannot prove that the story on the tablet refers to the Cain of the Bible and his descendants. However, we can be sure that the story of Cain was remembered for a long time, so this story could have been written after the flood about Cain and his descendants. (Sitchin, pp. 111-114).

The late professor Cyrus Gordon of Brandeis University noted the Mesopotamian tradition that science at the beginning of civilization was at a much higher level than it later became, declining from a higher level to a lower one. (Gordon, p.76).

In addition to this, artifacts have been discovered whose origin is placed so far back that they would have to come from the pre-flood world. If these artifacts are genuine, and they certainly seem to be, then the world before the flood was in many ways very advanced. Solomon wrote in Ecclesiastes; "The thing that has been is that which shall be, and that which has been done is that which shall be done, and there is nothing new under the sun. Whosoever speaks and says; look, this is new, should know that it has already been in the ages which were before us." (Ecclesiastes 1:9-10).

Mankind the thinker, mankind the builder, ever inventing something new, that which we have done is but the promise of the things that we will do, but the past calls to the future, and says there is nothing new.

Josephus tells us that Cain, "was the author of measures and weights, and whereas they lived innocently and generously

82

while they knew nothing of such arts, he changed the world into cunning craftiness." He first of all set boundaries about lands, he built a city, and fortified it with walls, and he compelled his family to come together to it, and called that city Enoch, after the name of his eldest son Enoch." (Josephus, pp. 42, 43)

Before we ask ourselves what our ancestors might have accomplished before the flood and what level of civilization they might have achieved, we should first recognize what we have accomplished in the last 900 years! We have gone from a mostly illiterate, agricultural society with no printing or gunpowder, to one with atomic energy, cars and computers. If our ancestors were as smart as us, what could they have accomplished in the same amount of time? Consider too that our ancient ancestors who lived before the flood were undoubtedly smarter than we are today. Scientists tell us that we only use a portion of our brains. Our pre-flood ancestors, on the other hand, with more oxygen reaching their brain, were able to use all of their brain, not just part of it as we are forced to do today. On top of that, humans lived so long before the flood that they could teach what they knew to many generations of their descendants. Adam would have known just about everyone mentioned in Genesis as living before the flood. Among those people mentioned by name, only Noah and his sons are recorded as being born after Adam's death.

Another account of the world before the flood originated with Berosus, an elderly native of Babylon. He knew Greek, and left Babylon when it was conquered by Alexander the Great. He wrote three books around 290 B.C. on the history and religion of Babylon. (Cory and Hodges, p. 43-46 & Gascoigne, p.4) The Babylonians taught that there were cities, armies, and wars in that antediluvian world. Their legends say that pre-flood humanity engaged in constant wars and became more and more wicked until they showed no kindness or courtesy to anyone and lost all reverence for the gods.

If ancient Sumerian histories are to be believed, other cities were built in the pre-flood world besides the city of Enoch. These histories are lists of the rulers of various cities, with a few remarks appended about each ruler and the time in which he ruled. They are known as "King Lists."

Five pre-flood cities are named in the Sumerian King Lists. (Jacobsen, Weld Blundell-144) A tablet found in 1914 in the excavated Sumerian city of Nippur names them: Eridu, Bad Tibira, Larak, Sitpar, and Shuruppak. (Kramer, "Sumerian Mythology," p.148) The Bible mentions the city of Enoch as having been built by Cain and named for his first-born son. Genesis 4:17 says, "And Cain knew his wife and she conceived, and bare Enoch and he built a city, and called the name of the city after the name of his son, Enoch." In the language of Sumer, the Hebrew name Enoch becomes Eridu. Bad Tibira, the second of the cities named as existing before the flood means "City of the Metal Workers." As already stated, the other three cities were Larak, Sippar, and Shuruppak. (Kramer, "Sumerian Mythology," p.151) Noah who was called Ziusudra by the Sumerians, is said to have lived in the last-named city, Shuruppak. (Daniken, p.62).

Please note that these names were later used by the Sumerians for cities built after the flood. This is much like people who are settling a new land naming a new city after a great or famous city in their home country. As an example, the Dutch, who founded a colony in what is today the state of New York, named the colony's capital New Amsterdam, after Amsterdam, the capital of their home country.

The fact that there was a city before the flood, at least according to the people of Sumer, that was named "City of the Metal Workers," is an indication that there was metal working before the flood. This agrees with the Bible, for one of Cain's descendants was named Tubal-Cain. The Bible calls him "a craftsman in every work of brass and iron," which tells us that pre-flood man engaged in metalworking. Josephus goes a step further and says that Tubal-Cain "invented the art of making brass." (Josephus, p.43).

In the Bible, people are not mentioned by name unless they are significant in some way. The first-born son is usually mentioned because he succeeded his father as head of the family. If you were not the first-born son, to be mentioned by name means that you were noteworthy in some way.

One of Cain's descendants, Lamech, had three sons and a daughter who are mentioned by name in the book of Genesis. His first son to be mentioned, Jabal, was called "the father of all who dwell in tents and are the owners of cattle." This is simply another way of saying that Jabal was the first to dwell in tents and to herd sheep. Lamech's second son, Jubal, is called the father of musicians. Lamech had a third son who is mentioned in scripture, Tubal-Cain whose name is translated by some as "smith of Cain." The bible calls him in Genesis 4:22, "an instructor of every artificer in brass and iron." "Smith of Cain" could mean that he made things out of iron and brass mainly for Cain.

Genesis 4:19-22 says,

> *"And Lamech took unto him two wives: the name of the one was Adah, and the name of the other Zillah. And Adah bare Jabal: he was the father of such as dwell in tents, and of such as have cattle. And his brother's name was Jubal: he was the father of all such as handle the harp and organ. And Zillah, she also bare Tubal-Cain, an instructor of every artificer in brass and iron: and the sister of Tubal-Cain was Naamah."*

We know that Cain's eldest son was Enoch. Josephus further tells us, "Now Jared was the son of Enoch; whose son was Malaliel; whose son was Mathusela; whose son was Lamech; who had seventy-seven children by two wives, Silla and Ada. Of those children by Ada, one was Jabal: he erected tents, and loved the life of a shepherd. But Jubal, who was born of the same mother with him, exercised himself in music; and invented the psaltery and the harp. But Tubal, one of his children by the other wife, exceeded all men in strength, and was very expert and famous in martial performances. He procured what tended to the pleasures of the body by that method; and first of all, invented the art of making brass (Josephus, pp.42-43).

It was quite common in ancient times, and in some cultures even today, to change a person's name any time something noteworthy was done by them or when something noteworthy happened to them. For example, the current Emperor of Japan took a new name, called in ancient times a "reign name," upon ascending the throne at the death of his father.

In the case of Tubal, he would not have been given the name "Smith of Cain," when he was born, since he was not a metal worker then. He would have been given the name much later in life, after he learned to work with metal, and then became a metal worker for Cain. Cain was Tubal's many times great grandfather, but considering that people normally lived for many centuries back then, and never showed any signs of aging, Tubal could most easily have worked for his ancestor. Though the Bible does not tell us the age to which any of Cain's descendants lived, if they lived on the average as long as the descendants of Seth, Cain's brother, then most of them lived to be past 900.

Today, scientists tell us that most of our brain goes unused. With more oxygen in our blood, as it was with a higher pre-flood atmospheric pressure, how much smarter would we be? How much faster and better we would think! Thomas A. Edison patented over 300 useful inventions. One of his inventions was the record player, from which humble beginnings the VCR came. Imagine what and how many workable inventions he might have come up with if he had been able to use all of his brain, instead of only a small portion of it! Imagine also what he might have accomplished if he had lived for centuries, building and improving on his inventions all that time! Is there any doubt then, that our ancestors before the flood, able to use all their brain, and living and improving on their individual inventions for many centuries, could have accomplished things that might rival and even surpass our achievements today?

There have been a number of unusual historical and archaeological discoveries made at different times and places around the world. There are artifacts that, because of their nature, are found in geological strata where they shouldn't be, and their appearance has baffled the minds of trained archaeologists. In plain, simple English, artifacts have been discovered that are far too advanced to have been made by any known civilization of the past. They are sometimes referred to as "out-of-place artifacts." They are manmade objects, sometimes found in rocks supposedly older than the human race, or they were relicts left by civilizations supposedly too primitive to make them. They are too authentic to dismiss as frauds, yet to accept them as genuine man-made artifacts would overturn the idea that all ancient people were primitive dwellers in a Stone Age world. Such artifacts first gained popular attention in the 1960s and 70s, when Erich Von Daniken wrote a series of sensational books, "Chariots of the Gods," "Gods From Outer Space," etc., which claimed that early man could not possibly have made such anomalous artifacts, and therefore aliens from another planet must have made them. Were our ancient ancestors far more scientifically advanced than we have realized?

Lamech had two wives. In the various Semitic languages, the prefix "Bar" can be added to a name to designate "son of." Since Lamech had two wives, people might have wanted to know which of those two wives Tubal-Cain was the son of. If he was the son of Zillah, they would have called him "Bar-Zillu," meaning the "Son of Zillah." The ending "u" was used to show that the person you were being called after was a woman. The ending "ah" was used if the person you were being called the son of was your father rather than your mother. In the language of Sumer, the first known civilization after the flood, the word for "iron" is Bar-zillu, leading us to think that Tubal-Cain was the son of Zillah, and that iron was named after him because he was well known for working with it, just as the Bible says. (Custance, p.6-7).

Lest we think that Tubal-Cain and the metal working ability of our ancient ancestors was on the scale of some primitive tribe, consider this. In 1968, Dr. Koriun Megurtchian of the Soviet Union unearthed what is considered to be the oldest large-scale metallurgical factory in the world, at Medzamor, in Soviet Armenia. Here, over 4,500 years ago, an unknown prehistoric people worked with over 200 furnaces, producing an assortment of vases, knives, spear points, rings, bracelets, etc. The Medzamor craftsmen wore mouth-filters and gloves as they labored and fashioned their wares of copper, lead, zinc, iron, gold, tin, manganese and fourteen kinds of bronze. The smelters also produced an assortment of metallic paints, ceramics and glass. But the most out-of-place discovery was several pairs of tweezers made of steel, taken from layers dating back before the first millennium B.C. The steel was later found to be exceptionally high grade, and the discovery was verified by scientific organizations in the Soviet Union, the United States, Britain, France and Germany. What makes this metal refining and casting site of special interest to us is that it is less than fifteen miles from Mount Ararat, where the Ark containing Noah and his family landed. (Noorbergen, p.32; see also Landsburg, p.21).

If the estimate of 4,500 years ago is correct for the operation of the above described metal working site, then it was in operation just shortly after the flood. The Jewish historian,

Flavius Josephus, who lived in the first century A.D., used manuscripts available during his time to calculate that Noah's flood occurred 1556 years after the creation of Adam. By adding the ages of the patriarchs in the bible at the time they had their first mentioned son, you yourself will come up with a roughly similar date. Likewise, Archbishop James Ussher, of Ireland, calculated that the creation of the world took place in 4004 BC. If 1556 is deducted from 4004 then the worldwide flood of Noah's time was around 2448 B.C. Scholars disagree slightly on some of the dates. But most agree that the flood took place between 2500 BC and 2300 BC.

Akkadian, one of the ancient languages of Mesopotamia, was no longer used after 1500 B.C. What is interesting is the fact that the Akkadians had a word for iron, centuries before man is supposed to have known how to smelt iron. (Victoria Institute, January 25, 2005) According to archaeologists, mankind first used stone, then discovered copper, then how to make bronze, and lastly discovered how to smelt iron. The age in which mankind learned to smelt iron is supposed to have come long after the culture and language of the Akkadians had ended.

It is also interesting that the name Brazil is spelled Brzl. This is the Akkadian word for iron. Nobody seems to know how Brazil, the country, got its name. There was an ancient Irish legend of a land across the Atlantic Ocean to the west. In the legend, the name of that land was Hy-Brazil. This land was supposed to be a rich source of iron. The country of Brazil, by the way, is a rich source of iron!

The sacred book of the Maya Indians, the Popol Vuh, says that the "first men" of the pre-flood era possessed great knowledge. "They were able to know all, and they examined the four corners of the earth, the four points of the arch of the sky and the round face of the earth." (Tomas, p.162) The Miao, an ethnic minority of China, tell that Adam, whom they call the Patriarch

89

Dirt, remember that Adam means dirt, was able to estimate the weight of the earth and to calculate the size of the heavenly bodies. (Traux, September 24, 2005).

Looking at the first achievements of the early post-flood earth gives us some idea of the scientific achievements of the pre-flood world. The earliest known civilization after the flood, that of Sumer, appears at the dawn of recorded history. It appears seemingly fully developed, that is, we can find no evidence that the civilization of Sumer started at a primitive state. (Ceram, p. 298, 302-303, 312) Supposedly, societies must start at a stage known as the hunter-gatherer stage, when people lived by hunting animals and by gathering seeds and vegetation that grew wild. People at this stage of development live in primitive tribal societies, not cities. The Sumerian civilization seems to have begun with cities and with farming, using irrigation to water their fields. They also had a written language.

It is only natural to assume that Noah and his family passed down most of their knowledge to the first generations of people after the flood. Since they had all lived before the flood, Noah and his wife lived for centuries before the flood, they had a great deal of knowledge about the scientific achievements and advances of the antediluvian world. They also lived for centuries after the flood, so they would have been walking libraries that their descendants could use to jump start civilization again.

It has often been suggested over the centuries that the people of the pre-flood world had writing. As one researcher put it, "It is now mostly admitted that alphabetic writing is as old as the human family that Adam knew how to write as well as we, and that he did write." (Seiss, p.23) Dr. Seiss has not been alone in his belief. Many other scientists and researchers have agreed with him.

"A system of writing was in effect in Europe as far back as the Stone Age." (Ripley, p.488) It is clear that the art of writing had been known for a long time, perhaps since the first dynasty of Kish, the first kingdom after the flood. (Fleure & Peake, p.22).

Have you ever wondered why we call our system of letters the alphabet? The word is actually the combination of the Greek names of the first two characters of the Greek alphabet, alpha and beta. But where did the Greeks get the names they used for the letters in the alphabet? They are merely the Greek variation of the Phoenician names aleph, beth, gimel, deleth, etc. These are actual words in the Phoenician language for ox, house, camel, door, etc. It has been suggested that the names were given to the letters because the shape of the letters were simplifications of earlier pictograms.

Most European alphabets are basically drawn from the earlier Phoenician one. The Phoenicians said that their alphabet was invented by a man named Cadmus, but Cadmus simply means "ancestor." Was this just a way of the Phoenicians saying that someone in ancient times, an ancestor in their national tree, invented writing? Who was this ancestor?

There are other symbols that seem to definitely be writing, that are very ancient as we count time. Some of these symbols, the same symbols, have been found in parts of Europe and in a number of sites in Egypt and China. In Egypt, this primitive form of writing predated the use of the hieroglyphics that the Egyptians later used. The same symbols have been found in Sumer, in caves in France and Spain, in the Balkans in the area drained by the Danube River and, quite surprisingly, in ancient China.

Cuneiform was a system of writing adapted by the Sumerians to the climate in which they lived. They did not have anything resembling paper on which to write. Instead, they developed a system of writing where they pressed wedge shaped

91

pieces of reed into clay. They then let the sun harden the clay and stored the resulting clay tablets. The older form of writing that they had obviously brought with them to Sumer did not have the shapes that reeds provided, so those symbols were mostly dropped.

It has been suggested that there must have been some very early contact between China and Sumer, for them to have begun writing using such similar letters. That is not necessarily so, at least the early contact could not have occurred through travel, but simply through their ancestors being in the same place at the same time. They and all the other peoples who seem to have used this system of writing could have learned it at the source where it was first used, whether that was the pre-flood world or in the early days after the flood.

In 1912, the famous archaeologist Flinders Petrie challenged the then prevalent idea about the origin of the alphabet in Egypt. (Moran and Kelley, p.3) Petrie pointed out the discovery of many similar signs in other lands and the possibility that those signs did not originate in Egypt. Our alphabet is supposed to have come originally from the Phoenicians.

In 1953, Hugh A. Moran developed the idea that the letters in the alphabet are based on the signs of a lunar zodiac of the Old World. (Moran, Gordon, p.94-95) David H. Kelley came up with the idea that New World zodiacs were related to those of the Old World. Moran and Kelley, in their stunning 1953 book, "The Alphabet and the Ancient Calendar Signs," presented a vast body of evidence suggesting that the Chinese system of writing and the alphabet were both inspired by an ancient twenty-eight sectioned lunar zodiac, or calendar, which Moran believed was Chaldean in origin. The book created a lot of excitement, but also generated opposition, as the ideas in it stirred a lot of controversy.

Flinders Petrie, Moran, Kelly and Seyffarth, all agreed that our alphabet was originally a reproduction of the zodiac. Seyffarth also thought the alphabet was aligned with the constellation of the planets at a point in time of 3446 B.C. He used the chronology of the Septuagint, which is slightly different from our present chronology. Seyffarth thought this alignment occurred at the end of the flood, possibly made according to the observation of Noah himself.

Seyffarth translated Phoenician, Chinese, Chaldean, Greek, and Roman myths which clearly related the formulation of the alphabet to the zodiac (Seyffarth, 1886, p.53-54).

There are a number of other sources of good information on the above topics. While none of these sources cover all of the topics above, they are still very informative.

Some of them are:

Petrie, William Flinders, "The Formation of The Alphabet," London, MacMillan and Company, 1912

Santillana, Georgio De, and Von Dechend, Hertha, "Hamlet's Mill," Boston, Gambit Inc., 1929

Sino-Platonic Papers, #196, 2009. On the Origins of the Alphabet

Pellar, Brian, http://sino-platonic.org/complete/spp196_alphabet, pdf June 16, 2014

Correspondences Between the Chinese Calendar Signs and the Phoenician Alphabet, by Julie Lee Wei, in the Sino-Platonic Papers

Early Contacts Between Indo-Europeans and Chinese, by Victor Mair, "The Columbia Anthology of Traditional Chinese Literature," Columbia University Press, 1996. p.35

"The Races of Europe," by William Z. Ripley, New York, D. Appleton & Company, 1899

"Sign, Symbol and Script," by Hans Jensen, G. P. Putnam and Sons, New York, 1969

"The Alphabet and the Ancient Calendar Signs," by Hugh A. Moran & David H. Kelley, Palo Alto, Calif., Daily Press, copyright 1969

We also have to wonder if the first great architectural achievement after the flood, the Tower of Babel, used ideas which came from before the flood. We do know that ancient people had a tremendous knowledge of mathematics and astronomy, and a number of accounts from ancient times say that much of this knowledge came from the world before the flood.

We know little from either legends or the Bible about the scientific advances before the flood. The only object other than cities that we know was built before the flood was the Ark. The Ark was the size of one of the great luxury liners of the early 1900s. The statement was made in 1869 that the ark was larger than any ship that had been built, up to and including that time. (Victoria Institute, "Faith and Thought," vol. 3, p.10).

We are also told in Genesis, chapter 6, verse 16, that God commanded Noah to put a "tsohar" in the Ark. Most translations refer to it as a window, but the meaning is actually "a light" and it can also mean something that is "dual." (Strong's New Exhaustive Concordance, number 6672 - tsohar – a light, dual, i.e. noon - midday, noonday) The word "tsohar" comes from another Hebrew word which means to "glisten." Many interpret this to mean that God commanded Noah to put a glistening dual object in the Ark, and that this object was comparable in brightness to the noonday sun. St. Jerome, in his commentary on Genesis, says that in the Hebrew, it states that you shall make a "noonday" for the Ark. (Jerome, p.38) Was this really some type of very bright artificial light, or was it in reality only a window? There was a window in the Ark (Genesis chapter 8, verse 6), but the word for this is "challown," which means a window, or a perforation or opening that can be used as a window. This word is used repeatedly in the Old Testament for window.

One piece of rabbinical literature states that during the time that Noah was in the Ark, "he had no need for the light of the sun by day nor for the light of the moon by night." Rather, he had a precious stone which he suspended from the ceiling of the Ark. "When the stone dimmed, he knew it was day, and when it glowed brightly, he knew that it was night." (Neusner, p.323).

It was perhaps with uncanny insight that historian Will Durant wrote, "Immense volumes have been written to expound our knowledge, and conceal our ignorance of primitive man, primitive cultures were not necessarily the ancestors of our own, for all we know they may be the degenerate remnants of higher cultures." (Landsburg, p.161).

There have been a number of unusual historical and archaeological discoveries made over the years at different places around the world. There are manmade artifacts that have been found where they shouldn't be, and their existence has never been adequately explained. Just two of those discoveries will be mentioned here.

An archaeologist, Dragoslav Srejovic, made a most unusual find in 1965, at a site now called Starcevo, on the Danube River. Excavating at this site on the Yugoslavian and Rumanian border, the first thing to be excavated was traces of a Roman road; beneath this were fragments of proto-Greek pottery, and below these were traces of Stone Age artifacts. Excavating yet deeper, something totally unexpected was found, the remains of a cement floor. Stone Age people were not supposed to have the knowledge to make concrete, yet they obviously did. There were actually many cement floors in the immediate area. It soon became plain that this had once been the site of a town in the Stone Age or before. The cement floors had been laid and then houses had been built on them. (Noorbergen, pp.159-60) Whether the town with the houses with concrete floors only dated back to the Stone Age, or whether it went back to before the flood is anybody's guess. What is your guess?

The Scientific American of June, 1851, Vol. 7, p.298, mentions a metallic vase that had been dynamited out of solid rock on Meeting House Hill in Dorchester, Massachusetts. The report described "a bell-shaped vessel, 4 1/2 inches high, 6 l/2 inches at the base, 2 1/2 inches at the top and about an eighth of an inch in thickness. The body of the vessel resembles zinc in color, or a composition metal in which there is a considerable portion of silver. On the sides, there are six figures; a flower, a bouquet, that are beautifully inlaid with pure silver, and around the lower part of the vessel, a vine or wreath, inlaid also with silver. The chasing, carving and inlaying are exquisitely done by the art of some cunning craftsman. This curious and unknown vessel was blown out of the solid pudding stone, fifteen feet below the surface."

The Creation Evidence Museum at Glen Rose, Texas owns a metal hammer that is imbedded in a piece of rock. The petrified wooden handle is broken, but part of the handle is still in place. This tool was discovered in June of 1936, near London, Texas, by Frank and Emma Hahn. The hammer head is 6.25 inches long, and the portion of the handle that remains is 4.25 inches long. Battelle Laboratories, the same laboratories that analyzed the moon rocks, analyzed this artifact as well. They found that the hammer head was 96.6% iron, 0.74% sulphur, and 2.6% chlorine. The only problem with this is that no one today can combine metallic iron with chlorine. To make a metal hammer head containing both iron and chlorine would require technology which we do not have. It would however be possible if the atmospheric pressure was greater than it is today. (Some of this information was obtained on a visit to the Creation Evidence Museum at Glen Rose, Texas, see also, Heffner, Heffner, and Baugh, p.30). In regard to this, you will recall that before the flood the earth's atmospheric pressure was nearly twice what it is today. (Baugh, p.56-57).

We have been taught to believe that early mankind lived in caves and had a very low intelligence, evolving over a long period of time to a higher degree of intelligence. If that is true then it would be logical to believe that early man had no scientific knowledge, that we began in a Stone Age type of existence and that only gradually did we begin to advance scientifically. However, science does not appear to have begun at a low state and to have only gradually evolved to what it is today. Rather, it appears that science evolved to great heights in the roughly 1,500 years before the flood, quickly rose again to great heights as population expanded after the flood, sank to a low level after the dispersion of the various ethnic groups at the Tower, began gradually rising again until suffering a setback with the barbarian invasions of Europe and the fall of Rome, and from that point to this has gradually risen once more. We do not know the heights to which civilization rose before the flood, but by all the evidence it was much higher than we have been taught. As to the civilization that existed between the flood and the Dispersion at the Tower, we must remember that knowledge of the pre-flood inventions would have been carried over to the post-flood world by the eight survivors on the Ark. It has been shown that very small and isolated populations do not produce inventions and innovations, rather they lose those they may have previously known. In an often-hostile environment, very small populations must concentrate on survival. In doing so, they discard and in time lose the knowledge of inventions and technological advancements they were once familiar with. Rock carvings in Africa show black men hunting with bows and arrows, yet they do not use nor even make bows and arrows today. The reason is that in most of Black Africa hunting is much easier with short throwing spears. Therefore, over time bows and arrows were discarded in favor of short hunting spears and now, today, the natives of that region no longer even make bows and arrows.

Likewise, in the mountain regions of Southeast Asia, the native tribes have a word in their language for boat, but they no longer make boats nor do they recall how they were made. Not being useful in the mountains, boats were first not made and then in time the very means of making them was forgotten.

## Away Up In Heaven

Away up in heaven,
I'm longing to be,
Where Gods' beauty and glory,
Unfold treasures to see,
Where the sweet scent of heaven,
Is fragrant and free,
In that land that's so high above me,

Away up in heaven,
It fills all the air,
The fragrance of incense,
That we call prayer,
Where all is glorious,
Wondrous and fair,
In that land that's so high above me,

I welcome each day,
For it is bathed in the light,
Of Christ's soon return,
Just as day follows night,
And I yearn for the songs,
Of the angels in flight,
As they circle above this earth, every night,

Heaven is just as close as a prayer,
Praise and worship,
Like wings, will carry us there,
Where all is beautiful,
Shining and fair,
Praise and worship,
Like wings, will carry us there,
Far away,
Yet so near and so fair,

Praise and worship,
Like wings, will carry us there,
Where the sweet scent of heaven,
Is fragrant and fair,
In that land that's so high above me.

- Dr. N. James Brooks, Jr.

*"There is a God shaped vacuum in the heart of every man*
*which cannot be filled by any created thing,*
*but only by God, the Creator, made known through Jesus"*

-    Blaise Paschal

# Chapter Six
# And the flood Swept Over the World

"The destruction of well-nigh the whole human race in an early age of the world's history, by a great deluge, appears to have so impressed the minds of the few survivors, and seems to have been handed down to their children, in consequence, with such terror-struck impressiveness, that their remote descendants of the present day have not even yet forgotten it. It appears in almost every mythology, and lives in the most distant countries, and among the most barbarous tribes." (Montgomery, p.23).

"The myth of a great flood which annihilates all humankind, leaving only a man and a woman who become the ancestors of all ethnic groups, is encountered in one or another form in virtually every part of the world" (Dang, p.304).

"There are many descriptions of the remarkable event (the flood). Some of these have come from Greek historians, some from the Babylonian records; others from the cuneiform tablets (of Mesopotamia)], and still others from the mythology and traditions of different nations, so that we may say that no event has occurred either in ancient or modern times about which there is better evidence or more numerous records, than this very one . . . It is one of the events which seems to be familiar to the most distant nations — in Australia, in India, in China, in Scandinavia, and in the various parts of America (Peet, p.203).

"Accounts of the flood exist everywhere in Polynesia, and are similar enough to the account in the Bible to merit attention" (Ellis, p.386).

"No tradition has been more widely spread among nations than that of a Deluge. It was the received notion, under some form or other, of the most civilized people in the Old World, and of the barbarians of the New World." (Prescott, p.581).

"Among all the traditions which concern the history of primitive humanity, the most universal is that of the Deluge" Lenormant, p.226). The story of the flood is "a universal tradition among all branches of the human race with the one exception of the black" (race) (Dod, quoting Lenormant, "Genesis," pp.33-34). (Lenormant is here speaking only of the Black tribes that live in Africa, for the Black tribes of the Pacific do have legends of the flood.)

Henry H. Howorth was a geologist who spent much time studying the evidences for the flood. He did not believe the Bible was divinely inspired. He was decidedly hostile to that idea. Even so, he declared that when the same traditions were found among many widely separately peoples, peoples between whom there had been no contact whatever, this was a suggestion that those traditions might be true. One of these traditions, he said, was the flood. Howorth felt that this common tradition, shared by many different people groups, suggested that something like the great flood had occurred in the past. (Nelson, pp.117-118).

The Bible says this about the flood, in Genesis chapter 7, "And God saw that the wickedness of man was great in the earth, and that every imagination of the thoughts of his heart was continually evil. And it repented the Lord that he had made man on the earth, and it grieved him at his heart. And the Lord said, I will destroy man whom I have created from the face of the earth; both man, and beast, and the creeping things, and the fowls of the air." The next verse, however, says that "Noah found grace in the eyes of the Lord." Verse 9 continues by saying, "Noah was a just man and perfect in his generation, and Noah walked with God.

Then we are told of God telling Noah that He intends to destroy mankind and everything on the earth that breathes.

However, God gives Noah specific instructions about a ship that he is to build. In this ship, Noah, his wife, their three sons and their son's wives, along with some of every kind of bird and animal will be saved.

In the seventh chapter of Genesis, we are told in verses 1 through 6:

*"And the Lord said unto Noah, Come thou and all thy house into the ark; for thee have I seen righteous before me in this generation. Of every clean beast thou shalt take to thee by sevens, the male and his female: and of beasts that are not clean by two, the male and his female. Of fowls also of the air by sevens, the male and the female; to keep seed alive upon the face of all the earth. For yet seven days, and I will cause it to rain upon the earth forty days and forty nights; and every living substance that I have made will I destroy from off the face of the earth. And Noah did according unto all that the Lord commanded him. And Noah was six hundred years old when the flood of waters was upon the earth.*

Genesis chapter 7:7-24 states,

*And Noah went in, and his sons, and his wife, and his sons' wives with him, into the ark, because of the waters of the flood. Of clean beasts, and of beasts that are not clean, and of fowls, and of every thing that creepith upon the earth, there went in two and two unto Noah into the ark, the male and the female, as God had commanded Noah. 10 And it came to pass after seven days, that the waters of the flood were upon the earth. 11 In the six hundredth year of Noah's life, in the second month, the seventeenth day of the month, the same day were all the fountains of the great deep broken up, and the windows of heaven were opened. 12 And the rain was upon the earth forty days and forty nights. 13 In the selfsame day entered Noah, and Shem, and Ham, and Japheth, the sons of Noah, and Noah's wife, and the three wives of his sons with them, into the ark; 14 they, and every beast after his kind, and all the cattle after their kind, and every creeping thing that creepith upon the earth after his kind, and every fowl after his kind, every bird of every sort. 15 And they went in unto Noah into the ark, two and two of all flesh, wherein is the breath of life. 16 And they that went in, went in male and female of all flesh, as God had commanded him: and the Lord shut him in. 17 And the flood was forty days upon the earth; and the waters increased, and bare up the ark, and it was lift up above the earth. And the waters prevailed, and were increased greatly upon the earth; and the ark went upon the face of the waters. 19 And the waters prevailed exceedingly upon the earth; and all the high hills, that were under the whole heaven, were covered. Fifteen cubits upward did the waters prevail; and the mountains were covered. 21 And all flesh died that moved upon the earth, both of fowl, and of cattle, and of beast, and of every creeping thing that creepith upon the earth, and every man: 22 all in whose nostrils was the breath of life, of all that was in the dry land, died. 23 And every living substance was destroyed which was upon the face of the ground, both man, and cattle, and the creeping things, and the fowl of the heaven; and they were destroyed from the earth: and Noah only remained alive, and they that were with him in the ark. And the waters prevailed upon the earth an hundred and fifty days.*

Josephus, writing in detail about the flood and Noah's preparation for it, after mentioning how Cain and all his descendants were extremely wicked, had the following to say about the descendants of Seth.

*Now this posterity of Seth continued to esteem God as the Lord of the universe, and to have an entire regard to virtue, for seven generations; but in process of time they were perverted, and forsook the practices of their forefathers; and did neither pay those honors to God which were appointed them, nor had they*

*any concern to do justice towards men. But for what degree of
zeal they had formerly shown for virtue, they now showed by
their actions a double degree of wickedness, whereby they made
God to be their enemy. For many angels of God accompanied (in
our terminology they mean sexual relations) with women, and
begat sons that proved unjust, and despisers of all that was good,
on account of the confidence they had in their own strength; for
the tradition is, that these men did what resembled the acts of
those whom the Grecians call giants. But Noah was very uneasy
at what they did; and being displeased at their conduct,
persuaded them to change their dispositions and their acts for the
better: but seeing they did not yield to him, but were slaves to
their wicked pleasures, he was afraid they would kill him,
together with his wife and children, and those they had married;
so he departed out of that land (Josephus, p.43).*

Josephus further tells us,

*Now God loved this man (Noah) for his righteousness: yet he not
only condemned those other men for their wickedness, but
determined to destroy the whole race of mankind, and to make
another race that should be pure from wickedness; and cutting
short their lives, and making their years not so many as they
formerly lived, but one hundred and twenty only, he turned the
dry land into sea; and thus were all these men destroyed: but
Noah alone was saved; for God suggested to him the following
contrivance and way of escape; that he should make an ark of
four stories high, three hundred cubits  long, fifty cubits broad,
and thirty cubits high. (In a footnote, we are informed that a
cubit is 21 inches.) Accordingly he entered into that ark, and his
wife, and sons, and their wives, and put into it not only other
provisions, to support their wants there, but also sent in with the
rest all sorts of living creatures, the male and his female, for the
preservation of their kinds; and others of them by sevens. Now
this ark had firm walls, and a roof, and was braced with cross*

*beams, so that it could not be in any way drowned or overborne by the violence of the water. And thus was Noah, with his family, preserved. Now he was the tenth generation from Adam, as being the son of Lamech, whose father was Mathuselah; he was the son of Enoch, the son of Jared; and Jared was the son of Malaleel, who, with many of his sisters, were the children of Cainan, the son of Enos. Now Enos was the son of Seth, the son of Adam. (Josephus, pp.43-44)*

*This calamity happened in the six hundredth year of Noah's government, age, in the second month, (Josephus, pp.44).*

Josephus further wrote, "Now all the writers of barbarian histories make mention of this flood, and of this Ark." Among them Josephus mentions Berosus, and quoted Berosus as describing the circumstances of the flood, and as writing 'It is said there is still some part of this ship in Armenia.' (Josephus, p.44-45).

The great German naturalist Baron Alexander Von Humbolt (1769-1859) penetrated far into the interior of South America, along the Orinoco River, in search of tribes that had had no contact with Europeans. Even among such tribes he found legends of the flood. (Montgomery, p.24).

There is a large collection of flood stories to be found in Sir James G. Frazer's book, "Folklore in the Old Testament," (1919), Vol. 1, pp. 146-330. There are a total of 143 flood stories from all parts of the world in his book.

There is so much evidence of a world-wide flood that there are scientists, who, while they may not believe in the Bible, do not deny that the flood took place. "There are, of course, flood stories in almost every folklore" (Ceram, p.276).

Scientist Rhodes Whitmore Fairbridge made the following statement in the Scientific American: "A deluge such as is described in the Book of Genesis occurs in the legends and folklore of almost every ancient people. Such agreement among the legends of so many peoples living in distant parts of the world has caused scholars in modern times to wonder whether mankind did, in truth, experience the worldwide catastrophe of a deluge" (Fairbridge, p.70).

Henry H. Howorth admitted that there are traditions of a great flood to be found among "widely separated peoples, between whom there has been no intercourse (i.e. no communication)" Nelson, p.117).

The ancient Greeks had different names and different places of origin for Noah, depending on which part of Greece or which Greek city you visited. The best known of the Greek names for Noah was Deucalion (Lenormant, p241), which means "New Wine Sailor," and of course the book of Genesis tells us that after the flood, Noah made and drank wine. (Wine was unknown before the flood, due to the different atmospheric conditions.) The flood involving Deucalion was, along with the flood legend of Ogyges, the principal flood legend of Greece. (Lenormant, p.241).

In Syria, and in parts of what is today Turkey, Noah was often called Noe. (Nelson, p.176). The Phrygian city of Apamea, a city in today's Turkey, caused coins to be struck that showed the ark with a man and a woman inside, with a dove bearing an olive branch flying towards them. The obverse side of this coin showed the couple leaving the ark. On the ark is the single word, Noe. (Lenormant, p.245).

The Sumerians called him Ziusudra, which is the name Berosus used for him. Berosus wrote the Babylonian account of the flood around the time of Alexander the Great. The name Ziusudra is often seen in its Greek form, Xisuthros. (Nelson, p.173). He was the king-priest of the city of Shuruppak. His name is sometimes seen as Ziusuddu. His name means "Life Days

Prolonged" or "Length of Days." Whatever he was called, the event and his part in it were the same. There was a great flood that covered the earth, and Noah and his wife, or Noah, his wife, and their family, were saved through a boat he had made. (Bryant, Vol. II, p.23).

Just as Noah, his wife, and their three sons and three daughters-in-law made eight people who were saved in the Ark, so in ancient Egypt there was a sacred object which consisted of a boat with the figures of eight people in it. They were described as the eight people who survived the flood. They were also referred to as the oldest gods of Egypt. (Bryant, Vol. III, p.9). There was also a custom in ancient times in Egypt that was practiced during the annual flood of the Nile River. They took, out of the temples, a boat with the figures of eight people in it. These figures were said to represent the Eight, the most ancient gods of Egypt. (Bryant, vol. III, p.9).

One of the most ancient complete maps of the constellations **is** found in the Temple of Hathor at Dendera, Egypt. It shows a map of the sky with the constellations reproduced in the Mazzaroth, or zodiacal circle. The symbol of the Ogdoad or "Group of Eight" (representing the eight persons saved in the Ark of Noah) is also shown. (Rolleston, Mazzaroth, Part Four, Astrology of the Ancients, last page, but unnumbered). It is shown as an oval with eight persons within it, four male and four females. They were said to have emerged out of the waters of Chaos and founded the regenerated world. After the flood, they appeared on the peak of a mountain which projected out of the waters. All the primeval rulers of Egypt traced their descent from them.

The Chinese in their early legends describe the earth as once being totally covered with water. (Jones, vol. ii., p.376). The Chinese also told of eight people being saved from the great flood that covered all the land. Sir William Jones declared: "The

Chinese, like the Hindus, believe the earth to have been wholly covered with water, which, in works of undisputed authenticity, they describe as flowing abundantly, then subsiding and separating the higher from the lower age of mankind; that the division of time, from which their poetical history begins, just preceded the appearance of Fu-hi on the mountains of Chin. (Jones, "Asiatic Researches," Vol. II. Discourse on the Chinese, p.376. quoted in Sacred Annals: or Researches Into the History and Religion of Mankind, vol.1, 4th Edition, George Smith, Carlton & Porter, New York, p.285,) Fu-hi is the first of the legendary first ten emperors of China (Campbell, p.411). Nineteenth-century Western scholars generally agreed with the Chinese that these legendary rulers were actual monarchs. (Campbell, p.383). According to the Chinese account, Fu-hi escaped the flood, accompanied by his wife, their three sons and three daughters. (Nelson, p.181). In this regard, it is interesting to note that traditionally, in China, when a girl married into a family, she was considered and treated as a daughter. Thus, the idea that Fu-hi had three sons and three daughters could mean that his three sons were married to the three women described as Fu-hi's daughters, which would put the Chinese version of the flood even more in line with that of the Bible.

Versions of the flood story come from Greek historians, from Assyria, from Babylonian records; from the cuneiform tablets of Sumer, from China, India, the Aztecs, Toltecs, and still other versions from many other nations, so that "We may say that no event has occurred either in ancient or modern times about which there is better evidence or more numerous records, than this one. It is one of the events which seems to be familiar to the most distant nations; in Australia, in India, in China, in Scandinavia, and in the various parts of America" (Peet, p.203.)

Literally hundreds of legends of a worldwide flood exist. One researcher of flood stories, James Perloff, wrote of some 250 flood legends that he was familiar with (Perloff, p.167). Other researchers mention hundreds more flood stories. (Baugh, p.72) Although the large number of such legends should be proof in and of itself that a worldwide deluge occurred, the similarities between most of the stories is equally impressive. Speaking of the some 250 flood legends that he had studied, Perloff writes that in 95 percent of them, the flood was worldwide; in 88 percent, a certain family was favored; in 70 percent, survival was by means of a boat; in 67 percent, animals were also saved; in 66 percent, the flood was due to the wickedness of man; in 66 percent, the survivors had been forewarned; in 57 percent, they ended up on a mountain; in 35 percent, birds were sent out from the boat; and in 9 percent, exactly eight people were spared (Perloff, p.168).

Ovid was a famous Roman poet who was born in 43 B.C. In his epic poem "Metamorphoses," he speaks about the flood, saying that blinding rain came down from heaven, ruining the crops. Next the seas rose and the springs poured forth water. Upon this happening, the rivers rose until everything on the earth was swept away, all mankind drowned, the birds and animals gradually tiring and drowning, until only limitless water remained. Deucalion, the name of this Greek flood hero, and his wife, in a raft, reached the heights of Mount Parnassus, the top of which remained above water. (Ovid, pp.9-10). Now compare Ovid's account of the flood with the following account kept alive orally by the Miao.

The Miao are a people who live in southern China near the border with Burma. The Miao tell that mankind grew so wicked that they ceased to return God's love or to live good lives. God therefore sent the flood to destroy them. There was one couple however, Nuah and his wife Gaw Bo-luen, who were righteous. Nuah and his three sons built a very big boat. In the boat, they put food and two of each kind of animal. When the flood waters began to subside, Nuah sent out a dove from the ark to learn if there was any dry land. Nuah and his family then sacrificed animals to God. "Their God then bestowed his good graces." (Truax, April 5, 2005).

The Miao have been scattered for centuries, with some settled in different parts of China, and other groups living in Southeast Asia. A different version of the flood story told by a different tribe of Miao, tells how a brother and sister escaped the flood waters in a large wooden drum and how all post flood humanity is descended from them. (Bernatzik, pp.302-306).

The Maya Indians, who live in Guatemala and the Yucatan Peninsular, dated their calendar from the flood. They believed that the world had once been destroyed by a flood, and would be destroyed again at a future date by fire. ("The Popul Vuh," p.19).

Studying the various accounts of the flood which exist around the world, the only logical explanation is that the story of the flood is the universal recollection of an event that occurred, and in which all mankind was concerned. The Jewish historian, Flavius Josephus, calculated that Noah's flood occurred 1556 years after the creation of Adam. By adding the ages of the patriarchs in the Bible at the time they had their first mentioned son, you yourself will come up with a roughly similar date. Archbishop James Ussher, of Ireland, calculated that the creation of the world took place in 4004 BC. If 1556 is deducted from 4004 then the worldwide flood of Noah's time was around 2448 B.C. Scholars disagree slightly on some of the dates. But most agree that the flood took place between 2500 BC and 2300 BC. This is in line with the flood date given by the Toltecs, a civilized nation once living in central Mexico. They said the flood came 1,716 years after Creation, as they counted time (Nelson, p.187).

Some of the Authorities Quoted In This Chapter

Baugh, Carl E. - Founder and Director of Creation Evidence Museum, Glen Rose, Texas

Scientific Research Director for world's first Hyperbaric Biosphere

Scientific Research Director for water reclamation and energized plant systems

Discoverer and Excavation Director of fourteen dinosaurs, including

Acrocanthosaurus in Texas and Diplodocus in Colorado

Co-discoverer and co-excavator of a unique South American ammonite that has not been described in the technical literature. Dr. Baugh is also the author of a number of books. This information was obtained mainly from the website:

http://www.creationevidence.org/about_us/directors_bio.php

Montgomery, John Warwick. - Professor of Law and Humanities at the University of Luton, England, and Director of its Human Rights Centre. He annually conducts the University's International Seminar in Jurisprudence and Human Rights in Strasbourg, France. He is also admitted to practice as a lawyer before the Supreme Court of the United States. Professor Montgomery holds eight earned degrees besides the L.L.B.: the A.B. with distinction in Philosophy (Cornell University; Phi Beta Kappa), B.L.S. and M.A. (University of California at Berkeley), B.D. and S.T.M. (Wittenberg University, Springfield, Ohio), M. Phil. in Law (University of Essex, England), Ph.D. (University of Chicago), and a further doctorate from the University of Strasbourg, France. He is Emeritus Professor of Law and Humanities, University of Bedfordshire, England, Distinguished Research Professor of Apologetics and Christian Thought, Patrick

Henry College, Virginia, U.S.A., and Director, International Academy of Apologetics, Evangelism & Human Rights, Strasbourg, France. His legal specialty is the international and comparative law of human rights. He is a U.S. and U.K. citizen, the author of some forty books in five languages, and is included in Who's Who in America, Who's Who in France, the European Biographical Directory, Who's Who in the World, and Contemporary Authors. (Much of this information was taken from Dr. Montgomery's website. http://www.jwm.christendom.co.uk/).

### We Are Walking In The Sunlight

All around us night is falling and the darkness grows apace,
Yet still the light is shining, bright as ever shone upon one's face,
We are walking in the sunlight, waiting the coming of the day,
The dawning of the glory that will drive the night away,

The coming reign of the only King whose reign will never end,
And the dawning of the glory that was before creation did begin,
We are walking in the sunlight that never will retreat,
We are basking in the glory that will never know defeat,

We are waiting for the dawning of the new world made for man,
Where God alone is sovereign and sin is banished from the land,
So though the darkness gathers and the trumpets sound retreat,
We know only victory awaits us, for our God knows no defeat,

-    Dr. N. James Brooks, Jr.

# CHAPTER SEVEN
# Various flood Stories From
# Around The World

Would you like to read a tiny handful of the hundreds of flood stories that abound throughout the earth? There are many hundreds of stories of a world-wide flood. In most of them either one man, or one man and his wife, are saved. The man's name is often not given. When it is given it is sometimes very similar in pronunciation to Noah.

Though there are hundreds of flood stories, most of them are so much like that, it would be tedious and boring to tell more than a few of them. Therefore, we will limit ourselves to only a handful of the flood stories, making sure that we tell some from all parts of the earth and that we describe some of the more unique and interesting ones.

Sumer, or Shinar, is the name of the civilization that grew up in southern Iraq after the flood. Our earliest written version of the flood story comes from Sumer. The name of the Sumerians for Noah was Atrahasis, which means "Exceedingly Devout." After the flood, his name was changed to Ut-napistim, which roughly means "He Found Life." This was the name by which the Babylonians knew him. It has been suggested that the name Noah may be found in the second syllable of Ut-na-pishtim, which according to some early scholars, such as C.J. Ball, should be pronounced as Nua. Still others have thought that instead of the first syllable being pronounced ut, it should be read as Nuh, making the name Nuh-na-pishtim. Nuh would be pronounced like Noah. (Rohl, p.46).

Among people living in the lands to the east of the Greeks, Noah was commonly called Noas, Nus, or Nuos . . . ." (Bryant, Vol.I, edition of 1807, p.13) Over two centuries before Christ, the city of Apamaea, in what is now Turkey, had coins minted showing Noah and the ark. Some of these coins still exist. On one side of each coin is a box like object with a man and woman looking out through a window. There is a dove flying towards them carrying an olive branch. The other side of the coin shows Noah and his wife leaving the Ark. On the Ark appears the word Noah which in Greek is spelled Noe. (Nelson, p.176)

One early Greek writer told how for a long-time people wherever they migrated named cities and towns after Noah. The people of India in particular were said to have named cities in Noah's memory. (Bryant, edition of 1807, vol.1, p.13 & pp.18-19)

From Wales comes the flood story of the Druids. It tells of Lake Ilion, meaning the "lake of waves" or the ocean, bursting its bounds and flooding the whole world. (Hislop, pp.242-243)

The oldest known Indian version of the flood comes from the Rig Veda, a collection of ancient Hindu poems, hymns, and stories. This legend can be dated earlier than the 9th century B.C. (Nelson, p.182) In the Rig Veda, a man named Manu also called Monu, built a boat and saved himself and seven companions from a worldwide flood. Monu is referred to as being "satya" which means righteous. The god who saved these people was Vishnu, whose name is the Sanskrit form of the Chaldean name Ish-Nuh, which is also Noah's name, as all three names (Ish-Nuh, Vishnu, and Noah, mean "man of rest." (Hislop, p.135)

The Sagaiye, people who live in eastern Siberia, say that God told a man named Noj to build a ship. Noj, his wife and family and all kinds of animals were saved when the flood came. (Holmberg, p.362)

From Lifou, one of the Loyalty Islands in the Pacific, comes a story of how the natives laughed at an old man named Nol because he was making a canoe far inland. He insisted that he would need no help getting it to the sea. He said the sea would come to meet his canoe. When he had finished building it, "rain fell in torrents, flooding the island and drowning everybody." Nol's canoe was lifted by the water and carried out to sea. (Gaster, p.107)

It is worthy of mentioning that some of the hieroglyphic inscriptions of Egypt call the god of water by the name of Noh, or No. This was the god who presided over the annual Nile flood, a title which plainly relates to some recollection of Noah presiding triumphantly over the flood. (Titcomb, September 2, 2005) The Egyptian historian, Manetho, who lived in the 3rd century B.C., also stated in his history of Egypt that there had once been a world-wide flood. (Nelson, p.177)

A flood legend told by the Nahau people of Mexico has Noah being called "Nata." He was instructed, by the Supreme God, to make a boat by hollowing out a cypress tree, so as to escape the coming flood with his wife Nena. (Mackenzie, p.198, see also Bancroft's "Native Races," vol. 3, p.69-70)

2 Peter 2:5 says,

*"God spared not the old world, but saved Noah, the eighth person, a preacher of righteousness, bringing in the flood upon the world of the ungodly."* Noah was one of eight people saved from the flood.

A few flood stories, such as the one from India, state that only eight people were saved in the flood. Two such flood stories are related here. One is from the Fiji Islands, which are located in the Pacific Ocean. The Fiji Islanders preserve a recollection of only one family, eight people in all, who alone were saved from the flood in a canoe. (Rawlinson, p.20)

The Chinese in their early legends describe the earth as once being totally covered with water. Associated with this flood is a man called Niu-va. (Jones, p.376) Byron Nelson says that the Hihking, he probably means the Shan Hai King, in an ancient Chinese classic compiled from even more ancient texts by Confucius, calls Noah "Fu-hi," and says that he, his wife, and his three sons and three daughters, eight people in all, were all saved from the flood, with Fu-hi becoming the first man of the post flood world. (Nelson, p.181) The Hihking also states that it was Fu-hi's three daughters who were saved. In the Chinese culture, when a girl marries into a family, she is considered a daughter, and that is what she is called. Therefore, when the story quoted above says that Fu-hi's three sons and three daughters repopulated the earth, it is probably daughters-in-law that it is referring to, rather than meaning that his sons married their sisters. An ancient temple in China has a wall painting that shows Fu-hi's boat in the raging waters of the flood. A dove with an olive branch in its beak is flying towards the boat. (Nelson, p.181-182)

In pre-Christian times, there were stories in different parts of Greece of a great world-wide flood. In each case the counterpart of Noah had a different name, according to the area or island of Greece where the story was told. (Donnelly, pp.90-91) The best known of these Greek stories and the name they most commonly used for Noah is that of Deucalion. (Donnelly, p.90) Bryant, in his Analysis of Ancient Mythology, page 21-23, mentions one of the historians of classical Greece who speaks of the flood as being worldwide, and as saying that "almost all flesh died." (Bryant, Vol. III, 1807. p.21) In some of the ancient Greek states the people would follow in processions a model of the ark of Deucalion. (Donnelly, p.111)

Of the ancient flood stories, "none approach so near to the Scripture narrative as Lucian, who, in his account of the Greek traditions, speaks of the Ark, and the pairs of different kinds of animals." (Prescott, p.581) Lucian was a famous Assyrian who wrote in the Greek language, and who lived in the second century after Christ. Lucian states that he heard the story about Deucalion from the Greeks themselves. Lucian relates that the entire earth was flooded, and all men perished. Deucalion and his family alone were saved, because of his wisdom and goodness. He and his family entered the boat he had built, which was of vast size. Some of all the animals of the earth came to him, all in pairs, male and female. They were harmless while on board the ark. They floated together in the ark as long as the flood remained. This, said Lucian, is the legend of Deucalion as told by the Greeks. (Lucian, pp.50-51)

The name Deucalion means "New Wine Sailor." This causes one to think of Noah, who was known for the discovery of wine. Wine was unknown until after the flood. The atmosphere of the earth before the flood was such that grape juice could not ferment. Another form of the name, Deucalion is Sisythes. That name is found in use in northern Syria at the city of Hierapolis, where there was a temple to honor him. (Nelson, p.175) Sisythes is a Greek corruption of the Chaldean name for Noah or Xisouthros.

According to Philo of Alexandria, a famous Jewish writer who lived around the time of Christ, said "the Chaldeans recognized that Noah and Xisouthros were one and the same person." Philo further relates "the Grecians call the person Deucalion, but the Chaldeans or Babylonians, called him Noe; in whose time there happened the great eruption of waters." (Bryant, 1807 ed. vol. III, p.23) Bryant adds that the Chaldeans likewise mention Noah by the name of Xisouthros. (Bryant, 1807 ed., vol. III, p.23)

A legend common among central Asian people who speak the Altaic language relates that there was once a good man named Nama, who had three sons. The god Ülgen commanded Nama to build a large boat. Nama entered the boat with his family and various animals and birds. After floating on the water for a time, the boat stopped in a group of mountains. On successive days Nama released a raven, a crow, and a rook, none of which returned. On the fourth day, he sent out a dove, which returned with a birch branch. (Holmberg, pp.364).

Polynesia is an area that covers most of the South Pacific Ocean. Its name comes from the Greek words poly or many and nesia which means islands. The name thus means many islands. Accounts of the flood exist everywhere in Polynesia and are similar enough to the account in the Bible to merit attention. (Ellis, p.386) One account from the Windward Islands tells of one couple, a man and a woman, who survived the flood along with animals which they had taken into their canoe. They rowed to the highest mountain they could see, where they landed and were safe. They then had children who repopulated the world. (Ellis, p.387-389)

Among the original natives of Cuba, now extinct, there was a legend that long ago an old man learned that a great flood was coming. He built a ship and entered into it with his family and many animals. After the flood was over, he sent out a crow to see if the flood waters had receded. (Montgomery, p.25) When it did not return, he sent out a pigeon, which returned with a branch in its mouth. (Titcomb, J.H., "On the Common Origin of the American Races With Those of The Old World," Faith and Thought, vol. 3, Victoria Institute, 1868. p.140).

Ixtililxochitl, a native Mexican historian and a descendent of the kings of the Toltecs, wrote that after tremendous rains the entire earth was submerged in water to a depth of 15 cubits. The few survivors escaped drowning in the flood by means of a toptlipetlocali, or closed chest. (Donnelly, p.103; see also Nelson, p.187)

The peoples of the New World had an almost universal belief in a worldwide flood. (Rawlinson, p.19) The natives of Mexico had "paintings representing the event, which showed a man and woman in a boat, or on a raft, with a mountain rising above the waters." (Rawlinson, p.19) Indeed, "of the different nations that inhabited Mexico prior to its discovery by the Spaniards, five had paintings representing the great deluge." (Titcomb, J. H., On the Common Origin of the American Races With Those of The Old World, "Faith and Thought," vol. 3, Victoria Institute, 1868. p.140) Paintings of the flood were discovered among the Aztecs, Miztecs, Zapotecs, Tlascaltecs, and Mechoacaneses (Prichard, p.359)

One survey of 120 tribal groups in North, Central, and South America, disclosed flood traditions among each of them. (International Standard Bible Encyclopedia, Vol. 2, p.822) There are two basic types of flood stories in the United States and Canada. One type has two or more people escaping from the flood in a canoe or in a floating building. The other type of flood story usually has one man and a mystical being, a demi-god named "Coyote," alone escaping the flood. The man then generally takes mud and recreates dry land with it. Likewise, he either recreates people, or a spirit or a god changes a bird into a woman, whom the man then marries.

The Pawnee, who live in Nebraska, believe in a Supreme Being whom they call the "Spirit Father." They also tell that there was a race of people previous to ours. This race was so evil that the "Spirit Father" destroyed them in a great flood. (Lang, p.255)

There are some accounts of the flood in North America, however, that are much closer to that of the Bible. A legend heard by a traveler in the Great Lakes region, told by some of the native tribesmen of that area, tells that formerly the father of the Indian tribes lived towards the east, where the sun rises. Having been warned in a dream that a flood was coming that would desolate the earth, he built a raft on which he placed himself and his family, and some of all the animals. After floating on the water for some months, land appeared and he, his family, and the animals disembarked. (Lenormant, p.264).

The flood stories of Central and South America are much more similar to that of the Bible than most of those in North America. Some of the most important of the American flood traditions are those of the more civilized nations of pre-Spanish Mexico, for paintings of the flood, and carvings depicting it existed there before any contact with Europeans. According to these documents, the Noah of the Mexican flood was called by most of the tribes Coxcox, by certain other people's Teocipactli or Tezpi, while by yet others he was called Nota or Nata. He had saved himself, together with his wife, in a ship, or according to other traditions, on a raft. Indeed, "of the different nations that inhabited Mexico prior to its discovery by the Spaniards, five had paintings representing the great deluge" (Titcomb, J. H., On the Common Origin of the American Races With Those of The Old World, "Faith and Thought," vol. 3, Victoria Institute, 1868. p.140 p.822) Paintings of the flood were discovered among the Aztecs, Miztecs, Zapotecs, Tlascaltecs, and Mechoacaneses. (Prichard, p.359) Those who call Noah, Tezpi, say he embarked in a large boat with his wife, his children, several animals, and grain. (Donnelly, p.99) Still another account calls Noah, Nota, and his wife, Nena. (Bancroft, p.69) The Peruvians believed that the rainbow was a sign that the earth would not be again destroyed by a deluge. (Kingsborough, "Mex. Antiq., "vol. viii; as cited by Donnelly, p.99)

Ancient paintings in Mexico often depict a boat floating on the waters of the flood. The boat floats beside a mountain, like the mountain the Biblical Ark landed upon, while the heads of a man and a woman, Coxcox and his wife, are shown in the air above the boat. A dove is also depicted. (Prescott, p.581) At least five Mexican nations, including the Aztecs and the Toltecs, had such paintings. Noah is known to these different nations by such names as Coxcox, Teo-Cipactli, or Tezpi. (Prichard, p.359) His wife is called Xochiquetzatl, and is identified as a woman with two tresses standing up like horns in her hair. (Prichard, p.359) A representation, such as the one described above of the Mexican Noah and his wife beside their ark, is found on an object in Mexico known as the "Calendar Stone." This Calendar Stone is known to have been made in 1478. (Donnelly, p.107) Their children who were born after the flood were given different languages by a dove. (Prichard, p.359) At least one account of a Mexican nation says that the world before the flood was inhabited by giants (Prichard, p.359), just as the Bible states in Genesis chapter 6, verse four.

The Michoacán, one of those Mexican nations, say that the boat in which Tezpi, their Noah, escaped the flood, was filled with various kinds of animals and birds. After the flood waters had receded, a vulture was sent out from the boat, but it stayed to feed on the dead bodies of those who had drowned. A humming-bird was then sent forth, which returned with a twig in its mouth (Prescott, "The Conquest of Mexico," p.582; see also Bancroft, pp.66-67)

Most flood stories are those of people who are not familiar with ships with hulls, or holds. Some of these stories describe the Ark as either a floating building, a building on a raft, or as some type of chest or box with a closed lid. Interestingly enough, the Hebrew word for ark (tebah) does not mean boat. It means a "box," or "chest." In actual fact, the ark was shaped more like a box or a barge than an ocean-going vessel. This was undoubtedly because it was not meant to travel, but only to keep those in it safe until the flood abated and they could leave the Ark. A boat shaped like a barge, a box, or a chest is much less likely to capsize than a regular vessel shaped for travel is. Barges, boxes, and chests have wide flat bottoms, which helps to stabilize them. Ships built for traveling any great distance do not have flat bottoms.

One version of the flood story from Peru says that the flood waters rose above the highest mountain in the world. All created things perished, except for a man and woman who floated in a box. When the flood subsided, the box lodged high on a mountain. (Gaster, p.127) The Thlinkuts, an Indian tribe living along Canada's Pacific coast, have a legend of a flood in which the only survivors escaped in a great floating building. (Bancroft, vol. 5, p.14)

Another flood story, told by the Bahnars, a primitive tribe in the Central Highlands of Vietnam, tells how the rivers swelled until the water reached the sky. The only survivors were a brother and a sister, who were saved in a huge chest. They took with them into the chest a pair of every sort of animal. (Berlitz, p.82) Other accounts of the Bahnar say it was not a chest, but a box). They floated until the flood waters abated and there was dry land again. (Gaster, p.98)

The Toltecs said their ancestors arrived in central Mexico 520 years after the flood, and 2236 years after creation. (Bancroft, Vol.5, fn., p.209) The native Mexican historian, Ixtlilxochitl, gives this as the Toltec legend of the flood: "It is found in the histories of the Toltecs that this age and first world, as they call it, lasted 1716 years; that men were destroyed by tremendous rains and lightning from the sky, and even all the land, without the exception of anything, and the highest mountains, were covered up and submerged in water fifteen cubits deep." They used the word caxtolmolatli to describe the situation. Here he adds that a few escaped this destruction in a "toptlipetlocali;" and that this word, "signifies a closed chest." (Donnelly pp.103-104. citing

Kingsborough's Mexican Antiquities, vol. ix. pp.321-322) A few of the flood stories, like those of China and Peru, mention that a rainbow appeared after the flood. The Peruvian version of the flood tells that the purpose of the rainbow was to assure the survivors that the earth would never again be covered by a flood.

Thus, we see that all over the earth there are not only stories of a great worldwide flood, but also that many of these stories are so much like that of the Bible as to make it a certainty that those stories have a common origin in fact.

*"Happiness is neither without us nor within us.*
*It is in God, both without us and within us."*

- Blaise Paschal

## Each Generation Must Pray and Serve

There is a land called Holland, much of it won from the sea,
Holland has dikes that were built to last, but dikes that must
tended be, For the sea would take the land back, and make it sea
again, The Dutchmen built with hearts of prayer, the Dutchmen
built to last, But the great dikes must tended be, today as in the
past, for if they are not tended, the deep wild sea will win at last.

Long ago, with hearts to serve, our forebears built to last, with
hearts of prayer, they built for us, dikes against the sea, Always
and always, we were warned, nothing untended will last, each
generation must tend and pray, this the warning from the past,
Each generation must tend the dikes with prayer, if freedom is to
last, For the dikes hold the wild sea back, but untended they will
not last.

Centuries passed, and the dikes went more and more untended,
We saw the growing waves, but though many men and women
pleaded, We lay at ease, and gave not the prayer and service that
was needed, For we had no heart to pray or serve – we had no
heart to save, The wealth that was stored up for us, we wasted it
with a wave, All that our forebears bade us believe, we did doubt
or we did deny, Still the dikes held the great sea back, the sea that
would cover all, Our forebears strove to serve and to pray, their
works did never fall, The wild sea is the mass of ungodly nations,
jealous and willing to wrong, Nothing we give them will satisfy,
no compromise will help us long, Each should work for what he
has, to take from others is always wrong, But those who pour in
among us would take and keep our land.

The dikes were built to keep those out who do not share our past,
Who care not for our culture, who do not wish to see it last, The
wild sea that cares not for service, are the nations that care not for
God, But now the tide is turning, we have weakened and failed
not they, For the great sea waves are restless, wilder they grow in

every way, And a nation that loses its moorings like Rome can fall in a day, Our forebears prayed and God was moved to hold the great sea back, Through the years the dikes stood firm, for guarding and tending they did not lack, We were born in a time of wealth, safe from the restless sea, But the time of our wealth and our safety long is past, The dikes are weakened by our neglect, the dikes that keep us free, Our forebears were right, untended the dikes will fail you see.

The truths we were taught are not useless, but life and death are they, And the greatest of all are to love, and to serve, and to pray, But now, from afar off, with the incoming tide, we hear an angry gale, As by a hurricane force, with mounting winds, seaward we are assailed, We are too far from the beach to see it, though we hear the angry roar, But we believe the dikes will hold, and last for centuries more, Those are the dikes our forebears made, and never have they failed, Time after time have the sea gales come, raging against the land, Time after time they have come, time after time they have passed, Slowly we've learned to ignore the gales, we ignore and are not afraid, For many centuries the dikes have stood, the dikes our forebears made, In spite of all our forebears said, untended we know they will last, This time the sea rises higher, the wind blows a greater gale, No one could live on the sea tonight, for the sea is a raging storm, Surrender forever, the great waves cry, tonight the dikes will fall, As we surrendered the work on the dikes, so our land is surrendered now, And dreadful is the cry of the sea, as the light and the dikes they fail, And now must our children live in the ruins of a land we did not guard,

Many feet over the dikes the pounding breakers stride, and it is more than ocean spray that lands on the landward side, like a runner leaping the hurdles, like a relentless evil thing, the very thing we were told to dread, the seas on the landward side,

Alarm bells ring and people flee, like frightened birds taken to wing, For what should we pray, for the break of day, We always had enough of light to show us the way, Enough to show us how to strengthen and tend the dikes, The dikes which we have justly lost, just as we lost our way, Time and again we were warned, time and again we failed, To teach and to show, what all should know, to guard, to serve, to pray, Those were the dikes our forebears made, this the land our folly lost, Run for your life, but where to run, as the land is covered with sea, The angry waves flood in, the dikes are broken, and we are undone, We failed to tend the dikes, and now the wild sea waves have won, We did not care to tend the dikes and pray, and now we inherit the sea, All that our ancestors built is lost, only ruins will greet the sun, We played a game called "Tend Not At All," and now the sea has won.

- Dr. N. James Brooks, Jr. (2008)

# CHAPTER EIGHT
# When All The World
# Spoke The Same Language

In describing life before the flood, the people of Sumer (southern Iraq) told how; "there was no fear, no terror, man had no rival, the whole universe, the people, in one tongue (one language) gave speech" (Kramer, p.107, note 2). The Bible tells us that both before the flood and for some time afterwards, everyone on the earth spoke the same language. Genesis 11:1 says, "and the whole earth was of one language, and of one speech."

Could there really have been a time when all mankind spoke the same language? That became the conclusion of a very famous linguist, Max Muller. Muller was considered by many in the later part of the 1800's to be the world's leading authority on languages. He argued that there was nothing unreasonable in the idea of there having once been a single language shared by all mankind. When asked if the different types of languages could be reconciled with a belief in one common original language, from which all other languages evolved, he answered, "Decidedly, yes!" (Muller, p.329)

Muller stated that while there were obviously language families which appeared to be quite distinct from one another, the derivation of one language family from another was not at all impossible (Muller, p.332). He declared, "If you wish to assert that languages had various beginnings, you must prove it impossible that language could not have had a common origin" (Muller, p.333)

By the term language family, Muller was referring to languages that are so closely related that it is obvious they sprang from the same parent language. Such languages originate as dialects. As dialects change and begin to differ more and more from each other, they become separate languages.

In time languages diverge and change so much that the speakers of sister languages (which are two or more languages in the same family), can no longer understand each other. "If a language community splits into two or more groups which are subsequently and immediately isolated from one another, the language of each group will continue to evolve. But because there is no fixed direction for linguistic change, these languages will gradually diverge from one another in both form and content, until, after a suitable time, they will have become quite distinct" (Albright & Lambdin, p.124)

For example, English originated from the same parent language as German. These two languages have changed so much that a speaker of English would have little reason to think of English and German as both originating from the same parent language. There are now such enormous differences between the two languages that people who speak one of the two languages cannot understand the other language at all. However, the two languages are both descended from an original Germanic language, which predated both of them. (Robinson, p.1)

For example, Cambridge University Professor H. Munro Chadwick stated, "Down to the fifth century, the German, English and Scandinavian languages differed but slightly from one another. In the fifth and following centuries differentiation took place very quickly within the northwestern group. English developed in general on lines about midway between German and Scandinavian, but with many special features of its own. Frisian (Dutch) seems to have differed little from English for a long time. (Chadwick, p.145)

131

Sir William Jones (1746-1794), who came to India as a judge of the Supreme Court at Calcutta, began the first systematic study of the relationships between human languages. Jones proposed that Greek and Latin, the classical languages of Europe, and Sanskrit, an ancient language of the people who had conquered India centuries before, had all descended from a common source. (Nehru, p.165). The evidence for this came from both the structure and vocabulary of the languages. A basic understanding of this can be had by looking at a couple of common words in those languages. An example is the word "father." It is "pater" in Latin, "patêr" in Classical Greek and "pitr" in Sanskrit. Words like these all plainly come from a common root word.

As research into the origins of Sanskrit, Latin, and Classical Greek continued, it gradually became evident that Jones was correct. This led to the discovery that the major languages of modern day India, Pakistan, Afghanistan, Farsi (the primary language of Iran), and virtually all the languages of Europe are related, and further that they descend from a common original language. Because the majority of the speakers of these related languages live in Europe and India, this newly discovered group of languages was named Indo-European.

The old Indo-European languages like Sanskrit and ancient Greek had complex declension and conjugation schemes, with an emphasis on tonal expression far beyond what modern languages use. (Declension is essentially a fixed pattern of endings or a set of endings. Conjugation is the way a verb changes form to show number, person, tense, etc.) Over many centuries the amount of declension and conjugation grew less, with today's modern Indo-European languages having far fewer cases of declension and conjugation. Even though the number of declensions and conjugations have dwindled, other parts of speech such as particles and auxiliary verbs have evolved to take

132

their place. This has had the effect of making Indo-European languages easier to learn. In other words, in the evolution the Indo-European languages, they started out harder to learn, but over time became simpler. This is hardly the type of linguistic evolution one would expect. It was a downward evolvement rather than an upward one.

We have talked about the relationship of the languages known as Indo-European, but what of the other main languages and language families of the world? Can they be proven to have had a common origin with Indo-European? Beginning in the 1800s, a growing number of linguists came to the conclusion that the language of the ancient Chinese had a common origin with Indo-European. Some of the evidence for the common origin of Chinese and Indo-European comes from the Hittite language. Hittite was the language of a kingdom that flourished on Turkey's Anatolian plain over four thousand years ago. (Gordon, p.86). (Just as an interesting side note, the Hittite word for water was "waa-a-tar" (Gordon, p.93)). Studying the ancient Hittite language, the oldest Indo-European language of which we have knowledge (Gordon, p.93), has led linguists to hypothesize that most of the present differences between Chinese and the Indo-European languages were nonexistent in the remote past. This indicates that the Chinese language had a common origin with Indo-European.

Because the period of time in which Chinese and Indo-European were the same languages and occurred even earlier and the formation of the actual Indo-European languages in which the common language from which Chinese and Indo-European came is called Proto-Indo-European. (See for example: Edkins, 1871; Chang, 1988; Hannas, 1997).

In the remainder of this article we will refer to Proto-Indo-European and all its related languages, such as Chinese, Japanese, Korean, etc. as the Japhetic languages. Japheth, Shem, and Ham

133

were the three sons of Noah. All the languages of the nations descended from Shem are called Semitic. The languages of the nations descended from Ham are called Hamitic languages. Therefore, it is reasonable to refer to all languages used by the descendants of Japheth as the Japhetic languages.

Comparing the Indo-European and Semitic language groups, the Semitic languages being primarily Hebrew and Arabic, Muller declared that the analysis of the grammatical forms in those families made it understandable how, in the course of time, languages so different in form as Hebrew and Sanskrit could have sprung from the same parent language. (Muller, p.333).

As far as finding a connection between the Korean and Japanese languages and Indo-European, the linguist Seymour Itzkoff relates that: "Koreans and Japanese speak a central Asian dialect to which visiting Finnish scientists, who themselves speak a Uralic-Altaic language related to Hungarian, have little difficulty adjusting." The similarities between the Finnish and Japanese languages are not very significant, but they are enough to show a common origin for the two languages, though it was far in the past. The Japanese have also traced their religious traditions to some of the early Indo-European deities in East/Central Europe, ca. 1500 B.C." (Itzkoff, p.39).

By tying the Chinese, Japanese, Korean, Indo-European, and Semitic languages together, showing the probability of a common origin for them all, basically only the Hamitic languages are left. By Hamitic are meant the languages spoken by the descendants of Ham. The descendants of Ham are the Egyptians, Libyans, a few of the tribes of the Arabian peninsular, and all the Black people of the world.

Most linguists agree that the Hamitic language families of Africa, of which there are three (Oliver, p.38), are derived from the same parent language. (Homburger, p.20). One researcher, Dr. Jan

F. Van Ordt, of South Africa, has shown a relationship between the Bantu languages of sub-Saharan Africa and the languages of most of the remaining Black peoples of the world. Dr. Van Ordt thinks that the Bantu speaking people who inhabit the greater part of sub-Saharan Africa had the same origin as the Dravidians who today inhabit southern India (Van Ordt, p.52-53). He also deduces a common origin for their languages. (Van Ordt, p.7).

Van Ordt states that a strong Semitic influence is found in the Bantu language family. This, he says, is commonly attributed to the influence of the Arabs. However, he says there is a yet much older Semitic influence in the Bantu languages which is far too old to be attributed to Arab traders. (Van Ordt, p.56). He believes this linguistic influence is traceable back to the time of the Assyrians, who spoke a Semitic language. (Van Ordt, p.56). Please note that Van Ordt believes that the Semitic influences in the Bantu languages can be traced back to the time of Assyria, not that those influences necessarily came directly from Assyria.

Since Van Ordt's time, though the Semitic and Hamitic language families have diverged greatly, their kinship has come to be generally recognized. It has been noted that Semitic and Hamitic share more root-words than can be explained by either of them adopting words from the other. Semitic and Hamitic languages also have some common grammatical peculiarities. (Bodmer, p.420ff)

Nearly all of the languages of the New World are related to some of the Asian languages. Those Asian languages in turn are Japhetic languages, being related to Proto-Indo-European. Thus, virtually all of the languages of the world can be tied to one of the three great language families of mankind. These three language families are, as we have seen, related to each other, thus having a common origin.

We can go further than this. The original language of mankind was apparently some form of Semitic. From this original language are derived not only the various Semitic languages (Arabic, Hebrew, Aramaic, etc.), but also the Japhetic or Proto-Indo-European languages, as well as the Hamitic languages. The linguist Franz Delitzsch believed that the ancient Syriac, Aramaic and Persian writers were correct in believing that an ancient Semitic language, known as Syriac or Nabatean, was the original speech of mankind. Delitzsch further believed that "in the confusion of tongues it remained as the language of Babylon" (Delitzsch, p.362).

What reasons are there for making such a statement as this? Though there are several, only one will be dealt with here. It has been proven that both the Japhetic and the Hamitic languages are anciently directly related to Semitic. It has not yet been proven that the Japhetic or Hamitic languages are directly related to each other. This would tend to say that neither of those two languages came from the other, but that since both are related to Semitic, that they came separately from the original Semitic language. By way of analogy, if A is directly related to B, and C is directly related to B, but A and C are not directly related in any way to each other, then the relationship between A and C is thru their separate relationship with B. By the same token, if the Japhetic and Hamitic languages are both directly related to Semitic, but are not directly related to each other, then their relationship is through their common but separate connection to Semitic. This would tend to indicate that both the Japhetic and Hamitic languages came from an original Semitic language. Some form of Semitic would thus have been mankind's original language.

"The science of language thus leads us up to that highest summit from which we see into the very dawn of man's life on earth. The words which we have heard so often from the days of our childhood, "and the whole earth was of one language and of

**136**

one speech," assume a meaning more natural, more intelligible, more convincing, than they ever had before" (Muller, p.391).

*"The supreme function of reason is to show man that some things are beyond reason."*

- Blaise Paschal

## Farewell Forever To The Church of The World

Farewell forever to the church of the world
Let fools and slaves submissively tremble
And lie down before the juggernaut car
But brave folk will rise in the strength of the Spirit
Following our God, who is calling from afar
We honor, yes honor, our spiritual forebears
Who launched forth before us on this uncharted sea
And though Satan howls and thunders distraction
We'll walk on the water and like Peter we'll be free
And while to the conflict others cry onward
We've learned to wait till our God says to go
He'll break the stronghold of evil's dominion
And raise His true Church to glory and might.

One day His true Church, in all of her glory,
Will see Him stand dazzling bright in the sky
With none to oppress us, no foes to oppose us
We'll praise Him forever, as He's seen by every eye.

Farewell forever to the church of the world,
No longer shall you trample on us, we are free
And we'll unfurl to the broad breeze of heaven
A banner of submission, submission to our king
Farewell forever to the Church of the World.

-    Dr. N. James Brooks, Jr.

# CHAPTER NINE
# When All The Earth Worshipped One God

*"Will the circle be unbroken, by and by, Lord, by and by,*
*In that better home awaiting, in the sky, Lord, in the sky,"*

Research shows that in ancient times all mankind believed in one and only one God. Because this God was always said to live either above the sky or in the sky, researchers began calling Him the Sky God. "The idea of the Sky-god as the universal spirit becomes such a basic assumption that it has every appearance of having been one of the fundamental religious concepts of mankind" (James, p.256)

Though most primitive peoples of ancient times left no written records detailing their beliefs about God, a very comprehensive and thorough study of the religious beliefs of primitive peoples was published by a German, Wilhelm Schmidt. His work was translated into English in 1931. Schmidt's monumental study provided conclusive proof that many primitive peoples have a concept of one all-powerful God, who created all things. (Custance, pp.125-128)

The evidence is that in ancient times mankind believed that the earth and all creation had been created and were sustained by one god and only one god. Their believing this is reasonable, for if Adam and Eve walked and talked with God, then naturally their descendants for many generations would have heard stories of that time, and would have known there was a God. Further, they would have known something about God, even though they did not know Him themselves.

A belief in one god is known as monotheism. Belief in many gods is known as polytheism, poly meaning many, and theism meaning of god. If the earliest civilizations of man believed in one god, what became of that belief, that we do not see widespread evidence of it throughout history?

Applying the beliefs of evolution to religion, there was a time when many accepted it as a given that mankind began their religious experience by belief in spirits, going from that to belief in many gods (polytheism) and finally to belief in only one god (monotheism). Both missionaries and archaeologists, however, reported that everywhere a belief in one god preceded belief in many. Religion had not evolved upwards from belief in many gods to believe in one. It had devolved downward, or degenerated from belief in one god to belief in many. There are several ways in which that typically happened, all of which will be discussed later.

Most civilizations and ethnic groups thus went from a belief in one god to a belief in many gods, and in praying to and seeking the help of those gods and of various spirits. However, they commonly retained the knowledge of one god who ruled over all, the creator and sustainer of everything. This one single god was generally said to live in or above the sky, sometimes in a place above the sky with a name of its own, a place like heaven. Since this God was said to live in or above the sky, modern researchers have come to call such a god a "Sky God." The Sky God of each ethnic group is generally so much like that of every other ethnic group that it would be easy to assume that there has never been but one Sky God, known by a different name in every language, but still only one god.

Missionaries and anthropologists alike found that tribes and ethnic groups around the world, ranging from the most primitive to the most advanced, believed in such a god. To all of them, this god was a vague impersonal being who could not be sought out and known by the peoples of the earth. Even so, the Sky-God was regarded as all-knowing and all wise. (Rose, p.55)

In addition, "The philological evidence, based on the vocabulary common to all branches of Indo-European speech, . . . . suggests that the original Indo-Europeans . . . . worshipped a Sky God." (Dawson, p.134)

Early Man . . . . appears to have been aware of a transcendent power external to the world, directly or indirectly governing its processes, and having his abode in the sky. (James, p.204)

So closely was the supreme god connected with the sky, that the ancient Babylonians used the same word for god that they used for the sky. (Kristensen, p.41). The same was true of other ancient peoples and of many peoples today. It is true of the Bonny tribe, who live at the mouth of the Niger River. Like the Babylonians, the ancient Aryan invaders of India, and a number of other ethnic groups, they use the same word for both "sky and "god" (Kristensen, p.41)

Among the Finns and certain related ethnic groups, the semantic elements "sky" and "god of the sky" are found to be such closely related terms that the association cannot be a recent thing. (Encyclopedia Britannica On-line, found under the topic – Sky-God). Though the Greeks came to worship more than one god, their pantheon, or collection of gods, was headed by an Indo-European sky god whom they called Zeus (Encyclopedia Britannica On-line). (Zeus is quite possibly a variant of the word Deos (bright or shining), which is related to the Latin word Deus, which means God.)

The Sky-God was normally regarded as all-knowing and all wise. (Rose, p.55)

In Mesopotamia, the supreme god was Anu, the god of heaven. In fact, his name in Sumerian was the same as "the sky," and the high esteem in which he was held as the most potent force in the cosmos long after his cult had fallen into obscurity suggests his great antiquity going back to prehistoric times. (James, p.213)

Among the Romans, Jupiter was the pre-eminent deity, "father both of gods and of men" (Bulfinch, p.4). Jupiter was also the Roman sky-god. According to Roman belief, Jupiter ruled from heaven, while his brothers, Neptune and Pluto, ruled the ocean and the underworld, respectively. There are two themes of stories about Jupiter. One theme has Jupiter being the supreme god who created "both gods and men," while the other theme says Jupiter was born of a goddess and that his father was supreme god before him. There is no reconciliation between these two themes about Jupiter, and even in the days of the early Romans, men such as Cicero stoutly defended the first theme, while deriding the second, which gave Jupiter the worst passions and vices of mortals.

Jupiter may well mean "Father Jove." Jove was the chief god of the Etruscans, a people who lived in northern Italy and for several hundred years ruled the Romans. Jove in Etruscan means "He who was and is and is to come," and may itself have had a common origin with the name Jehovah. (Rolleston, p.83)

The Aztecs and the other tribes of Mexico that spoke the same language, though they had thirteen principal gods, believed in one Supreme Being, whom they termed simply Teotl, or God. They also called him "He by whom we live." They believed him to be invisible. Their knowledge of him and of how he should be worshipped was obscure and largely lost. Nevertheless, behind a screen of thirteen lesser but important gods and more than 200 even lesser ones, those nations retained a knowledge from their past of one Supreme God. (Prichard, p.362)

Spirits who must be propitiated and whose aid may be sought for the success of an enterprise are not the same as a god and should not be considered as such. The famous African explorer of the very early 1800s, Mungo Park, reported that everywhere he went he found a prevalent belief in many spirits, but in only one god. "Belief in one God and in a future state of reward and punishment is entire and universal among them," Park said of the many natives he questioned. (Lang, p.241)

"One instance of a contemporary co-existence of higher and lower religious belief is to be seen in Madagascar, where the natives, though they were found in the 17th century worshipping their departed ancestors, and reverencing charms and idols, yet possessed the knowledge of a Supreme and Supernatural Deity, whose attributes directly connected religion with morality" (Titcomb, Prehistoric Monotheism, p.143)

Robert Drury, an Englishman, was shipwrecked on Madagascar in 1702, remaining there as a slave for fifteen years. He reported that the natives there referred to the Supreme Being as "the Lord Above." One of their sayings was "God alone bears rule." Another was, "Better be guilty with men than guilty before God." (Titcomb, "Prehistoric Monotheism" p.144). The Zulus likewise have knowledge of a Supreme Being. They call Him "The Great Great One" (Titcomb, "Prehistoric Monotheism" p.145). Titcomb was in this instance quoting the man who at that time was Bishop of Natal, a province in British South Africa.

Andrew Lang, speaking of the Australian tribes, says that though they believe in spirits, usually malevolent ones, they believe also in one god and only one. All over the continent of Australia, the natives, though they roam only in small bands and have no formal rulers other than headmen over each small band, believe in a God in Heaven who is omniscient, moral, all-seeing and who cannot die. (Lang, p.201, 204). Interestingly, they also believe that mankind was not intended to die, that death came

**144**

into the world but that that was not the original intention of God. (Lang, p.203, 205)

Professor Evans-Pritchard records that among the Nuer in Nilotic East Africa, God is considered a being of pure spirit, and because he is like wind or air "he is everywhere and being everywhere he is here now." He is far away in the sky yet present in the earth which he created and sustains. "Everything in nature, in culture, in society and in men is as it is because God made it so." Although he is unknowable and invisible he sees and hears all that happens. The Sky God of the Nuer is responsive to the pleas of those who call upon him. Since the Sky God can be angry he can and does punish wrongdoing. Punishment for wrongdoing can be stopped or lessened by repentance and reparation, and by prayer and sacrifice. (James, p.207)

"The idea of the Sky-god as the universal spirit becomes such a basic assumption that it has every appearance of having been one of the fundamental religious concepts of mankind" (James, p.256). James felt that the existence of a sky-god is firmly established and deeply rooted in the history of religion from the time of the Stone Age onwards. (James, p.209)

Mircea Eliade, for thirty years head of the History of Religions Department at the University of Chicago, and editor-in-chief of MacMillan's Encyclopedia of Religion, concluded from his study of the history of comparative religions that a supreme being who lived in the sky was believed in by most primitive societies. He concluded that worship of the Sky-God was at one time the very center of religious life, though he felt that in time the Sky-God had been superseded by other deities and religions. (Peters, p.72)

It was Eliade and other researchers who began to use the term "sky god," in speaking of these gods. (We say "gods," but if those peoples who believe in the sky gods are to be believed, there is only one sky god, with every culture that believes in him having their own separate name for him in their own language (Peters, p.72). The Sky God was generally believed to not involve himself in the affairs of people or the world, remaining passive and aloof from the affairs of mankind. Nevertheless, societies that believe in a sky god also believe that he created the world and all that is in it. These societies typically also believe that the sky god created other gods and goddesses. They also generally believe that the sky god has no interest in the world or mankind. Because of his perceived lack of disinterest in their lives, most ethnic groups who believe in the sky god actually pay little attention to him, mainly worshipping other gods, or spending their time attempting to appease spirits. Eliade came to feel that belief in the sky god was in ancient times widespread and at the very center of religious life. (Peters, p.72). "The philological evidence, based on the vocabulary common to all branches of Indo-European speech, . . . . suggests that the original Indo-Europeans . . . worshipped a Sky God." (Dawson, p.134). Early Man . . . . appears to have been aware of a transcendent power external to the world, directly or indirectly governing its processes, and having his abode in the sky (James, p.204)

Typically, in a people's history the time would come when they would begin to worship other gods and goddesses besides the Sky-God. Those other gods would begin by being in a subordinate position to the Sky-god, but many times, one of them, usually the sun-god, would in time be treated as if it were the Supreme Being, rather than the Sky God. The Incas of Peru, some of the Algonquin tribes in North America, the Chinese and Koreans, are just a few of the peoples who over time relegated the Sky-God to a lesser position, and exalted other gods in his place. None of those people though, ever completely forgot the god who lives in the sky. (James, p.257)

Overtime most of those people began to ignore the Sky God more and more. Other gods sprang up, and in time the Sky God was either ignored or virtually forgotten, or he became the supreme god of a large and often growing number of gods and goddesses. A few ethnic groups however, retained a much more vibrant recognition of this god. We will learn more about them at the end of this article.

Among the Finns and certain related ethnic groups, the semantic elements "sky" and "god of the sky" are found to be such closely related terms that the association cannot be a recent thing. (Encyclopedia Britannica On-line, found under the topic – Sky-God)

Though the Greeks came to worship more than one god, their pantheon, or collection of gods, was headed by an Indo-European sky god whom they called Zeus (Encyclopedia Britannica On-line). (Which may be a variant of the word Deos (bright or shining), which is related to the Latin word Deus, which means God.) The original god of the Indo-Europeans was Dyaus Pitar, by some felt to be Deus Pitar (*Overland Monthly and Out West Magazine*, Volume 12, Current Literature, a book review of "Primitive Culture," by Edward B. Tylor, Henry Holt and Company, New York, 1874. p.386). Deus Pitar or Dyaus Pitar, whichever way one spells it, was the same name and appears to have meant "Shining Father." At one time he seems to have been the only god the Indo-Europeans had. Because he lived above the sky, he is usually classified as a "sky god."

"Nowhere does sky worship seem to be so consistently elaborated as in the ancient Chinese religion." There the sky-god was not only the supreme god, his title/name of Shang-ti (or Shang-di) actually means supreme emperor. (Brede, p.42). The sky god of ancient China, the supreme being, was also known as the 'Lord on High'. (Maisels, p.295). One description of Him, found in an ancient Chinese book, says He is "a Being who knows all things; the secrets of the heart are not hid from Him" (Titcomb, Prehistoric Monotheism, p.140). Confucius said of God that there was only one. (Titcomb, Prehistoric Monotheism, p.141)

The founder of the philosophy of Taoism, Lao-tzu, who lived in China in the 6th century BC, made the following statement concerning the existence and being of God:

> "Before time, and throughout time, there has been a self-existing being, eternal, infinite, complete, omnipresent. Outside this being, before the beginning, there was nothing." (Cooper, p.13)

> ." . . . sky worship in the literate religions does indeed exhibit traits which are held in common and may rightly be considered characteristic" (Kristensen, p.41)

> "As in China, so in Korea, behind all the Shamanism, Buddhism, and Confucianism of the people is a dim background of theism -- the worship of the one great god, Hananim, whose name like that of Shang Ti has been adopted by the Protestant missionaries for God" (Saunder, p.161)

> "The Routledge Dictionary of Gods and Goddesses, Devils and Demons" says 'Hananim is the "Old Korean god of the sky, and supreme god: he moves the stars, rewards good and punishes evil" (Lukar, p.73)

> "The sky god of India, in particular of the Vedic religion, is Varuna. He too is the supreme god, who is called the "universal king" (samrāj). His exalted rest contrasts sharply with the industrious nature and display of power of the other Vedic gods, such as Indra. There are no myths about him, and he has little personification. His will and essence is the universal order . . . . " (Kristensen, p.44)

148

Though the Creator God who lives in the sky is considered invisible and is often not worshipped, He is believed in by many primitive peoples. Each such tribe or nation has a name for him in their own language, and believe that He is good, all-wise, all-knowing, and that He has laid down laws by which mankind is supposed to live. (James, pp.206-07, 227, 257; see also Richardson, p.137)

The Creator God in the sky did not remain alone forever though. As time passed, people began to conceive of other gods, gods and goddesses more in line with their own desires. In time, these new gods began to displace the Sky God, though he was apparently never forgotten. One writer, speaking of the Aryan invaders of India, writes, "In the Vedic pantheon, where Dyaus Pitar held pre-eminence as the Sky-father and personification of the heavens, . . . . gradually he was displaced . . . . by the Vedic nature gods and goddesses (James, p.258). In the quotation above, Pitar is the Sanskrit word for father. Though in Sanskrit, Dyaus Pitar was a title by which the Sky God was called, He was also known by the name Varuna. The origin and exact meaning of that name is debatable. But He is represented in the Rig-Veda as a clear example of a Sky-God. "Of his earliest history, we have no information -- in the most ancient records he is already fully formed. In the Rig-Veda, he embraces the whole of life -- he is absolute ruler and moral governor, he punishes sin and forgives the penitent. (Toy, p.313)

Among the Romans, Jupiter was the pre-eminent deity, "father both of gods and of men" (Bulfinch, p.4). Jupiter was also the Roman sky-god. According to Roman belief, Jupiter ruled from heaven, while his brothers, Neptune and Pluto, ruled the ocean and the underworld, respectively. There are two themes of stories about Jupiter. One theme has Jupiter being the supreme god who created both gods and men, while the other theme says Jupiter was born of a goddess and that his father was supreme god before him. Between these two themes about Jupiter, and even in the days of the early Romans, men such as Cicero stoutly defended the first theme, while deriding the second, which gave Jupiter the worst passions and vices of mortals.

It is agreed without question that three of the world's four oldest civilizations are those of Sumer, Egypt, and China. The evidence is that all three of these peoples originally believed in only one god. (Virtually nothing is known of the fourth civilization, Hurrappa.)

Virtually all archaeologists and historians believe that the oldest human culture is that of Sumer. Stephen Langdon, of Oxford University, an early authority on the Sumerian culture, stated: "The evidence points unmistakably to an original monotheism," (Langdon, p.114). Speaking of the conclusions he had reached through his studies and research, Langdon wrote, "In my opinion the history of the oldest civilization of man is a rapid decline from monotheism to extreme polytheism and widespread belief in evil spirits. It is in a very true sense the history of the fall of man". (Langdon, p.114)

"In the early days, the Egyptians worshipped one only God, the maker of all things, without beginning and without end. To the last the priests preserved this doctrine and taught it privately to a select few." ("American Encyclopedia," vol. vi. p.463; cited by Donnelly, p.212). Plutarch, in his book upon Isis and Osiris, alludes to an underlying and earlier national belief in one Supreme God. He says, "The end of all the religious rites and mysteries of the goddess Isis was the knowledge of that First God who is the Lord of all things" (Titcomb, On The Antiquity of Civilization, "Faith and Thought," vol.3, p.7).

An ancient hymn of the Egyptians says: 'He is not graven in marble; He is not beheld; His abode is not known; there is no building that can contain Him; unknown is his name in heaven;

He doth not manifest his forms; vain are all representations (of Him)'. (Rawlinson, p.322)

"To the great and supreme power which made the earth, the heavens, the sea, the sky, men and women, animals, birds, and creeping things, all that is and all that shall be, the Egyptians gave the name neter. This word survives in the Coptic, but both in the ancient language and in its younger relative the exact meaning of the word is lost". (Budge, p.lxxxiii)

James Legge, a distinguished translator of Chinese classics, wrote that the Chinese once believed in only one God. (Legge, p.28). Their name for God was Shang Ti (or Shang Di), which means "Supreme Heavenly Ruler" (Custance, p.9). Legge described the Chinese concept of Shang Ti by saying: "Shang Ti is self-existent. He existed before the heaven and the earth and sun. He created them. He rules over them. His years have no end" (Legge, p.32). For many centuries, the Chinese people worshipped only Shang Ti. (Kang and Nelson, p.14). This lasted until 255 B.C.

Chinese writing was originally pictographic. That is to say, each character was a picture or diagram describing the object it pictured. These characters were usually made up of other characters, or radicals, as they are generally called. Thus, the earliest Chinese word for Heaven was composed of two radicals. One radical meant man, while the other meant above. Heaven thus was written as "the man above." (Custance, p.9)

From China comes this ancient prayer: "Of old in the beginning, there was the great chaos, without form and dark. The five elements (the planets) had not begun to revolve, nor the sun and moon to shine. In the midst thereof there existed neither form nor sound. You, O Spiritual Sovereign, came forth in your presidency, and did first divide the grosser parts from the purer. You made heaven. You made earth. You made man. All things with their reproducing power got their being. You have vouchsafed, Heavenly Ruler, to hear us, for You regard us as a Father. I, Thy child, dull and unenlightened, am unable to show forth my dutiful feelings. Your sovereign goodness is infinite. As a potter, You have made all living things. Your sovereign goodness is infinite. Great and small are sheltered (by You). Engraven on the heart of Your poor servant is the sense of Your goodness, so that my feelings cannot be fully displayed. With great kindness, You do bear with us, and not withstanding our demerits, do grant us life and prosperity". (Legge, p.29)

The prayer just above was a prayer to Shang Ti, one that the Emperor of China traditionally prayed at the time of the "Border Sacrifices," when the Emperor worshipped and made offerings to Shang Ti in the name of the Chinese people. In ancient China only one god, whom they called Shang-Ti, meaning Supreme Heavenly Ruler, was worshipped. At that period in its history, the Emperor of China would make an annual sacrifice to Shang-Ti at the western border of China. This was known as the border sacrifice. The Shu Ching, or Book of Documents, is one of the oldest Chinese books. It was found hidden in the walls of the home of Confucius when it was pulled down in 140 B.C. (Kang & Nelson, p. 11 & 12). This manuscript tells that in the year 2230 B.C. at the border sacrifice, the Emperor Shun, in sacrificing to Shang-Ti, offered the prayer.

For many centuries, the Chinese people worshipped only Shang Ti. (Kang and Nelson, p.14). This lasted until 255 B.C. Gradually however, worship of Shang Ti began to die out among the Chinese people. (Kang & Nelson, p. 14)

The earliest account of religious worship in China is that found in the Shu Ching (a Book of History compiled by Confucius). In it, he records of the Emperor Shun in 2230 B.C. that "He sacrificed to Shang Ti." This is in reference to the ceremony known as the "Border Sacrifices" (Legge, p.14)

152

The oldest known examples of Chinese writing are found inscribed on what are called "oracle bones." In these inscriptions, God is referred to as a single and all-powerful deity. (Custance, pp.121-123)

Nor were the peoples of Sumer, Egypt, and China alone in ancient times in believing in only one God. George Rawlinson, in his "History of Phoenicia," speaks of the original monotheism of the early Phoenicians. "There is sufficient reason to believe that originally, either when they first occupied their settlements upon the Mediterranean or before they moved from their primitive seats upon the shores of the Persian Gulf, the Phœnicians were Monotheists . . . . in the earliest times, the religious sentiment of the Phœnicians acknowledged only a single deity--a single mighty power, which was supreme over the whole universe" (Rawlinson, p.321). "Originally, the Phoenicians were Monotheists" (Waddell, p.263)

The ancients typically had no doubt that creation was the result of divine purpose, and therefore did not occur by chance. Some doubted that there could be a creation without a Creator and based their reasoning on logic alone. Cicero declared: 'is it not a wonder that anyone can bring himself to believe that a number of solid and separate particles by their chance collisions and moved only by the force of their own weight, can bring into being so marvelous and beautiful a world?' (Cicero, p.161). Cicero goes on to say that if anyone thinks that is possible, they should also be able to believe that if letters were dumped out onto the ground, it would be possible for them to fall in such a way as to spell out all the words of a book.

Cicero continues, 'How can these people bring themselves to assert that the universe has been created by the blind and accidental collisions of inanimate particles . . . . If these chance collisions of atoms can make a world, why cannot they build a porch, or a temple, or a house or a city? A much easier and less laborious task.' (Cicero, pp.161-62.)

The sacred book of the Maya says that at one time, people "did not invoke wood nor stone, and they remembered the word of the Creator and the Maker, the Heart of Heaven, the Heart of Earth." (Goetz, Morley, & Recinos, p.172). The Maya describe that time by saying that "the speech was all the same." It also mentions both black and white people living together somewhere to the east, the place from which the Maya came to the lands where the Spanish found them. (Goetz, Morley, Recinos, p.172)

Though the Hindus revel in a profusion of gods, numbering in the thousands, Max Muller, the great 19th authority on the religions of east Asia, writing of the Rig Veda, which most scholars date to 1500 B.C., stated that "There is a monotheism that precedes the polytheism of the Veda, and even in the invocation of the innumerable gods, the remembrance of a God, one and infinite, breaks through the mist of idolatrous phraseology like the blue sky that is hidden by passing clouds". (Muller, p.559)

"In the early ages of mankind," says Wilkinson in his "Ancient Egyptians," "The existence of a sole and omnipotent Deity, who created all things, seems to have been the universal belief". (Hislop, p.14)

Though the Greeks in classical times had many gods and goddesses, that was not always true. Xenophanes, Plato, and Aristotle, three well known Greek philosophers, all used Theos in their writings as a personal name for God. (Richardson, p.49), just as it is believed that Deos was anciently used in the time before Greek and Latin diverged and became separate languages. (Encyclopedia Britannica, 15th ed., vol. 13, p.951, and vol. 14, p.538). The Septuagint, a Greek language translation of the Old Testament, also uses Theos in place of God, as do the oldest known copies of the New Testament, from which our modern versions are translated.

Hierocles, a disciple of the Platonic school, wrote: "Most men are bad, and under the influence of their passions; and, from their propensity to earth, are grown impotent of mind. But this evil they have brought upon themselves by their willful apostasy from God, and by withdrawing themselves from that communion with him, which they once enjoyed in pure light". (Deane, p.27-28)

The famous Roman orator and statesman, Cicero, speaking of "the lord of the universe, who sways all nature by his nod," quotes another philosopher, Ennius, as declaring God to be "the father both of gods and men." Cicero goes on to declare God to be "a present and a mighty God. If anyone doubts this, then so far as I can see he might just as well doubt the existence of the sun. For the one is as plain as the other." (Cicero, p.124)

Xenophanes, a famous Greek playwright, said: "there is one God, greatest among gods and men, similar to mortals neither in shape nor in thought" (Barnes, p.95). "He sees as a whole, He thinks as a whole, He hears as a whole" (Barnes, p.96). "Always He remains in the same state, changing not at all". (Barnes, p.97)

The ancient Scandinavians believed in "a Supreme God, master of the Universe, to whom all things were obedient and submissive; called in the old Icelandic literature, Author of everything that exists, the Eternal, the Being that never changeth" (Titcomb, Prehistoric Monotheisim, p.154)

Though we commonly think of the chief of the Norse gods as being Odin, they anciently had another and older god who was considered supreme. The Edda says that he was the first and oldest of the Norse gods. He was called the Alfadir, (All-Father). "He lives from all ages, governs all realms, and sways all things, great and small. He created heaven and earth, and the air, and all

155

things pertaining to them. He also made man, and gave him a soul which shall live and never perish, though the body molders away". (Sturluson, p.8-9)

Elsewhere in the Edda, the Norse god Odin is referred to as the "All-Father," however, for several reasons, not least of which is that Odin is also said to have been a man who eventually died, it appears that the All-Father mentioned above is not Odin, but rather an older conception of God. Since Odin was a real man who lived and died, it appears obvious that he was never the real All-Father. It seems plain that it was only at some period after his death that he was given the title of All-Father, and worshipped as the real All-Father, the creator god of the Scandinavians. (Sturluson, p.xviii)

Sturluson says that the All-Father, or Father of All, "lives from all ages, he preserveth all realms, and swayeth all things great and small." "He hath made man and given him a soul which shall ever live and never perish. And all the righteous shall dwell with Him in the place called Gimli; but the wicked shall go to Hel" (Titcomb, "British-Israel How I Came To Believe It," pp.190-191).

There is evidence that the Incas of South America at one time were also monotheists, for though they came to believe in many gods, and though it is generally thought that their greatest god was the Sun God, whom they named "Inti," they knew of a greater god, who ruled over all. One of their names for him was Kon-Tiki, which means "The Eternal." He was also known as the Creator and the Ruler of the World. The knowledge of this god predated the Inca Empire. (Herrman, p.182-83, 185)

Another of their names for the creator god was Virakocha. He was sometimes referred to as Pachacamac, and sometimes called "Virakocha Pachacamac" (Prescott, p.43-44, footnote). It is not known what the meaning of Virakocha is, though under both names he is described as the "Supreme Being, the Creator and Ruler of the Universe" (Prescott, p.43). Pachacamac is said to mean "He who sustains and gives life to the universe" (Prescott, p.43, footnote 6). One Inca description of Virakocha said that he was: "The everlasting Lord, symbol of the world, and its eternal first cause, master and ruler. He is the Sun of suns. He is the creator of the world . . .." (Herrman, p.185). He was, according to Garcilasco De La Inca, (who was both an Inca and a noted authority on his own people), a god who was worshipped only inwardly, as an unknown God. (Prescott, p.44, footnote 2)

The knowledge and understanding of the Creator God which was had by the nations mentioned, can be called a general understanding of God. They did not claim to know specifics things about God, nor did they have specific laws or rituals relating to His worship. They had only a vague and general understanding of God and His requirements for them. Are there any of the world's peoples in modern times who still retain such a knowledge of God? There definitely are!

Though little is known today about the Lisu, who live in Communist China, the other peoples mentioned are now predominately Christian. They are only a small number of the many peoples of the world whose ancestral religion focused around the idea of a typical Sky God, a Creator God who is good, who requires obedience from mankind, and who lives in a place above the sky. All of these peoples, and many others, were primed to accept Christianity, since its teachings about God and the early days of mankind were so similar to their own. The spiritual beliefs of such peoples as these, held long before they met the first European, gives us pause to wonder if once all people did not share these beliefs. If they did, then later developments of religion, such as ancestor worship and belief in a multiplicity of gods, were a divergence from the age old religious beliefs of mankind.

Though most primitive peoples of ancient times left no written records detailing their beliefs about God, a very comprehensive and thorough study of the religious beliefs of primitive peoples was published by a German, Wilhelm Schmidt. His work was translated into English in 1931. Schmidt's monumental study provided conclusive proof that many primitive peoples have a concept of one all-powerful God, who created all things. (Custance, pp.125-128)

Many of the most primitive peoples on the earth, such as the Australian aborigines, the Bushmen of South Africa, the African pygmies, and the Fuegian people of Patagonia, believe in a supreme god, who had created all things. In many cases they think of this supreme god as distant and unknowable, but they believe he exists. Further, even though they may speak of good and evil spirits, they do not conceive of these spirits as gods. (James, p.206; see also Richardson, pp.138- 140)

Hananim is the "Old Korean god of the sky, and supreme god: he moves the stars, rewards good and punishes evil". (article titled Hananim, by Lukar, p.73)

In both China and in Korea, behind all the Shamanism, Buddhism, and Confucianism of the people is a dim background of theism -- the worship of the one great god, Hananim, whose name like that of Shang Ti has been adopted by the Protestant missionaries for God. (Saunder, p.161). For many centuries missionaries had gone to China. They always made converts, but unfortunately, they chose names for God that were unfamiliar to the Chinese people. When Protestant missionaries reached China, they copied the Catholics by using an invented name for God. The Chinese already had a name for God, as we have seen, the name of Shang Ti or Shang Di.

The first missionaries to reach Korea were also Catholic. They reproduced what had occurred in China by inventing

Korean names for God. Later, in 1884, the first Protestant missionaries reached Korea. These missionaries had a much greater and quicker success than those in China had had. This was largely because they did not teach the Koreans about a foreign god, but about the ancient god of their ancestors, Hananim. Hananim, which means "The Great One," was the name for the "sky god" of Korea. Telling the Korean people that they had come to teach them about the ancient god of their forefathers caused Koreans to flood the church buildings erected by these missionaries. That is why today a large portion of the Korean people are Christian. They are mostly Presbyterian, to be exact, for it was the Presbyterians who first taught them about the ancient God of Korea, Hananim. This was the god of their forefathers, a god whom they had never understood much about, but whom they were eager to learn about.

Snorri Sturluson, an 11th century A.D., Icelandic historian and writer, recording the myths, legends, and history of the ancestors of the Norse, described their pre-Christian ancestors knowledge of God as someone who "liveth" . . . . "from all ages ; he preserveth all realms and swayeth all things great and small." "He hath formed" . . . . "heaven and earth, and the air, and all things thereunto belonging." "He hath made man and given him a soul which shall live and never perish. And all that are righteous shall dwell with him in the place called Gimli; but the wicked shall go to Hel . . . .". (Titcomb, "British-Israel; How I Came To Believe It," p.191)

Sturluson said that as time passed after the flood, the great majority of mankind, loving the pursuit of material things, left off paying homage to God. Snorri wrote that they came to avoid any mention of God, and in time their descendants knew nothing at all about their Creator. In the end, he said they forgot the very name of God and in most of the world there was not to be found anyone who knew about God. (Sturluson, p.1)

## God of Grace And Glory,

God of grace and glory,
Father of the free,
How shall we extol You,
Who are born of Thee,
Greater and still greater,
Shall Your kingdom be,
God of grace and glory,
We praise and honor Thee,
Not for power or greatness,
Not for self and not for fame,
But for Your glory only,
Did our ancestors own Your name.

And we in this day also,
For us may it be the same,
For Your glory and Your honor,
Will we serve and praise Your name.

- Dr. N. James Brooks, Jr.

160

*"It is the heart which perceives God and not the reason.*
*That is what faith is: God perceived by the heart, not by the reason."*

-   Blaise Paschal

# CHAPTER TEN
## The Tower of Babel

Genesis chapter 11 tells that when everyone on the earth spoke the same language, they decided to build a city and a tower, a tower so tall that its top would reach high into the heavens. We are told that their purpose in doing this was to help keep themselves united, so that they would not be scattered across the earth.

> *"And it came to pass, as they journeyed from the east, that they found a plain in the land of Shinar; and they dwelt there, and they said, "Go, let us build us a city and a tower, whose top may reach unto heaven, and let us make us a name lest we be scattered abroad upon the face of the whole earth."* (Genesis 11:2-4)

The expression, "whose top may reach unto heaven," simply means that the Tower would be tall and would reach towards heaven. It did not mean that the builders were trying to build a tower high enough that they would reach heaven and could enter it by way of their pyramid. Deuteronomy 1:28 has the Hebrews saying when they heard of the size and power of the inhabitants of the land of Canaan, "Our brethren have discouraged our heart, saying, the people is greater and taller than we; the cities are great and walled up to heaven." Though they heard that the cities of the Canaanites were "walled up to heaven," they did not take this to mean that the top of the cities' walls reached into heaven. The Israelites correctly took this to mean simply that the walls of the cities were very high, reaching towards heaven. Likewise, the Tower of Babel did not reach up into heaven. The expression that was used in planning the building of the Tower, "whose top may reach unto heaven," meant that they planned for the Tower to reach high into the sky.

Their reason for building the pyramid was as a rallying place, "lest we be scattered abroad upon the face of the whole earth." Built on a wide flat plain, a high tower would be seen for many miles and would indeed serve as a grand rallying point for the earth's peoples. Their actual reason for building the pyramid is "lest we be scattered abroad upon the face of the whole earth."

Not spreading out over the earth was in deliberate disobedience to a direct command from God (Genesis 9:1). The Tower was built on a wide flat plain. A tall tower would therefore easily be seen from a great distance and would serve as a rallying point for the earth's people as long as they lived on that flat plain.

Genesis 11:1-4 (KJV) says,

*"And the whole earth was of one language, and of one speech. And it came to pass, as they journeyed from the east, that they found a plain in the land of Shinar; and they dwelt there. And they said one to another, Go, let us make brick, and burn them thoroughly. And they had brick for stone, and slime had they for mortar. And they said, Go, let us build us a city and a tower, whose top may reach unto heaven; and let us make us a name, lest we be scattered abroad upon the face of the whole earth."*

The Bible describes God's reaction to the building of the Tower thus: "And the LORD came down to see the city and the tower, which the children of men builded.  And the LORD said, Behold, the people is one, and they have all one language; and this they begin to do: and now nothing will be restrained from them, which they have imagined to do.  Go to, let us go down, and there confound their language, that they may not understand one another's speech. So the LORD scattered them abroad from thence upon the face of all the earth: and they left off to build the city" (Genesis chapter 11, verses 5-8, KJV).

Following are a few of the many accounts of the Tower that are scattered over the earth, just as the descendants of the builders were scattered.

The Apaches have a legend that after a great flood, from which a man named Montezuma and the coyote alone escaped. Montezuma became then very wicked, and attempted to build a house that would reach to heaven, but the Great Spirit destroyed it with thunderbolts. (Bancroft's "Native Races," vol. iii, p.77)

From the island of Hao, part of the Tuamotu islands in Polynesia, comes a story of the Tower that says after a great flood some of the survivors made an attempt to erect a high building by which they could reach the sky and see the creator god. "But the god in anger chased the builders away, broke down the building, and changed their language, so that they spoke divers tongues." (Williamson, p.94)

The Tower was built on a wide flat plain in what is now southern Iraq. That area was anciently known as Sumer, or as the Bible calls it the land of Shinar. The people of ancient Sumer told of a golden age when everyone spoke one language, then the god Enki changed their speech (Wenham, p.236). The Sumerian account of the Tower, called "Enmerkar and the Lord of Aratta," describes the rebellion that resulted in the building of the Tower, and the confusion that followed when every tribe or nation received a separate language and was dispersed across the earth. The Sumerian account ends with the words, "the leader of the gods changed the speech in their mouths, [brought (?)] contention into it, into the speech of man that, until then, had been one". (Kramer, pp.108-9)

Josephus says that after descending from the mountains, the descendants of Noah, led by his three sons, settled in what became Sumer. Josephus calls it Shinar. (Josephus, p.46) Josephus goes on to say that God commanded the people, not once but twice, to spread abroad and people the earth, but they did not obey God, instead they built a tower of burnt brick, "cemented together with mortar, made of bitumen which is tar, that it might not be liable to admit water" (Josephus, p.46)

The actual words of Josephus are:

*"Now the plain in which they first dwelt was called Shinar. God also commanded them to send colonies abroad, for the thorough peopling of the earth that they might not raise seditions among themselves, but might cultivate a great part of the earth, and enjoy its fruits after a plentiful manner. But they were so ill instructed that they did not obey God, for which reason they fell into calamities, and were made sensible, by experience, of what sin they had been guilty, for when they flourished with a numerous youth, God admonished them again to send out colonies; but they, imagining the prosperity they enjoyed was not derived from the favor of God, but supposing that their own power was the proper cause of the plentiful condition they were in, they did not obey him. Nay, they added to this their disobedience to the Divine will, the suspicion that they were therefore ordered to send out separate colonies, that, being divided asunder, they might the more easily be oppressed."*

*"Now it was Nimrod who excited them to such an affront and contempt of God. He was the grandson of Ham, the son of Noah, a bold man, and of great strength of hand. He persuaded them not to ascribe it to God, as if it was through his means they were happy, but to believe that it was their own courage which procured that happiness. He also gradually changed the government into tyranny, seeing no other way of turning men from the fear of God, but to bring them into a constant*

**165**

*dependence on his power. He also said he would be revenged on God, if he should have a mind to drown the world again, for that he would build a tower too high for the waters to be able to reach! And that he would avenge himself on God for destroying their forefathers"!*

*"Now the multitude were very ready to follow the determination of Nimrod, and to esteem it a piece of cowardice to submit to God, and they built a tower, neither sparing any pains, nor being in any degree negligent about the work, and, by reason of the multitude of hands employed in it, it grew very high, sooner than any one could expect, but the thickness of it was so great, and it was so strongly built, that thereby its great height seemed, upon the view, to be less than it really was. It was built of burnt brick, cemented together with mortar, made of bitumen, that it might not be liable to admit water. When God saw that they acted so madly, he did not resolve to destroy them utterly, since they were not grown wiser by the destruction of the former sinners, but he caused a tumult among them, by producing in them divers languages, and causing that, through the multitude of those languages, they should not be able to understand one another. The place wherein they built the tower is now called Babylon, because of the confusion of that language which they readily understood before, for the Hebrews mean by the word Babel or confusion."* (Josephus, p.46-47)

A further result of each of the earth's extended families suddenly speaking a different language was that the command God had given them was finally obeyed. They began to spread abroad over the earth.

Of the many stories of the Tower that come from sources outside of the Bible, one reason given for the building of the Tower was to protect themselves in case God sent another flood upon the earth. The idea of using the Tower as a rallying point to keep the world's people together is also given as a reason for building the Tower. Babylon and the Tower were built on a wide flat plain. A tall tower would therefore easily be seen from a great distance and could serve as a rallying point for the rebellious people, even after they had settled widely over the vast plain.

The book of the Quiche Mayas, the "Popol Vuh," describing the creation of the first men "in the region of the rising sun," (Bancroft's "Native Races," vol. v., p.548), says that all spoke the same language. (Bancroft, vol. v., p.547) It goes on to say that their language changed, and "not being able to understand one another any longer, the people scattered across the earth" (Bancroft, vol. v., p.547). The translation of the Popul Vuh referred to by Bancroft is that by Brasseur de Bourbourg.

Ixtlilxochitl, a Mexican historian and a descendent of the Toltec kings, wrote that after the flood a zacuali, or tower of great height, was erected as a place of refuge should there be a second flood. (Donnelly, pp.103-104). He further said that all mankind was dispersed by being given different languages so that they could no longer understand each other. (Nelson, p.187). The Toltecs said that after being given different languages, the different peoples of the earth went to different parts of the world to live. Their ancestors, they said, reached central Mexico 520 years after the flood. (Nelson, p.187)

The Romans had what were called the Sibylline Oracles, which were a long series of legends and stories from the far distant past. They were kept in one of the temples of Rome. No one knows their actual origin for certain. One of the stories in the Sibylline Oracles, quoted by Josephus, says: "When all men were of one language, some of them built a high tower as if they would thereby ascend up to heaven, but the gods sent storms of wind and overthrew the tower, and gave everyone his peculiar language and for this reason it was that the city was called Babylon". (Josephus, p.46-47)

Another translation of the Sibylline Oracles says:

> When are fulfilled the threats of the great God,
> With which He threatened men, when formerly
> In the Assyrian land they built a tower,
> And all were of one speech . . . .
> Then rose among mankind fierce strife and hate,
> One speech was changed to many dialects,
> And earth was filled with diverse tribes and kings
> (Eusebius, "Theophilus To Autolycus,"Book II,
> chapter XXXI).

The Babylonian account, as transmitted by Abydenus, a Greek historian, tells that, "once men who being puffed up by their strength and great stature, and proudly thinking that they were better than the gods, raised a huge tower, where Babylon now stands and when they were already nearer to heaven, the winds came to the help of the gods, and overthrew their structure upon them, the ruins of which were called Babylon. And being up to that time of one tongue, they received from the gods a confused language". (Abydenus, p.416)

In the Chinese language, the written word for tower is composed of symbols that say, "mankind, of one speech, united, undertook to build with bricks of fired clay" (Kang and Nelson, p.106) This is comparable to Genesis 11: 3-4, as quoted on page one of this chapter.

An Assyrian writer, Abydenus, is quoted as saying,

> "They say that the first inhabitants of the earth, glorying in their own strength and size, and despising the gods, undertook to raise a tower whose top should reach the sky, in the place in which Babylon now stands: but when it approached the heaven, the winds assisted the gods, and overthrew the work upon its contrivers and its ruins

*are said to be still at Babylon and the gods introduced a diversity of tongues among men, who till that time had all spoken the same language and a war arose between Cronus and Titan. The place in which they built the tower is now called Babylon, on account of the confusion of the tongues; for confusion is, by the Hebrews, called Babel"* (Cory and Hodges, p.55; see also Eusebius, "Preparation for the Gospel," Book IX, Chapter XIV.)

Many of the stories that tell of the Tower maintain that it, or at least its top, was damaged or destroyed by a violent wind. Moses Charenenses, a famous Armenian historian of antiquity, states that God overthrew the Tower by a terrible storm. (Quoted in Josephus, "Antiquities of the Jews," p.46) In the Jewish "Book of Jubilees," it is said that "the Lord sent a mighty wind against the tower and overthrew it upon the earth". (Charles, p.26)

In the traditions of several of the ancient nations of Mexico it is told that those who survived the catastrophe of the violent winds that destroyed the Tower lost "their reason and speech". (Bancroft, vol. III," p.64)

In another part of the world are the Miao, a people who live in southern China. They say that after the flood the descendants of Noah's sons multiplied and all spoke the same language.

*"Their speaking was all with the same words and language.*
*Then they said let us build us a very big city;*
*Let us raise unto heaven a very high tower.*
*This was wrong, but they reached this decision;*
*Not right, but they rashly persisted."*

Their oral history then tells how God changed their language from one language into many, causing them to separate

**169**

and spread around the globe. They refer to the earth as a ball i.e. round. (Traux). (It is interesting that even at that early age, there were people groups who knew that the earth was round.) And so, the Tower was destroyed, and its builders, their speech changed into many languages, no longer able to communicate with each other, began the process of scattering across the face of the earth.

Review again the account in the Bible, it says in Genesis chapter eleven, verse 1.

> *And the whole earth was of one language, and of one speech. 2 And it came to pass, as they journeyed from the east, that they found a plain in the land of Shinar; and they dwelt there. 3 And they said one to another, Go to, let us make brick, and burn them thoroughly. And they had brick for stone, and slime had they for mortar. 4 And they said, Go to, let us build us a city and a tower, whose top may reach unto heaven; and let us make us a name,* **lest we be scattered abroad upon the face of the whole earth.**

In reading the account in the Bible, one error that people often make is the assumption that the purpose of building the Tower was to find a way to reach heaven on their own. That idea has been taught so much and by so many that it will not hurt to say again that to go to heaven by means of the Tower was never the plan of the builders. Their plan in building the Tower is plainly stated in verse four, as shown above. It says their purpose in building the Tower was to prevent themselves from being "scattered abroad." The Wycliffe Translation says plainly, "and they said, Come ye, and let us make a city, and a tower whose height shall stretch up to the sky; and make we our name well-known, or else we shall soon be parted from each other into all the earth" (Genesis 11:4).

This was in deliberate disobedience to a command from God to the descendants of Noah, that they spread themselves across the earth. Genesis chapter 9:1, "And God blessed Noah and his sons, and said unto them, "Be fruitful and multiply, replenish the earth."

Genesis 11:5-9 states:

> *And the Lord came down to see the city and the tower, which the children of men builded. And the Lord said, Behold, the people is one, and they have all one language; and this they begin to do and now nothing will be restrained from them, which they have imagined to do. Go to, let us go down, and there confound their language, that they may not understand one another's speech. So the Lord scattered them abroad from thence upon the face of all the earth and they left off to build the city. Therefore is the name of it called Babel, because the Lord did there confound the language of all the earth and from thence did the Lord scatter them abroad upon the face of all the earth.*

God said, in the above verses, that He does not want the various peoples of the earth to be united as one. The reason being that united there is nothing we can imagine that we cannot do. God does not want us to have either that unity or that power. He therefore forced us to scatter over the earth by giving every extended family a different language.

This is in line with mankind wanting to have things their way and being eager to justify doing whatever they want. There are two stories that are completely different from the others in this chapter. They are stories however that directly express the feeling of most people for God and His demands on them. A story from Polynesia says the heavens were once very close to the earth. Heaven and earth were so close that people were oppressed by the closeness of heaven. They could not walk. They were forced to crawl. A hero arose with a solution. He took long poles and pushed heaven away from the earth. This made the gods mad, and they send a great flood in which most of the people on the earth drowned. However, the hero, for his successful liberation of mankind, was declared by his followers to be a god. (Hislop, p. 52-3)

At first this may not seem much like the flood story in the bible, but think about it for a moment. Pushing heaven away from the earth is just a way of saying that some of the earth's people rebelled and refused to have anything to do with God. They did this because they did not like heaven interfering in their affairs. The Snohomish tribe, mentioned previously, also tell that once heaven was so close to the earth that the people could not walk upright. Here also the people came together with long poles to force heaven away from the earth. All the people of the world were brought together and given long poles. At an agreed upon signal they all pushed, and after several attempts, the sky was pushed away from the earth. (Velikovsky, pp.182, 190)

These stories sound much like the Greek Titan, Atlas, who, when the heavens pressed to closely upon people, lifted the heavens upon his shoulders, and standing upon the Atlas Mountains of North Africa (Morocco), held the heavens away from the earth. We will discuss the Titans in more detail later. They were the foremost followers of the man who is said to have built the Tower. He was the first or leading Titan.

All of these legends, and there are more like them, appear to be a remembrance of what Cush and Nimrod did in leading a rebellion to push God out of the affairs of mankind, thus doing man the great favor (a favor if you support rebellion against God), of attempting to push God out of the affairs of men. To put it more simply, Nimrod supposedly got God off of people's backs.

Berosus, a priest of Babylon, wrote, "They say that the first inhabitants of the earth, glorying in their own strength and size and despising the gods, undertook to build a tower, whose top should reach the sky, upon the spot where Babylon now stands. But, when it approached heaven, the winds assisted the gods, and overturned the work upon its contrivers. These ruins are said to be at Babylon, and the gods introduced a diversity of tongues among men, who until that time had all spoken the same language". (as quoted by Cory & Hodges, p. 55)

For instance, on the island of Hao, part of the Puamotuor or Tuamotu islands in Polynesia, the people used to tell that after a great flood the sons of Rata, who survived, made an attempt to erect a building by which they could reach the sky and see the creator god Vatea (or Atea). "But in anger, the god chased the builders away, broke down the building, and changed their language, so that they spoke diverse tongues" (Williamson, vol. 1, p.94). Williamson wrote, "As to the question of Biblical influence, I can certify that this tradition contains many ancient words which today are no longer understood by the natives."

## Just As It Was Meant To Be

The world in its sleep lies slumbering on,
No signs of awakening they see,
But we're gathered together to greet the dawn,
Just as it was meant to be,
We know that the fig tree is leafy and green,
All the signs of Your coming we see,
And soon Your great glory will dawn and be seen,
Just as it was meant to be,
Like a new born babe just opening its eyes,
Like the first glimmer of light on the sea,
We hear a voice saying arise, arise,
Just as it was meant to be,
The red dragon is falling from the skies,
The beast will soon rise from the sea,
But God's on the throne, so open your eyes,
Just as it was meant to be,
Now Father, oh Father, show us the sign,
Which for ages we've waited to see,
A new day will dawn and Your glory will shine,
Just as it was meant to be,
And forever and ever Your word will be law,
Forever and ever Your reign we will see,
Yes all the world over Your word shall be law,
Just as it was meant to be,
The future belongs to Thee,
The future belongs to Thee,
A new day is dawning and we will be free,
Just as it was meant to be,

- Dr. N. James Brooks, Jr.

"There are only three types of people;
those who have found God and serve him;
those who have not found God and seek him,
and those who live not seeking or finding him.
The first are rational and happy;
the second unhappy and rational,
and the third foolish and unhappy."

- Blaise Paschal

# CHAPTER ELEVEN
## Where Was The Tower of Babel

"Now the plain in which they first dwelt was called Shinar". (Josephus, p.46)

"The place wherein they built the tower is now called Babylon". (Josephus, p.46)

Berosus, a priest of Babylon, wrote that the ruins of the Tower "are said to be at Babylon". (Cory & Hodges, p.55)

"And the Lord sent a mighty wind against the tower and overthrew it upon the earth, and behold it was between Asshur and Babylon in the land of Shinar". (Charles, p.82)

The Tower itself is referred to as the Tower of Babel. This is because it was built, the Bible tells us, at the city of Babel. Babel in Hebrew means "confusion." In the rest of the Semitic languages however, it means "Gateway of God." The sentences above make it clear that the Tower of Babel was built in the land of Shinar. Shinar forms the southern part of Iraq. In ancient times that part of the world was known as Mesopotamia. The Tower was built at or near the city of Babylon, which the Bible says was at one time called Babel by the Hebrews. "The place in which they built the Tower is now called Babylon, on account of the confusion of the tongues; for confusion is, by the Hebrews, called Babel". (Cory and Hodges, p.55)

It seems that this should make it easy to determine where Babel was. The matter is not that simple however. There are at least three cities that are believed by various people to be the city

176

of Babylon, and likewise there are three pyramids that vie for the title of Tower of Babel. Further, as you will see, we cannot be certain that the name of the city of Babel or Babylon was not changed at some time in the past.

However, what about the thought that the Tower was actually a pyramid? Any thinking person might here ask how the Tower could have been a pyramid? The pyramids of Mesopotamia, and indeed all the pyramids in the world, with the exception of most of Egypt's pyramids, are what are known as "step pyramids." They are so-called because they are built in levels, or steps, with each level being a little smaller than the one directly beneath it. They also have actual steps going up the sides so that anyone who wished to could ascend to the top of the pyramid, where there was often a temple to a god.

There are many pyramids in Mesopotamia, of which Shinar is a part, but there are only three that are considered for the title of Tower of Babel. The question becomes, which is the actual Tower?

As already stated, in Hebrew, Babel means "confusion" (Catholic Encyclopedia on-line). At one time however, the city known today as Babylon was known as Tintir, which means "Place of the Tree of Life" (Catholic Encyclopedia on-line). Borsippa, the twin-city of Babylon, is located about six miles from its sister city. Like Babylon it was abandoned about 300 years before the birth of Christ. It is the site of a ruined step pyramid. This ruined pyramid has long been known to the locals as Birs Nimrud, meaning "Tower of Nimrod." This is also translated as "ruins of Nimrod." According to inscriptions found on cylinders, deposited, one on each level of the pyramid, the pyramid doubled as a temple, and was repaired by King Nebuchadnezzar. The inscriptions further read that this pyramid was the most ancient monument of Borsippa, built by a long-ago king, who was unable to finish the top of the pyramid, where the temple itself was supposed to be. (Jones, p.3)

Borsippa was once called "the second Babylon." And its temple tower was named "the supreme house of life" (Pinches, p.24). Borsippa means, in Assyrian, "The Tower of Tongues." The ancient cuneiform texts use another word for Borsippa. This word means "the town of the dispersion of tribes" (Lenormant, pp.131-132.). The pyramid at Borsippa is one of three pyramids in the area. Differing authorities claim one or the other of them as the original Tower of Babel. The pyramid at Borsippa is held by most to be the remains of the Tower of Babel. (Sayce, p.112-3, 405-7)

The reason that the cuneiform tablets deposited at the pyramid of Borsippa gave for the pyramid never being completed in that long-ago day when its construction was begun, is as follows. "People had abandoned it, without order expressing their words". (Jones, p.3)

Near the center of this city, in ancient times there was a pyramid known as the Temple of Marduk. An ancient tablet was found there that reads in part, "The building of this illustrious tower offended the gods. In a night, they threw down what they had built. They scattered them abroad and made strange their speech" (Halley, p.84). That pyramid no longer exists. Where it once stood there is now only a vast hole 330 feet square. The pyramid itself was dismantled and carried away brick by brick by people seeking easily obtained bricks for building. (Ceram, p.285; see also Halley, p.84)

Herodotus, the famous Greek geographer, visited the city that we commonly know as Bablyon, and the temple/pyramid there. This was about the year 458 B.C. Herodotus left a description of the pyramid from his own observation. He described it as being composed of seven levels, with each level dedicated to a different god, and painted in that god's color. There was a large temple on that first level, furnished with pure gold. (Ceram, p.287-290)

Herodotus described the Tower thusly:

> *The temple of Jupiter Belus occupies the other, whose huge gates of brass may still be seen. It is a square building, each side of which is of the length of two furlongs. In the midst a tower rises of the solid depth and height of one furlong; on which, resting as a base, seven other turrets are built in regular succession. The ascent on the outside, which, winding from the ground, is continued to the highest tower;* ("Herodotus," vol.1, p.135)

Ceram writes that the base of the Tower was 288 feet on a side, the total height of Tower and temple also 288 feet. The first stage was 105.6 feet in height; the second, 57.6 feet; the third, fourth, fifth, and sixth, 19.2 feet each; and the Temple of Marduk 48 feet in height. The temple housed the most important god in the Babylonian pantheon. The walls of the temple were plated with gold, and decorated with enameled brickwork of a bluish hue, which glittered in the sun, greeting the traveler's eye from afar. (Ceram, p.289)

The Babylonian ruler Nabopolassar, and his son, Nebuchadnezzar, each left an inscription telling of their work of restoration on the Tower. (Ceram, p.288). The inscription left by Nabopolassar has been translated thus: "At that time Marduk (Babylonian god of war), commanded me to build the Tower of Babel, which had become weakened by time and fallen into disrepair . . . . " (Ceram, p.288)

Pinches felt that the temple tower of E-sagila in Babylon is the most likely of the pyramid temples to have been the Biblical Tower of Babel. This temple had a shrine upon it called "The temple of the foundation of heaven and earth" (Pinches, p.23). We do not know for certain when the above-mentioned city was built, nor do we know if it is the true Babylon or not. Ferrar Fenton, in a footnote to his translation of Genesis 10, says that the above city was built by King Nebuchadnezzar, which would make it not nearly old enough to have been the original Tower of Babel. (Fenton, p.9, fn.). Likewise, we do not know when the tablet was placed there. It could, for all we know, have been placed there many centuries after the destruction of the Tower of Babel, and could have been placed at the wrong pyramid simply by mistake. The wrong pyramid might have been chosen because the very city that was thought to be Babel could have been the wrong city. The inscription reads in part that this was "The tower of Borsippa, which a former king erected and completed to a height of 42 cubits, whose summit he did not finish, fell into ruins in ancient times". (Halley, p.83)

Sir Henry Rawlinson saw and described the tower/step pyramid of Borsippa, and included his belief that the inscription on it was correct about it being erected "in the remotest antiquity by one of the primitive Babylonian kings," and later rebuilt by Nebuchadnezar. (Hilprecht, p.186)

Of the three pyramids mentioned as contenders for the title of Tower of Babel, the pyramid at Borsippa is held by most to be the remains of the Tower of Babel. (Sayce, p.112-3, 405-7)

In many an inscription of Nebuchadnezzar, the temple-towers at both Babylon and Borsippa are referred to as having been restored by him. Thus, in what is known as the great cylinder of Nebuchadnezzar, the following statement occurs – "I caused the fanes (sacred towers) of Babylon and Borsippa to be rebuilt and endowed." (Pinches, "The Old Testament: In the Light of the Historical Records and Legends of Assyria and Babylonia," p.138)

There are those who call Borsippa "the second Babylon" (Pinches, "The Religion of Babylonia and Assyria," p.24). The great temple at Borsippa "may have disputed with the 'House of the High Head,' E-sagila in Babylon, the honor of being the site of the confusion of tongues and the dispersion of mankind". (Pinches, "The Religion of Babylonia and Assyria," p.24)

Though most scholars believe that the ruined pyramid at Borsippa is the Tower of Babel (Sayce, p.112-3, 405-7), there is also speculation that a pyramid at the city of Eridu is the true Tower. The ancient city of Eridu is referred to as the original "Babylon" by the historian Berossos. Berosus, or Berossos, was a priest of Bal who lived during the time of Alexander the Great. (Verbrugghe and Wickersham, p.70)

So, which of the three pyramids was the real Tower of Babel? You decide. You be the judge.

## You Illuminate My Way

Once I walked in darkness and the darkness held sway,
Then You came and chased the dark away,
You are the light that forever holds sway,
You are the light Who illuminates my way,
How could I have been so blind,
You do more than chase the night away,
You do more than keep the dark at bay,
You illuminate the night, You illuminate the day,
And whenever I will let You, You illuminate my way,
The darkness is not dark to You, the dark is like the day,
Without You I am blind, but with You to illuminate the way,
I can see where I am going, I can see the way,
For you illuminate the darkness, You illuminate my way,
No gifts of myrrh and incense brought on a silver tray,
No gifts that kings would appreciate,
have I gained in my earthly stay,
But I know Him who keeps the dark at bay,
He who illuminates the day,
And I worship before Your throne,
for you illuminate my way,

- Dr. N. James Brooks, Jr.

*"Noble deeds that are concealed are the most esteemed."*

-    Blaise Paschal

# CHAPTER TWELVE
# The Builder of the Tower of Babel

In the last chapter, we discussed which of the step-pyramids of Mesopotamia might be the actual Tower of Babel. In this chapter, we are going to discuss the man who took the lead in the building of that Tower.

First let us look at Noah's three sons, Shem, Ham, and Japheth. One of Ham's sons was Cush. Because in ancient times a person's name meant something and was supposed to tell something about them or their life, it behooves us today when reading about such people to know what their name meant. In the case of Cush, his name means literally "Burnt Face," i.e. Cush was black. All black people were called Cushites in Hebrew. The scripture that asks, "Can the Ethiopian change his skin, or the leopard his spots" (Jeremiah 13:23), says literally, "Doth a Cushite change his skin and a leopard his spots?" ("Young's Literal Translation of the Bible").

Not all of the descendants of Ham are Black. This is because Ham, according to legend, had several wives. Though he had only one wife with him in the ark, he is said to have married other women later. Those women would have been nieces and other close relatives, since the only people immediately after the flood were the children of Noah's three sons and several generations of their descendants. In saying that Ham over a period of time married more than one woman and that they were all his close kin, it must be remembered that the survivors on the ark lived for several hundred years after the flood, while the first six generations born after the flood lived for several centuries. (See Genesis 11:10-23).

According to a Roman work called the Fabulae, men lived for centuries after the flood under the government of God, with no laws or cities, and with one common language. Then Mercury, also known as Hermes, arose. The Fabulae says that because of Mercury (or Hermes) the various languages began, ethnic groups were divided, and disagreement and discord began. In Egyptian, Hermes means "the son of Ham." This legend is thus speaking of Cush. (Hislop, p.25-26). Ham had a number of sons. However, only one of them, Cush, was worshipped as a god. Therefore, the god Hermes, also called Mercury, was Cush.

Some ancient historians ascribe to Cush the building of the Tower and the first movement after the flood to get people to rebel against God. It seems logical, after studying all that is said, to believe that Cush began the rebellion and the building of the Tower (Hislop, p.31). If Ham's progeny were mainly responsible for leading mankind away from obedience to God and into the worship of false gods, the historian Gregorius Turonensis laid most of the blame for this on Cush (Hislop, p.25, note 4).

It was another however who brought both the rebellion and the Tower to their completion. That other was Cush's son Nimrod. He brought the rebellion that Cush began to its fullness (Hislop, p.31). The Jewish Encyclopedia says that Nimrod "made all the people rebellious against God" (The Jewish Encyclopedia, vol.9, p.309). Nimrod is also the one who completed the city of Babylon and the Tower. "The king who built both the city and the Tower of Babel was Nimrod" (Pinches, p.126). Properly speaking the "land of Nimrod" (Micah v. 6) is Babylon . . . . the land whose great cities he was regarded as having founded . . . . and the land where . . . . he ruled when he was king upon earth". (Pinches, p.126)

"Now it was Nimrod who excited them to such an affront and contempt of God. He was the grandson of Ham, the son of Noah, a bold man, and of great strength of hand. He also said he would be revenged on God, if he should have a mind to drown the world again; for that he would build a tower too high for the waters to be able to reach and that he would avenge himself on God for destroying their forefathers!" (Josephus, pp.46-47)

Genesis 10:8-9 says "Cush begot Nimrod; he began to be a mighty one on the earth.  He was a mighty hunter before the Lord; therefore it is said, "Like Nimrod the mighty hunter before the Lord." The Hebrew word translated "before" can also mean "against," meaning that Nimrod was opposed to God. (Clarke, p.86). Genesis 10:10-12 continues, "And the beginning of his kingdom was Babel, Erech, Accad, and Calneh, in the land of Shinar. From that land, he went to Assyria and built Nineveh, Rehoboth Ir, Calah, and Resen between Nineveh and Calah (that is the principal city)."

"Nimrod son of Chus was the first to seize despotic rule over the people, which men were not yet accustomed to; and he reigned in Babylon". (St. Jerome, p.40).

Nimrod prided himself on his physical strength. He is represented by Homer (in the Odyssy), as a giant, and as being continually in pursuit of wild beasts. (Bryant, edition of 1874, vol. I, p.9). The better to remind people of his strength, he liked to be depicted with the horns (Hislop, pp.65, 229), tail, and cloven hoof of a bull or ox. The following example well explains what the Anglo-Saxon ancestors of today's English people came to think of Nimrod. Most of the English people today are of Anglo-Saxon descent. Though they do not know why, they commonly think of Satan as black. More than that, he is generally depicted as having horns, a tail, and a cloven hoof, just as Nimrod was depicted in ancient times. The English today probably think of Satan in this manner because their ancestors spoke of an evil deity who looked exactly like the present day English idea of Satan. They called him "Zer-Nebo-Gus." Zer-Nebo-Gus is not a Saxon name. It comes from ancient Babylonia. It means "the seed (descendant) of the prophet Cush". (Hislop, p.34)

It is of further interest that today in the English language we have a word for someone or something that is not what it is pretended to be. That word is "bogus." Nimrod offered a bogus god, his father Cush, to the peoples of the world. He also offered them a bogus high priest for that god, himself. Bogus (Zer-ne bogus) has become our word for something fake, an imposter or a fraud that is passed off as the real thing, which it is not.

Saint Jerome, who lived in the 4th and early 5th centuries, wrote that Assyria was settled by people from Babylonia, which people also founded Nineveh. He further said that Nineveh was named for "Ninus, the son of Bel" (Saint Jerome, pp.40-41). Nineveh actually means "the habitation of Ninus". (Hislop, p.24)

When reading that Ninus was the son of Bel, we must remember that most of the titles by which Nimrod was known were also used for his father. Bel was one of those titles or names. The only title or name that was used exclusively for Nimrod was the name Nimrod and the name or title of Ninus, "The Child." Ninus was a very common name for Nimrod in parts of the ancient world. There is no question that Ninus and Nimrod are the same individual. Indeed, the Roman historian Apollodorus, who was born in 180 A.D., stated that "Ninus is Nimrod" (Hislop, p.54). Ninus, meaning "The Child," is a name Nimrod's widow gave him after his death. Yet another early Christian writer, named Clement, wrote that "a certain king Nimrod . . . . whom the Greeks also called Ninus, and from whom the city of Nineveh took its name". (Clement, "Recognitions of Clement," Book IV, chapter XXIX)

The Plain of Shinar (southern Iraq) was itself once known as the Land of Nimrod. The city of Babylon was founded by Nimrod, who called the city Babel. You will recall that some feel

Babel should be translated as the court or gate of God. Bab-El, they feel, comes from babah, a gate, and El, meaning God. (Bullinger, p.507)

Jacob Bryant said of Cush, "His sons were the first rebels upon record. The building of the Tower called Babel is supposed to have been effected under their direction, for Babel was the place of habitation, where their imperious prince Nimrod, who was called Alorus and Orion, resided" (Bryant, "New System or an Analysis of Ancient Mythology," Vol. 3, p.148). Ancient Irish records, predating the arrival of Christianity to Ireland, also state that "Nimrod and his kinsfolk" were the builders of the Tower. (Keating, Vol. II, p.2.)

Some ancient historians thus state that Nimrod's initial help in building the Tower came from other Black people, other descendants of his father Cush. Much of Nimrod's later help in his attempt to spread his authority through war also came from other descendants of Cush (Cushites). If this is true, where did these Cushites, these Black people live? Some undoubtedly lived in the area where Babylon was built. Sir Henry Rawlinson, the first translator of primitive Babylonian documents, declares the vocabulary employed in those documents to be 'decidedly Cushite or Ethiopian,' and states that he was able to interpret the inscriptions chiefly by the aid which was furnished to him from published works on the Galla or Abyssinian and the Mahia or South Arabian dialects' (Rawlinson, "Egypt and Babylon," p.8). Though no Black people live in the area of old Babylon today, there are Black people, known as Marsh Arabs, who live in the marshes in the delta of the Euphrates River, south of the ruined city of Babylon, but still in the land of ancient Sumer.

There is also evidence that many Black people, Cushites, lived in what is now the southern part of the Arabian Desert. At that time, it was not a desert. Rawlinson observed that linguistic evidence showed the early existence in Arabia of at least two races, one in the north and central part of Arabia, who were a Semitic people, and the other in the south, who were non-Semitic. The one in the south possessed a language resembling the dialects of the aborigines of Ethiopia. (McClure, p.31). "The ancient home of the Cushite race was .... Arabia" (Garnier, p.281).

Support for this idea comes from a discovery in the Arabian desert of ancient rock carvings of tall black cattle herders, looking like the Watusi and Masai, who live today in Africa. This find suggests that the people of East Africa may be living descendants of those ancient Black herdsmen who lived in southern Arabia when it was a fertile, well-watered land (McClure, p.80). In addition, there are still Black people living in the coastal part of southwestern Arabia today. This region is known as the Hadramaut.

Legends concerning the origins of the Yoruba, a tribe that lives in Nigeria, relate that in the second millennium B.C. a people known as Kishites began to enter Africa from Arabia, landing first on the Ethiopian coast along the Red Sea and later gradually spreading south and west (Murray, p.76). It has been speculated that these Kishites, from whom the Yoruba descend, came from the city of Kish in Sumer. According to Sultan Bello of Sokoto, the Yoruba are of the tribe of Nimrod. (Murray, p.76). In the late nineteenth century, Sultan Bello was a chief of the Yoruba.

Kish was about eight miles from Babylon. The Sumerians tell us that Kish was the first city built after the flood. The city of Kish was indeed founded, according to most archaeological estimates, shortly after the flood. One version of the Sumerian King List opens the history of post flood civilization with the following statement: "After the flood had swept over the earth and when kingship was lowered again from heaven, kingship was first in Kish". (Pritchard's "Ancient Near Eastern Texts," p.265)

Some early histories refer to Nimrod as "King of the World." This was a title which the rulers of the Babylonian Empire later took for themselves. It was from their rulership of Kish that the Babylonian emperors claimed their royal title as "King of the World" (Unger, p.53). It is quite possible that they modeled themselves after Nimrod, taking the title "King of the World" because they ruled the city of Kish, just as Nimrod perhaps had, for he may have ruled from Kish before he built the city of Babylon.

Among other reasons for thinking that Cush and his son Nimrod were originally from the city of Kish, there is a Hungarian legend that says the father of Nimrod was Tana. (Legend of The White Stag). Etana was according to Sumerian mythology the earliest known ruler of the city of Kish. The Kishites believed that their city was founded by Etana. Etana could be Cush under a different name. You will recall that in those times, and for thousands of years afterwards, people's names changed from time to time because of events in their lives.

How long ago did Nimrod rule? The Roman historian Velleius Paterculus, recorded that between the reign of Ninus (Nimrod) and the conquest of Philip II, King of Macedonia, by the Romans, lay an interval of nearly 2000 years (1995 years to be exact). (Velleius Paterculus, vol.1, p.15). Paterculus further states that Ninus was king of the Assyrians, and that he was the first to hold world power. Philip was defeated by the Romans in 197 B.C. If Paterculus is accurate in his chronology, Nimrod began his reign in 2192 B.C. Another writer says of Nimrod that "according to the common chronology he was contemporary with the Emperor Shun, of China" (Legge, p.54). According to the Encyclopedia Britannica, Shun was Emperor of China twenty-three hundred years before the birth of Christ.

Nimrod had other names besides those already mentioned. He was known under the name of Alorus as the first king of

Chaldea. Additionally, he was known as Orion. (Editor's note – Chaldea here refers to the southern half of Iraq). The Greeks often referred to Nimrod as Nebrod. (Bryant, vol. I, p.9)

So far in this article we have seen that Nimrod had at least five names with different meanings, two of those names being Nimrod and Ninus. In ancient times, a person's name might change several times during his or her lifetime. A child's name usually changed as he or she grew older and something noteworthy happened in their life. Even as an adult, people would have name changes to symbolize a noteworthy change or event in their life. Even today that still occurs at times in some cultures.

When the late Emperor Hirohito of Japan died and his son prepared to ascend the throne, the son gave himself a new name. Important people would also be known by a different name in countries where a different language was spoken. Sometimes an individual would have a number of name changes. If we do not know what different names an individual had, the history of their life and times can become very confusing. Name changing sometimes makes it hard to keep up with people of the ancient world, for we are often not told of a name change, we simply stop hearing about someone by one name and then begin hearing about what appears to be another person. A different name is being used, but it may be the same person.

When we know that a name change has occurred, it behooves us to look at the meaning of the new name. Looking at the meanings of the names of ancient people will usually tell us something about that person. Ham, for example, means "Dark" (referring to his complexion), and also "Hot" as in hot tempered. Ham is a Hebrew word, and Hebrew is a member of the Semitic language family. In the language of the ancient Semitic peoples many personal names were intended to have two meanings.

Many names in ancient times, in both Semitic and in many other languages, were intended to have a double meaning. Vowels were not used in spelling, which made it easier to give names a double meaning (Garnier, p.21), as a number of words would have been spelled alike. As an example, in English, bell, bill, and ball, would all have been spelled bll.

The name Nimrod is one of those words that has a double meaning. Nimrod is said to have tamed leopards and to have begun their use in hunting, as is still done on a small scale in India, today. Therefore, one meaning of his name is leopard tamer, or "tamer of the leopard" (Kautzsch, p.137 2b) as it is usually rendered. The spelling of Nimrod, nmr, is the way that leopard tamer was spelled. Leopard is spelled mrd. To spell tamer of the leopard, one adds the letter n in front of the word leopard. Since Semitic words were commonly spelled with only three letters, when a letter was added in front of a word, the last letter was then dropped. The word leopard tamer would thus be spelled nmr, the exact way that Nimrod was spelled.

What a name meant could often be determined only by its relationship to the words around it, so if the context did not tell you what a name meant, you would be hard pressed to discover it, since virtually all words were spelled with only three letters and none of them were vowels.

The other meaning of Nimrod's name comes from marad, (see Strong's Exhaustive Concordance of the Bible, #4775). Marad means "to revolt," or "to rebel," pointing to violent resistance to God (see Kiel and Delitzsch's Old Testament Commentary). The name fits Nimrod, because "he was a rebel against God, as is generally said, and because he caused all the world to rebel against God, by the advice he gave to the . . . builders of Babel" (Gill, comments on Genesis 10:8, p.68). Like the word leopard," to rebel" is also spelled mrd. If an "n" is added before the "m," the spelling then becomes "nmr," and the word now means "The

192

Rebel." (Kautzsch, p.137, 2b). Nimrod's name thus has the meanings of both "Leopard Tamer" and "The Rebel."

In addition to names often having more than one meaning, the same person might be known by one name in one country, while in another country that same person might be called by a different name. This was true even when two small countries bordered each other.

For example, you will recall that one of the three pyramids considered as possibly being the original Tower of Babel is a pyramid at the city of Eridu. The ancient city of Eridu was referred to as the original "Babylon" by the historian Berossos, a priest of Bal who lived during the time of Alexander the Great. (Verbrugghe and Wickersham, p.70.) Associated with this pyramid is a Sumerian hero and ruler named Enmer-kar. In Sumerian, the suffix "kar" means "hunter," so "Enmer-kar" is in fact "Enmer the Hunter," just as Nimrod is referred to as a mighty hunter in Genesis 10.

Furthermore, Enmerkar is named in the Sumerian King List as "the one who built Uruk," just as Nimrod is described in Genesis 10:10 as having a kingdom that began in Babel (Eridu) and Erech (Uruk)... in the land of Shinar. Further, Enmerkar would have been spelled nmr, just as Nimrod was. After Enmerkar's death he was worshipped by the Sumerians as the god Nimurta. (Here we have nmr again, which you will recall means to rebel, like the name of Nimrod.) In time, the Babylonians also came to worship Nimurta. All the above makes it very likely that Enmerkar and Nimurta were two additional names for Nimrod.

Yet another name for Nimrod is Marduk. (Pinches, p.141). Marduk was the Babylonian god of war. In time, the worship of Marduk became part of the state religion of Babylon. (Verbrugghe & Wickersham, p.70. Merodach was the chief god of Babylon, and according to the Babylonians, the city of Babylon was built by him. (Pinches, p.126). Merodach was also another name for Nimrod. (Pinches, p.13). Like people, gods and goddesses were often worshipped under different names in ancient times.

Nimrod had a crown made that he used as the symbol of his authority, for another ancient writer, Pherecydes of Syros, a Greek writer of the 6th century B.C., recorded that Nimrod was "the first before all others that ever wore a crown" (Cory and Hodges, p.173). This was the time, when, "according to the Greek historian Hyginus, the first kingdom upon earth was constituted, and when one language only prevailed among the sons of men" (Cory and Hodges, p.173).

Many ancient writers say that Nimrod got the idea of wearing a circular crown of gold upon his head from a circular constellation in the night sky known as the Northern Crown. (Rolleston, p.131). There was an ancient prophecy involving the Northern Crown. This prophecy said there was coming a ruler who would be born of a virgin. (Rolleston, p.16-17). The prophecy said the Northern Crown belonged to that coming ruler and king. Nimrod claimed that crown and that status for himself, though it in no way fit him. Nimrod said he was the prophesied king who was to come. After the scattering of the world's people at the Tower, Nimrod used war and a false religion to try and reestablish his control over the various ethnic groups of the earth. We are told that Nimrod began the first post flood wars, subduing all the peoples then living in the East. (Hislop, p.25). Ninus "conquered all the nations from Assyria to Libya" (Garnier, p.25). It was however through the false religion that he started that Nimrod made his biggest and most lasting attempt to gain control of the earth's people.

Thus, ends this article on the Tower of Babel and its builders. Our story about Nimrod does not end here though, for the next article will tell of the attempt by Nimrod to entice people to serve him though the false religion that he began, the first organized false religion on the earth, which involved the idea of reincarnation and the worship of his father Cush.

*"The heart has its reasons which reason knows nothing of."*

-   Blaise Pascal

## A Stone in God's Temple

Christian, mid your daily duties,
When cares oppress your heart,
When no matter what your efforts,
Troubles form life's greatest part,
Do not let your heart be tempted,
From its hold on truth and light,
Do not let your footsteps falter,
In the pathway of the right,

Yes, tho your way seem weary,
Never halt you in the fight,
For step by step will bring you,
The reward that awaits the right,
And perseverance in the conflict,
Make you a stone in God's temple of light.

- Daniel Allen Johnston

# CHAPTER THIRTEEN
## The First Organized False Religion

We are shortly to read how Nimrod founded the world's first organized false religion. There had been people before Nimrod who were prayed to and worshipped as gods after their deaths, but until Nimrod began it, there was no organized religion. Both God and false gods had been worshipped, but again, there was no organized religion. You will remember that people often had their names changed in ancient times when they did something unusual or noteworthy. We have also learned that the gods and goddesses of the heathen were people who had done some noteworthy deed and for that were declared to be gods after their death. Let us look at one of the oldest gods of mankind, the first at any rate to be worshipped after the flood. In English, his name means Heaven. His name in Greek is Ouranos.

Another form of Ouranos is Uranus. Uranus and his wife were the most ancient of the Greek gods. (Robbins, p.17). Euhemerus was a Greek philosopher who lived about 330-260 B.C. Euhemerus is quoted as saying that Uranus was the first who honored the heavenly gods with sacrifices, upon which account his name was changed to Heaven. (Eusebius, p.60). Uranus's earlier name, according to Eusebius, was Epigetus or Autochthon. (Eusebius, p.36). (Eusebius, circa 275 A.D. to 339 A.D., from whom I am quoting, was bishop of Caesarea in Palestine and is often called the father of church history.) Autochthon means indigenous or native, and formed or originating in the place where found, according to the Merriam-Webster Dictionary. As we have seen, Eusebius translated it as "Earth Born" (Eusebius, p.36).

Euhemerus is quoted as saying that Uranus was "honored by all and universally acknowledged as a god" (Cory and Hodges,

p. 172-174). Uranus's wife's name means Earth. (Robbins, p.17). The Romans in their own language of Latin called Uranus by the name of Coelus, which means Heaven, and his wife they called Terra, which of course means Earth. The wife of Uranus was first known as Titea. (Cumberland, p.292). Later her name was changed to Gaia or Ge (Cumberland, p.292), which means "Earth" in Greek (Cumberland, p.292). Some accounts say she was renamed after the earth because she was held to be as beautiful as this earth, our world. (Cumberland, p.292). If Heaven and Earth were real people who were renamed and then worshipped as Gods after their deaths, who were they?

We may learn something more about them from the names of their children. An ancient pre-Christian history of great note in the ancient world was called the "Sibylline Oracles." These writings were held in the highest esteem by the Romans. They are sometimes held to be the writing of one woman, but more commonly they were thought to have been a history written and preserved by a group of priestesses called the Sibyls. Copies of these writings existed in temples in many cities in the ancient world. Following is a portion of those writings in which three sons of Heaven and Earth are named. "Twas the tenth age successive, since the flood ruin'd the former world: when foremost far amid the tribes of their descendants stood Cronus, and Titan, and Iapetus, offspring of Heaven and Earth" (Bryant, p.99). If these men, said to be the descendants of Heaven and Earth, were real people who were declared to be gods after their deaths, who were they and how can knowing who they were tell us who their parents were?

The Greek writer Eupolemus specifically said that Cronus was the father of Canaan (Cumberland, pp.118), and in the Bible, we learn that Ham was Canaan's father. ("Ham was the father of Canaan," Genesis 9:18). Thus, we know that Cronus was Noah's son Ham. Iapetus is a Greek way of spelling Japheth, for Japetus

**199**

and Iapetus are Greek forms of Japheth (Cory & Hodges, p.76) as is Iapetos, a variant spelling of Iapetus. (Rouse, vol. XXXVIII, p.126. Noah and his wife had three sons. Genesis 9:18, "And the sons of Noah that went forth of the ark were Shem, and Ham, and Japheth: and Ham is the father of Canaan." Now we know who the couple were who were renamed Heaven and Earth by the ancients. They were none other than Noah and his wife.

Since Canaan was the son of Ham and Noah was the father of Ham, Uranus would have been Noah. Further, Uranus is described as having been the first in the world to offer sacrifices to heaven, and Noah was the first person after the flood -the first in the new world that existed after the flood, to offer a sacrifice to the God of heaven. Thus, we see that after the flood, among the first gods of the pagans were our ancestors, Noah and his wife.

In the Rig Veda, an ancient writing of India, it is stated that the first and most important of the Indian gods are the Sky God, Dyaus Pitar (Murdoch, p.22), which means Heaven Father (Garnier, p.22), [or Father Heaven]. His wife was the Earth Mother, Mata Prithivi. They are called the Father and Mother of the gods (Murdoch, p.22).

In the religion of the native New Zealanders, Heaven and Earth are said to be the parents of us all. They are called Rangi and Papa, or Heaven and Earth (Grey, p.1). Rangi and Papa are also the names by which the peoples of New Guinea refer to the supreme god and his wife. These people, just like the Greeks, the Romans and some other ancient peoples, claimed that Heaven and Earth were our remote ancestors, the parents of us all. Do you understand why?

We have now learned something of one of the first false religions of mankind. But what of Nimrod and the false religion that he founded? He and many of Cush's other descendants at first refused to leave the site of the Tower when the confusion of languages occurred. "They stood their ground at the general migration of families, but were at last scattered over the face of the earth" (Bryant, vol. 1, p.vii). "Nimrod would still obstinately stay". (Hislop, p.233)

Though God scattered the peoples of the earth by giving each extended family a different language, not all left the area around the Tower or Nimrod's control. Nimrod also sought to find new ways to reunite the earth's people, to make them one again. As part of his effort to do that, Nimrod founded a religion that he hoped would draw the peoples of the earth together and unite them against God like the Tower had done. Nimrod declared his deceased father, Cush, to be a god, thus beginning his new religion. He gave Cush the title of Bal, or Ba-al in some dialects, meaning Lord or Master.

Another title Nimrod gave to Cush was Bel. Bel has a double meaning. It means "The Confounder," because his followers believed him responsible for confounding the language of mankind and turning one language into many. In addition to meaning the Confounder, Bel also means "The Mingler" (Hislop, p.40). Bel was called "The Mingler," because according to the Greek playwright Aristophanes, Bel mingled all things. (Hislop, p.40) This could be a reference to the attempt to undo God's dispersion of the extended families of the earth. God commanded the peoples of the earth to disperse and spread out over the earth. Instead, Cush and Nimrod built the Tower, hoping to use it to keep the earth's people in one place.

After his own death, Nimrod's wife declared him to be a god like his father. She gave Nimrod the same titles that he had given his father, Bal or Baal, and Bel. The title of Bel, the Confounder and the Mingler, might suit Nimrod more than his father, especially the title of the Mingler, for Nimrod not only took a major part in the construction of the Tower, he also began the world's first organized religion in a further attempt to get the earth's people to remain in Shinar and intermarry instead of dispersing. God said in Genesis that he did not want the earth's people to be one people. Nimrod attempted in vain to make them one. Perhaps he thought of the reason God said He did not want mankind to be one people.

*And the Lord said, Behold, the people is one, and they have all one language; and this they begin to do: and now nothing will be restrained from them, which they have imagined to do. 7 Go to, let us go down, and there confound their language, that they may not understand one another's speech. 8 So the Lord scattered them abroad from thence upon the face of all the earth: and they left off to build the city.* Genesis 11:6-8 (KJV)

The Greeks referred to Cush as Belus, which is a combination of Bel and Bal, having both their meanings. This title was also given to Nimrod after his own death. There is an additional title that was only given to Nimrod. That title was Ninus and means "The Child." Saint Augustine writes:

> *And so, this Chus (Cush), the father of the giant Nemrod (Nimrod), is the first-mentioned of the sons of Cham (Ham) . . . . mention is made of his kingdom which began with the famous city of Babylon and the other cities or regions in that neighborhood.*
>
> *It is mentioned that Assur went out from that land (that is, the land of the Sennaar (Shinar) which belonged to the kingdom of Nemrod, and built Nineve (Nineveh), and the other cities mentioned with it. All this happened later, but it was mentioned here because of the greatness of the kingdom of the Assyrians after its expansion by Ninus, the son of Belus, the builder of the great city of Nineve. Babylon took its name from Belus, just as Nineve from Ninus. Assur (from whom the Assyrians take their name) was not among the sons of Cham*

*(Ham), the middle son of Noe (Noah), but among the sons of Sem (Noah's son Shem), the oldest son of Noe. Thus it is clear that those who later gained the kingdom of the giant and from there proceeded to build other cities (like Nineve, built by Ninus) were descendants of Sem.*
(St. Augustine, p.491)

This agrees with what has already been said. The city of Babylon and the Tower were built primarily by the descendants of Cush. (The reader will recall that the bricks with which the city of Babylon was built were stamped with writing, the language of which was identified as being of Hamitic origin.) These Hamites, descendants of Cush, were later defeated and the land of Babylon was taken over, as St. Augustine says, by descendants of Shem.

Nimrod set himself up as the high priest of the worship of Cush. As high priest, he was known as Bal-cahn), "Bal's priest" (Hislop, p. 232). The sun was declared the personification of Cush, for just as the sun enlightens the physical world, so Cush was said to have enlightened the world spiritually, by turning many from the service and worship of God. As part of this new religion Nimrod taught reincarnation, and that the fires of Bel/Bal/Baal would purify those whose bodies were burned in them, thus rendering them ready for another and a better incarnation. (Hislop, p. 229-232). Indeed, the very name of the land Nimrod ruled, Shinar, means Land of the Regenerator, or Land of the Re-incarnater. Nimrod was said to cause his followers to be reincarnated or reborn, all of them into a better station in life, as a reward for following him. That is why the land he ruled was called Shinar, Land of the Re-incarnater, or Regenerator.

The Greek writer Apollodorus said that "Ninus taught the Assyrians to worship fire." The sun, as the great source of light and heat, was worshipped under the name of Bal. As the sun in the heavens was the great object of worship, so fire was worshipped as Bal's earthly representative. Ab, the 5th month of

203

the Syrio-Chaldean calendar, was devoted to the worship of Bel the Fire-god, and was called by the Sumerians "Month of Bil or Gi-Bil" (Waddell, p.273)

Since we have already seen that fire was worshipped as the enlightener and the purifier. Nimrod is singled out by the voice of antiquity as commencing this fire-worship. The identity of Nimrod and Ninus has already been proved; and under the name of Ninus he is represented as originating the worship of fire.

Before the invention of footnotes, scribes literally wrote between the lines of documents when they wanted to add additional or clarifying information. That is where we get our expression "reading between the lines." The additional information written between the lines was called a "gloss." The Sumerian cuneiform sign for the sun is defined in glosses as meaning "Bel." (Waddell, p.267). Bel was said in the oldest Sumerian hymns to have "settled the places of the Sun and Moon" (Waddell, p.267) Both comments show of course that Bel was more than a name for the sun, and that he was more than the sun god. The sun and fire simply personified Bel. The name of Bel has been discovered to be derived from the Sumerian word for "Fire, Flame or Blaze," namely Bil, for which the written word-sign is a picture of a fire-producing instrument with tinder sticks. (Waddell, p.267)

Fire was worshipped as the enlightener and the purifier. Nimrod is singled out by antiquity as commencing this fire-worship. The identity of Nimrod and Ninus has already been proved; and under both names he is represented as originating the worship of fire.

Nimrod's creation of a false religion as a means of keeping people under his control was like many another tyrant who has used religion to control the masses. It was the policy adopted by Jeroboam, King of Israel, when he set up his golden calves at Dan and Bethel, urging the ten tribes that he ruled to worship the two calves. He did this in hopes that the Israelites under his rule would stop going to Jerusalem to worship at the temple.

Followers of the new religion believed that the spirit of Cush, "The Great Enlightener," as he was sometimes called, had gone into the sun. That at least was believed by later generations. It was never believed that Cush had bodily gone into the sun, for a tomb was erected for him at Babylon. (Diodorus Siculus, Book XVII, 112.3)

The sun and fire were worshipped as personifications of Cush. Since Cush was called The Great Enlightener, it was perhaps logical to associate him with fire and with the sun, as both give light to the physical world, just as Cush was said to have enlightened his followers. This enlightenment was done by awakening them to the idea that they did not need to follow God. Fire and the sun were taken to be merely symbols of the god Cush.

As already stated, after his own death Nimrod was also declared to be a god and was given the same titles as his father Cush. It was only after his death that he was deified. Then, retrospectively, he was worshipped as the child of the Sun, or the Sun incarnate. (Hislop, p.229). Over time, Nimrod gained many other names and titles. He was given different names for the different attributes he was credited with having. Likewise, in different languages he quite often had a different name peculiar to that language.

The Greeks often referred to Nimrod as Nebrod. (Bryant, vol.1, p.9) Bryant speaks of the author of an account called the Paschal Chronicles as saying that it was Nebrod or Nimrod who first taught the Assyrians to worship fire. (Bryant, vol. III, p.39). The fact that Nimrod and Ninus were the same person has already been proven; and under the name of Ninus, Nimrod was represented as originating the practice of fire worship. In a fragment of the writings of Apollodorus, it is said that "Ninus taught the Assyrians to worship fire." (Hislop, p.226). "There is the strongest evidence that apostasy among the sons of Noah began in fire-worship." (Hislop, p.226)

There began to be a tendency towards idolatry; and the adoration of the Sun was introduced by the posterity of Ham" (Bryant, p.7). The Romans identified Bêl with Jupiter and called him Jupiter Heliopolitanus (Robinson, p.8)

As the sun in the heavens was the great object of worship, so fire was worshipped as its earthly representative. Earthly fires would purify those whose bodies were burned in them, thus rendering them ready for a new and a better incarnation. The title given to Nimrod, as the first of the Babylonian kings, by Berosus, indicates the same thing. That title is Alorus, "the god of fire." In his own life-time, however, he set up no higher pretensions than that of being Bal-Khan, or Priest of Baal.... Infants were the most acceptable offerings at his altar. (Hislop, p.231)

Where and in what region of the earth was the first act of sun-worship performed?

> *All are agreed that this form of worship took its rise in the same region to which philology has already conducted us and identified as the father-land of mankind. On the plains of Shinar rose the great tower or temple of Bel, or the Sun. There was the first outbreak of a worship which quickly spread over the earth, continually multiplying its rites and varying its outward forms, becoming ever more gorgeous but ever the more gross, by exhibiting in every land, and among all peoples, the same seminal characteristics and root-affinities which were embodied in the first act of sun-adoration on the Chaldean plain. (Wylie, p.29)*

The worship of fire is associated with Baal even in the Bible. There is the familiar story of Elijah and the prophets of Baal in I Kings 18, where Elijah challenged the priests of Baal, the God of Fire, to have Baal send fire to devour the sacrifice to him. The title given to Nimrod, as the first of the Babylonian kings, by Berosus (a priest of Baal), indicates his great involvement with fire worship, for that title is Alorus, "the god of fire." (Hislop, p.229)

A further example from the Bible of Baal's involvement with fire worship is the word Baal-peor, which is found twice in the Bible. Peor, though it is found in the Old Testament, is not a Semitic word. It is the Hittite word for fire. It is similar to the Greek word for fire, "pyr." The Greek word "pyr" is the word from which our English word "fire" is derived (Mendenhall, p.109). Baal-peor simply translated means the "Master or Lord of Fire."

Everywhere he went, Nimrod was accompanied by dancing and singing, by music, song and revelries. By these means he attempted to excite people and to gain their allegiance to his newly created religion. (Hislop, p.55) Those who danced and sang the praises of Nimrod were led by nine women. The nine muses of Greek mythology were modeled directly on the nine women who led the singing and dancing in honor of Nimrod.

As already said, after his death Nimrod was joined with Cush in being worshipped as a god, usually known by one of the three names of Bal, Bel or Belus. (Hislop, p.226) "He, Nimrod, was likewise styled Belus, but as this was merely a title, it renders his history very difficult to be distinguished." (Bryant, vol. 1, p.11) That means it was difficult to distinguish him from his father Cush, who carried the same title.

To the Canaanites, Phoenicians, and Israelites, Cush and later Nimrod were both known as Baal, which has the same meaning as Bal. Nimrod inherited the titles of Bal, Baal, Bel, and Belus, after his death, when he began to be worshipped. After his death, his widow also gave him a new name, Ninus, which when applied to Nimrod is usually interpreted to mean "The Child." She gave him this title because of the ancient prophecy that included the constellation called the Northern Crown. That prophecy was believed by the Hebrews, the Arabs, and the Persians, to date back to the time of Adam and Eve's third son, Seth. (Josephus, p.43). Many prominent astronomers of the 1800s calculated that the constellations and the accompanying astronomical ideas of the ancients originated around 4,000 years before Christ. (Rolleston, p.6.) (This would place them within the lifetime of Seth.) The prophecy said that the Coming King to whom the Northern Crown belonged would be born of a Virgin.

From ancient times until the 1800s, there were only forty-eight named constellations. (Rolleston, p.2). The first of these is that of a young woman. This constellation was and is known as "The Virgin" (Rolleston, p.97). It is commonly known today by its Greek name, Virgo, which means "The Virgin." The second constellation was and is that of Coma (a Greek word). This is usually translated into English as "The Desired One," or "The Child." Two years after the death of Nimrod, Semiramis gave birth to a blond, blue-eyed son. She claimed that Nimrod was this boy's father. She said further that Nimrod had gotten her pregnant with this child after he had died and become a god. You will recall the baby was born two years after the death of Nimrod and further that Nimrod was black. In addition to the above lies, Semiramis further claimed that the baby was Nimrod reborn or reincarnated.

The ancient just-mentioned prophecy said that the Coming King to whom the Northern Crown belonged would be born of a Virgin, which, believe it or not, Semiramis now claimed she was!

After the death of Nimrod, not content with proclaiming herself to be both a virgin and the mother of a reincarnated Nimrod, called Ninus, Semiramis encouraged the worship of herself, declaring herself to be a goddess. In the ancient Mid-East and in the Roman Empire, there was a goddess with many names, so many that she was called the "Goddess of A Thousand Names," Nimrod's wife, Semiramis, is generally thought to be the original of that goddess. (Garnier, p.274). She apparently took over the statues of pre-existing goddesses, claiming that they were really her. Semiramis was often called Cybele and as Cybele was often depicted with a circular crown on her head. This crown was turreted, that is, it had towers on it. This was to show that it was a statue of the woman who put towers along the walls of Babylon. Regardless of the name associated with any goddess and despite who a depiction of a goddess showed her to be, if she wore a turreted crown it is commonly felt that that statue, painting or carving is of Semiramis.

The statue of Diana at Ephesus is one such statue that depicts Semiramis. We know that it depicts her because the statue has a turreted crown on its head. It was a statue that was said to be of Diana, but those who worshipped Semiramis knew this was really a statue of her. That is why in Acts 19, verse 27, Demetrius the silver smith cried out that "the temple of the great goddess Diana should be despised, and her magnificence should be destroyed, whom all Asia and the world worshippeth." All the world did not worship her under the name of Diana, but people throughout much of the Roman Empire and adjoining parts of the Middle East worshipped her as Semiramis, under many varied and diverse names.

Her father-in-law, Cush, began the construction of Babylon. Her husband, Nimrod, surrounded Babylon with a wall and continued the work on the Tower of Babel, the work that his father had probably begun. It was Semiramis, however, who constructed the towers that strengthened and enhanced the walls of that city.

In her own lifetime, just as she promoted the worship of her dead husband Nimrod, so she also promoted the worship of herself. Now when you hear something about one of the leading gods of the ancient Greeks or Romans, perhaps you will remember both that they were real people and also that they were known by many different names in different countries and in different languages. They were real people, often not very nice people, but real people who were declared to be gods and goddesses after they died. Real people just like you and me.

Nimrod had set himself up as the high priest of the worship of Cush. Nimrod taught reincarnation, and that the bodies of worshippers of Cush should be cremated. He taught that the fire would purify those whose corpses were burned in it, thus rendering them ready for another and a better incarnation. (Hislop, pp. 229-232)

It appears that the practice of cremating the dead began with Nimrod and the worship of Cush which he created. Prior to that time, burial seems to have been the normal mode of treatment for the bodies of the dead. Many people, including the Romans, adopted the practice of cremation. The early Christians reversed this practice, insisting on burying their dead. Only in recent years has cremation been making a comeback in the Western world.

In 1887, a German archaeological expedition in southern Iraq found mounds at two different sites in Babylonia. Both mounds were discovered to contain dwellings for the dead. People on dying had been cremated and then placed in small houses, where it was apparently assumed their spirits would dwell. (Hilprecht, pp.283-84)

It seems logical to connect the cremation and burying of the bodies of all these thousands of ancient Babylonians, who found their last resting place around the sanctuary of their god, with the ziggurat of Bêl itself, remembering that at El-Hiba, the German archaeologist Koldewey also excavated a two-staged ziggurat, or, according to his theory, "the substructure of an especially important tomb" around the base of which, exactly as at Nippur, nothing but "ashgraves" occurred (Hilprecht, p.456). Ashgraves means the ashes of those who have been cremated.

Though Nimrod taught that fire would purify those whose bodies were burned in it, rendering them ready for another and better incarnation, not all those whose bodies were burned in the flames of Baal were already dead. Some were burned alive as a sacrifice to their god. Babies were often sacrificed. These were generally the result of unwanted pregnancies, though parents sometimes sacrificed older children to Bal/Baal in hopes that it would cause him to hear and answer their prayers.

Some of those who died in the flames of Baal worship, especially infants and children, were then eaten by the priests. This is where the word cannibal comes from. Cahn is the Babylonian word for priest. Cahna means "the priest." Cahna-bal therefore means "The Priest of Bal." In English, the spelling has been changed to cannibal. (Hislop, p. 232). "Infants were the most acceptable offerings." (Hislop, p.231)

Sacrifice of infants and young children was often a means of getting rid of those who were unwanted. Devotees surrendered their children to Baal in the flames and "the children's screams were drowned out by the trumpet and drum". (Wright, p.75)

Child sacrifice was a prominent feature of Baal worship. (Hislop, p.231). This was especially true among some peoples, such as the Phoenicians and Carthaginians. (Waddell, p.270). The Carthaginians spoke a dialect of the Canaanite language and

**211**

called themselves Canaanites. (Quigley, p.253). The sacrifice of infants and young children was practiced by them as offerings to their god Moloch, which was another name for Baal. (Quigley, p.254). At the final defeat and conquest of Carthage by the Romans, the horrified Romans reported that the Carthaginians were sacrificing their young children alive to Baal, in hopes that it would induce Baal to intervene and save their city from the Romans. (Quigley, p.253)

Bal/Baal came to be worshipped over most of the world. "The extraordinary prevalence of the worship of the fire-god in the early ages is proved by legends found over all the earth, and by facts in almost every clime." (Hislop, p.230) The Roman historian Pliny, writing in the first century A.D., stated that in his time, the worship of Baal extended as far east as India. (Cicero, end notes, p.199) The Phoenicians are thought to have carried Baal worship to the western and northern coasts of Europe. Baal may have given his name to many localities in the British Isles, such as Belan, and the Baal hills in Yorkshire. (Donnelly, p.67). "Bel, or Belus, meaning Lord or Ruler, is to be met with from India to Scandinavia as the name of a deity, in Irish and in Punic, in Babylon and Assyria". (Rolleston, p.77)

Sir James G. Frazier writes that there are signs of past Bal worship that prevailed "from Ireland on the west to Russia on the east, and from Norway and Sweden on the north to Spain and Greece on the south" (Frazier, p.396).

Seumas MacManus, author of "The Story of the Irish Race," says that Bal is the name by which the ancestors of the Irish worshipped the sun-god when they lived in Asia long ages before. They brought this worship with them when they came to Ireland. The Irish name for May Day is Baltine, meaning "the fire of Bal." MacManus goes on to recount that Saint Patrick had to preach against sun worship in Ireland. (MacManus, p.98)

212

In the Western Hemisphere, the Incas and the Aztecs also worshipped the sun, though they worshipped it by names in their own languages. This does not prove or disprove that they began or did not begin their worship of the sun as Bal worship. However, they not only worshipped the sun, they worshipped the sun using great stepped pyramids, like the stepped pyramids of Mesopotamia.

The Aztecs also sacrificed people to the sun god. Additionally, they practiced cannibalism as a part of their religion, just as Baal worshippers of North Africa and the Middle East did. (Wright, p.41). The Aztecs of ancient Mexico would fatten a captive and eat him as an offering to one of their gods. (Frazer, p.607) The Incas dropped the practice of human sacrifice when a solar eclipse occurred just as the high priest was about to offer someone as a sacrifice to the sun. The solar eclipse caused them to think that the sun god was no longer pleased with human sacrifice.

Most of us have at some point in time read or studied Greek mythology. In the mythology of Greece, that fabulous creature, the Centaur, half-man, half-horse, figures a great deal. That imaginary creature was intended to commemorate the man who first taught the art of horsemanship. The Greeks themselves admitted that the centaurs did not originate as a Greek myth. (Hislop, p.298)

If the myth or idea of the Centaurs did not originate with the Greeks, where did the name Centaur come from and what does it mean? It was originally a Chaldean word. Centaur or Kentaur is derived from Kehn, "a priest," and Tor, "to go round" (Hislop, p.297). "Kehn-Tor," therefore, is "Priest of the Revolver," that is, of the sun, which, to all appearances, revolves daily around the earth. Since Nimrod began the worship of his father Cush with the adoration of the sun, it seems reasonable to make Nimrod the first of the Kentaurs or Centaurs, the priests of the revolver. Centaurs were supposed to have only one eye. This appears to have meant that they were focused solely on the revolver, the sun, who symbolized their god, first Cush and then additionally Nimrod. They had an eye only for their god. Further, just as the sun was in ancient times called the eye of heaven, so the one eye of the centaurs symbolized the sun, as a representation of their god, and their focus on him.

Sir James G. Frazier explains the once widespread custom in much of Europe of pushing a burning wheel down a hill on the longest day of the year. He says the burning wheel represented the chariot wheels of Bel. (Frazier, p.396)

Images of a man in a chariot carrying the sun were sometimes drawn and were meant to represent Bal/Bel. With the passage of time, people took to drawing only one of the wheels of Bal/Bel's chariot, and eventually they would save time by drawing only part of the wheel. By leaving part of the rim of the wheel off, people ended up with the swastika symbol. The sun wheel, as it is called, has been found carved in stone across Europe and North Africa. (Fell, "Bronze Age America," p.280; Fell, "America B.C.," p.68. fn., p.73) Thus, even in America we have found evidence of the worship of Bel, the Sun God. (Fell, "America B.C.," pp.6, 8-9)

**Let Me Dwell in The Land Where God Moved in His Might**

Let me dwell in the land where God moved in His might,
Where so many lived who fought the good fight,
The land that is blest with a trust from the past,
Awaiting the day of God's triumph at last.

Let me dwell in the land that is blest by the dust,
And made bright by the deeds of the righteous and just.

**214**

Who lived by their faith, and unwavering did act,
Made covenant with God, and stood by their pact.

Let me dwell in the land where past victories fierce blasts,
Have placed on the future the imprint of the past.
Give me the land where great triumphs were made,
And victories won, that toppled schemes Satan laid.

Let me dwell in the land that has story and song,
That tell of the triumph of right over wrong.
Give me the land that has God in each spot,
Where the promise He made, will n'er be forgot.

Let me dwell in the land where the Spirit's past waves,
Are remembered by others than those in their graves.
For out of the past, the promise will come.

Just as night heralds the light that is yet to be born,
So with the dark comes the promise of morn.
And the prayers of the dead, with faith which were sown,
Will yet get an answer from Heaven's own throne.

As step after step in the pathway of right,
Results in a stone in the temple of light,
So the things that were promised, we surely shall see.
For out of the past, the promise is born,
And the word that was spoken results in our morn.

-     Dr. N. James Brooks, Jr.

*"Be true, kind and generous, and pray earnestly to God to enable you to keep His commandments and walk in the same all the days of your life."*

-   R.E. Lee

# CHAPTER FOURTEEN
# How Did We Go From One God To Many?

Where our ancient ancestors believed in one God, mankind later believed in many gods. This happened primarily in two different ways. One way was that of famous or renowned people being worshipped as gods after their death. As an example, we have already seen how Noah and his wife were worshipped after their deaths, and where Nimrod had his father Cush worshipped as a god after his death. We know that Nimrod likewise was worshipped as a god after his own death, due to the efforts of his wife, Semiramis.

You will recall that Saturn was a title that was first held by Ham. (Garnier, p.20, 25). As Saturn, and under other names, Ham was worshipped as a god. Ham and all the eight survivors of the flood were worshipped to some degree. Noah seems to have been worshipped very little. His wife was worshipped a great deal in the ancient past. She is still worshipped to the present day in a few remote areas and by some feminists. It has already been said that Noah and his wife were full brother and sister. We also know the name of Noah's wife.

Though we know the name of Noah's wife, we know nothing of the wife of Shem or of Japheth. Japheth was worshipped by some of the peoples descended from him. Ham was likewise worshipped, both by his own descendants and by many other peoples. By reading the legends associated with the gods we can determine accurately who the leading gods of the Greeks and Romans were. Many them were descendants of Cain. The worship of some of the descendants of Cain was begun before the flood. Some of Cain's descendants began to be worshipped because of their prominence before the flood, where many of them are described in Genesis as great inventors. This practice continued after the flood, perhaps in part because of Ham's first wife, the one who survived the flood with him on the Ark.

Cronus, we have learned, was one of the titles that Ham was given. The Roman writer, Plutarch, noted that one wife of the god Cronus (he later had other wives – Cumberland, p.332), was called Nemaus. (Cumberland, p.107). Nemaus is the Greek form of Naamah. (Garnier, p.196). Naamah is mentioned in the Bible. Her name and her lineage are given in the book of Genesis, where in Genesis 4:22 we read, "And Zillah, she also bare Tubal-cain, an instructer of every artificer in brass and iron: and the sister of Tubal-cain was Naamah." Naamah was worshipped under many different names after the flood. (Johnson, pp.20-22).

She was often depicted with the tail of a fish, or with the lower part of her body being like that of a fish (Cumberland, p.338). This was to show that she was one of those who had escaped the flood. Her earliest post flood name was Nammu (Johnson, p.20), the name by which the people of Sumer called her. (The civilization of Sumer or Shinar is the oldest post flood civilization known.) She was worshipped under other names in different countries and in different languages. (Johnson, p.20).

Persaeus (307/6–243 BC) a Greek Stoic philosopher and a pupil of the famous philosopher Zeno, said that men who had made some great and useful contribution to civilized life often came to be regarded as gods (Cicero, Book One, section 38, p.17).

The famous Roman orator Marcus Tullius Cicero, mentioned that men in his own time tell us, "brave, or famous, or powerful men attained, after death, the rank of gods, and that it is these very men whom we are accustomed to worship, and pray to, and venerate". (Cicero, Book One, section 119, p.44)

In "Roman History" by C. Velleius Paterculus, (Book One, 15), the author states that Alexander the Great was descended from Hercules, who had been declared, after his death, to have become a god.

Tertullian, one of the fathers of the Early Church, in writing to the heathen, reminded them of their god Saturn, one of their oldest gods. Tertullian said, "neither the Greek Diodorus, or Thallus, neither Cassius Severus or Cornelius Nepos, nor any writer upon sacred antiquities, have ventured to say that Saturn was anything but a man" (Tertullian, "Apology," p.26) "It becomes sufficiently certain that Saturn and all his family were human beings" (Tertullian, "Ad Nationes," p.142, given by Tertullian as Book 2, chapter xii.) Tertullian also quotes Cicero as saying, "there are many men and women among the number of the gods" (Tertullian, "The Divine Institutes," p. 27). He says also of Saturn, who was sometimes called the father of the gods that, "he was a king on earth". (Tertullian, "The Divine Institutes," p.25) To digress for a moment, Saturn was one of the titles or names that were carried by each of three men in turn. Ham was the first man to be known as Saturn. After his death, the title or name of Saturn was passed on to his son Cush, and after Cush's death it passed to Nimrod. Another of those names, or titles, was Belus and yet another was Cronus. (Garnier, pp.20, 25). Thus, each of these three men were known in turn by the titles of Saturn, Belus, and Cronus.

According to the Greek writer Diodorus Siculus of Sicily, the Egyptians taught that the gods had "originally been mortal men, but gained their immortality because of their wisdom and their public benefits to mankind, some of them having also become kings". (Eusebius p.44)

Likewise, "Alexander the Great, when he was in Egypt with his army, wrote to his mother that the chief priest of Egypt had confided to him that even the highest gods, such as Jupiter,

Juno, Saturn, etc. were human people who had been declared to be gods" (Cumberland, p.348). Diodorus said that "knowledge of this was a secret that the priests of Egypt kept from the general public". (Diodorus of Sicily, Book I, 27, In the Loeb Classical Library vol. I, it is p.89-91)

Diodorus additionally noted that the Greeks also had knowledge that the gods had originally been men. He quotes a Greek, Euhemerus (circa 330 B.C. to 260 B.C.), as relating how he had been blown ashore on an island called Panchaea, where he found a temple in which was the information that the gods had originally been mortal men (Eusebius, p.59-60). Diodorus Siculus the Sicilian taught in Book VI sec. 1 of his Library of History that Euhemerus taught thusly.

"As regards the gods, then, men of ancient times have handed down to later generations two different conceptions: Certain of the gods, they say, are eternal and imperishable, such as the sun and the moon and the other stars of the heavens, and the winds as well and whatever else possesses a nature similar to theirs; for each of these the genesis and duration are from everlasting to everlasting. But the other gods, we are told, were terrestrial beings who attained to immortal honor and fame because of their benefactions to mankind."

Diodorus not only gave a detailed description of Euhemerus' theory, he also called Homer, Hesiod, Orpheus, and many other Greeks, liars and writers of myths, concerning many of the stories they told about the gods (Diodorus of Sicily, "The Library of History," Book VI of the Loeb Classical Library, see also Book III of the Loeb Classical Library). Diodorus also wrote that prior to worshipping deceased heroes and benefactors as gods, the Egyptians and Greeks had worshipped the sun, moon, and stars. (Eusebius, p.60)

Athenagoras (ca. 133 – 190), an Athenian philosopher and a convert to Christianity, is likewise quoted as saying,

> "We owe to Orpheus, Homer, and Hesiod, the fictitious names and genealogies of the Pagan Daemons, whom they pleased to style gods, and I can produce Herodotus for a witness to what I assert. He informs us that Homer and Hesiod were about four hundred years prior to himself, and not more. These, says he, were the persons who first framed the theogony of the Greeks and gave appellations or names to their deities. (Bryant, p.160-162) Theogony is the origin and genealogy of the gods.

Studying the history of various people groups, it becomes plain that what was said of the gods of the Egyptians and the Greeks was also true of the gods and goddesses of other people groups, that they also were mortals who had been declared gods after their deaths.

The Phoenicians made statues of Hercules, and worshipped him, but Herodotus tells us that Hercules was merely a deified man who was such a hero to the Phoenicians that after his death they declared him to be a god (Waddell, p.266). This fact was also noted by the late Prof. George Rawlinson (Rawlinson, pp.321-22).

In the first two Sumerian dynasties, which had their seats at the cities of Kish and Erech, we see so-called gods mingling with people upon the earth. Tammuz, the god of vegetation, for whose annual death Ezekiel saw women weeping beside the Temple at Jerusalem, is here described as an earthly ruler. He appears to be described as "a hunter," a phrase which recalls the death of Adonis in Greek mythology. According to a Sumerian king list, he reigned in Erech for a hundred years. (King, p.28; see also Fleure & Peake, p.29)

In time, the sun, moon, and the five planets that were known to the people of the ancient world came to be considered the abode of some of the gods, who were said to have taken up residence in one of those heavenly bodies when they died. Thus, the Pharoahs of Egypt, who were considered gods, were said to each take up their abode in the sun when they died. Each of the five planets known to the ancients was given the name of the god or goddess associated with it. With the passage of time, the sun, moon, and the five planets just named were no longer thought of as an abode for gods and goddesses but rather those objects came to be worshipped by the mass of the people as if the objects themselves were actual divinities.

The names by which those planets are known today show which god or goddess was associated with each of them. Following are the names by which those planets are known to us. The five planets are: Mercury, known as Hermes (meaning son of Ham) to the Greeks, Venus was Aphrodite to the Greeks, Mars was known to the Greeks as Ares, Jupiter to the Romans was Zeus to the Greeks, and Saturn, also called Cronus by the Romans, was called Helius by the Greeks. (Diodorus, Book II, sect. 30) Some of these names were actually titles borne by more than one person (Cumberland, p.291). Saturn is an example. There was a real person called Saturn (Eusebius, p.40), but after his death the title went to at least two of his descendants, each in turn. The Greeks knew Saturn as Cronus, and Cronus was first used as a title for Ham (Cumberland, p.151, 199, 296). With the Greeks and Romans, Saturn and Cronus (or Kronus), were used interchangeably (Cory, pp.82, 110). Saturn and Kronus are actually identical terms (Gascoigne, quoting the Greek author Abydenus, who lived about 200 B.C. p.14).

In Egyptian, Hermes means "Son of Ham," so it is easy to see that this was another name for Cush (Hislop, p.25-26). Hermes was the Greek god of shepherds, flocks, herds, merchandise, weights and measures, and thieves. The Romans knew him as Mercury.

One of Egypt's gods was Imhotep. He was the god of scribes and the god of medicine, not only for the Egyptians, but also for the Greeks, who called him by the Greek name, Aesculapius (Landsburg, p.91-96). Imhotep was the Prime Minister of the second pharaoh of Egypt, who is said to have ruled around 2700 B.C. (Landsburg, p. 91). Other sources date his reign as being around 2300 B.C. Not until around 300 B.C., nearly two thousand years after his death, did he become a god in the minds of the Egyptians. (Landsburg, p.96)

Another Egyptian who came to be worshipped was Ahmose-Nefertari, the widow of Pharaoh Amosis III. She and her son were worshipped in the Theban necropolis and were adopted by the royal necropolis workmen of Deir el Medina as their special patrons and protectors (David, p.3). Deir el Medina is an ancient Egyptian village that was home to the artisans who worked on the tombs in the Valley of the Kings during the 18th to 20th dynasty.

Hawaii is a one of many island groups scattered over a wide expanse of the South Pacific. Collectively, these island groups are known as Polynesia. Wakea, whom Hawaiian genealogies list as the ancestor of all the Hawaiian people, is regarded as a man in historical Hawaiian tradition, but is considered a god in the more southern island groups of Polynesia. (Beckwith, p.294)

A similar example is that of the Norse god, Odin or Woden. He was an early Scandinavian king who led a migration north from Thrace to Scandinavia, where he settled on the island of Odense, in the Baltic Sea. After his death, he was worshipped as a god. (Sturluson, p.xviii)

The Encyclopedia Britannica, Ninth Edition (1894), vol. 2, page 594 under the topic "Asgard," states the following.

*"The historical explanation of Asgard, as given by the early northern authorities, is that, in the country called Asaheim to the east of Tanagvise on the Tanais or Don River in Asia, there was a city called Asgard in which ruled a great chief, known as Odin or Woden, who presided over religious sacrifices which were held there. At that time, the Roman generals were marching over the world, and reducing nations to subjection, and Odin, foreknowing that he and his posterity would occupy the northern lands, and unwilling to encounter the Romans, left Asaheim with a vast multitude of followers, and wandered first westward to Garderike in Russia, and afterwards to Saxland in North and East Germany. After some time, he proceeded northward, till at length he came to the Malar Lake in Sweden, where they settled at a place known as Sigtuna, the present Upsala. His twelve diar, or chief priests, in the course of time founded states for themselves, and everywhere set up the laws and usages which they had followed in Asaheim. Here we have a historical link with the Mythic story of Odin's halls in Asgard, and his twelve-attendant priest but we have no means of fixing the date of the events referred to. It has been conjectured that Odin may have lived at the time when Mithridates Eupator was defying the armies of Rome, 120-80 B.C.; and that, to avoid subjection to either power, he and other Sarmatians or Caucasian chiefs left their settlement on the Black Sea, and wandered forth in search of new and independent homes, to the north and west of the primary Asiatic seat of their tribes. It is not improbable that records of such earlier migrations had lingered among the people dwelling on the shores of the Euxine or Black Sea, for it is certain that, whatever may be the age of Odin's appearance in Scandinavia, previous waves of population had passed from the Black Sea to the Baltic, and cleared the way for the reception of*

*that highest phase of Aryan civilization brought to Northern Europe by Odin and his followers."*

We can see from this that Odin is not a myth or an imagined god, but a real historical person.

Seumas MacManus, in his history of Ireland, mentions the "Dagda," who reigned over Ireland. His daughter, Briget, was a woman of wisdom, who became the Irish goddess of poetry. (MacManus, p.6)

Isaac Preston Cory quotes an extract from a "History of the Phoenicians. "It says: Of these were begotten were two brothers who discovered iron, and the manifold uses of it. One of these called Chrysor, whom he says is Vulcan, exercised himself in words, and charms and divinations; and he invented the hook, and the bait, and fishing-line, and coracles, or light fishing boats; he was the first of all men that sailed by using sails to propel ships. Wherefore men worshipped him after his death as a God, and they called him Diamichius, the great inventor. (Cory &Hodges, pp.7-8)

Many nations made their own founding ancestor one of the chief gods they worshipped. In the Aneid, the king of Latium tells refugees from the city of Troy that Dardanus, their ancestor and the founder of the city of Troy, "has been received and enthroned in a golden palace of the star-glittering sky, and his altar lengthens the roll of deities". (Virgil, p.181)

In "The Lost Cities of Africa," Basil Davidson tells of a Hungarian who was one of the first white men to visit the Bushongo tribe. "For the benefit of this European, one of the first they had ever set eyes on, the elders of the Bushongo recalled the legend and tradition of their past. They traversed the list of their kings, a list of one hundred and twenty names, right back to the

225

god-king whose marvels had founded their nation.' (Davidson, p.3)

Thus, we see that in antiquity people were declaring important and noteworthy people to be gods and goddesses. That is one way, though not the primary one, by which the world gained the multiplicity of gods that we read of today.

A second and much less significant way in which gods were created has also been described in this article. That was when inanimate objects like the sun, the wind, the moon, came to be worshiped as gods.

There was yet another way by which mankind went from a belief in one God to a belief in many. This was by treating each attribute of a god or goddess as if it were a separate god. In time, the common people would forget that they were only praying to a known god in one of his attributes. They would come to think of each attribute as a separate god. By this method many new gods and goddesses were added to an ever-lengthening roll of deities known and worshipped by mankind. Gods and goddesses were also added to the ever-lengthening roll of deities by the fact that when a god or goddess began to be worshipped in another country, or by a people of a different language, the name of that god was often changed, perhaps with the passing of time, into a name that was more easily pronounceable by its new worshippers. The god's name might also be translated into the language of the new country or people. In this manner, Adam's name became different in the Miao language than it was in Hebrew. Its meaning, however, remained the same. It still meant Dirt.

## Revival Is Near

The great times are upon us, the great times long foretold,
When God will visit on us, days of glory, days of gold,
And save many, indeed all, who will fall upon their face,
Take repentance when it's offered and receive His saving grace.

Long ago predicted, the time foretold at last is near,
And a season of God's mercy soon will once again appear,
Just as once He came and visited, in power from above,
So here at the end of the Ages, He will shower us with His love,
All we must do to receive Him, is not to turn and walk away,
For repentance scorned may never come to us again that day,
There is power to believe, and divine forgiveness to be had,
No one who comes to Jesus will ever be turned away sad,
Times of rejoicing are upon us, times of pleasure are now here,
Open wide your hearts, receive Him, for Christ the Lord is here,
Just as He sent at Pentecost, and has often sent again,
So now at last in the fullness of time, revival comes again.

We must open our lives to receive it, we must not turn away,
For though strange it may be to us, we need it much today,
For all our world is weary, and all our lives are worn,
As living in this world of sin leaves our hearts sad and forlorn,
But now at last that's ending, for revival is almost here,
And our great God who sends it, He Himself is near,
Eager to enlighten, and most eager to end it all,
The sin, the darkness, the misery, that has cast on the earth its pall.

-    Dr. N. James Brooks, Jr. (2010)

*"In all my perplexities and distresses,*
*the Bible has never failed to give me light and strength."*

-    R.E. Lee

# CHAPTER FIFTEEN
## How Did We Go From One God To Many
## Part Two

There are several different ways in which primitive peoples in ancient times fell from a belief in one god to a belief in many. We have discussed two of them. We saw that great and famous people were sometimes worshipped as gods after their death. We have mentioned a second way in which gods were made. This was when the same god was worshipped in different countries under different names. The third way in which gods were created was when people who had been declared to be gods were worshipped under different titles, with each of those titles representing a different attribute of a god. To express this idea slightly differently, different titles would be given to a god. Each title would reflect a different attribute of that god. In time however, each title or attribute would come to be thought of and treated as if it were a separate god.

"Divers names were anciently given to the same man as titles of honor, especially after consecration into the number of the gods, or persons to whom religious worship was to be given" (Cumberland, p.291). Certain attributes of a god would be emphasized, then that God would be prayed to under a title or name that stressed that attribute. Over time each particular attribute of a god would come to be thought of as if it were a new and separate god. In this way one god would become many gods, as the various attributes turned into new gods. (McCrady, p.55).

It is as if we took certain attributes of the Lord God and treated them as if each attribute was a separate God. Exodus 15:26 says in part "I am the LORD that healeth thee." Psalm 107:13 says, "Then they cried unto the LORD in their trouble, and he saved them out of their distresses." When we are sick we pray and ask God to make us well. Suppose when we were praying to be made well we prayed to God as "Our Healer." When trouble comes upon us or bad things happen, we pray to God to end those troubles. Suppose we prayed to Him sometimes as God the Healer and sometimes as the God who saves people from trouble? To someone who didn't know any better it would sound as if we were praying to two different gods. Suppose further that we made no effort to explain to others that we were praying directly to one God, and were just mentioning different attributes of His, meaning Savior from trouble, God the Healer, etc. If they were not taught otherwise, it is easy to see how future generations could end up with the belief that each separate name was a separate god. This was the third way that new gods were formed.

As an example, the Aztecs thought of Quetzalcoatl (the Plumed Serpent) as the Creator God. Under a different name he was worshipped as the Wind God. Under yet another name he was the god of the planet Venus. Under still other names he was worshipped as a number of other gods. Only the priests knew that he was really a single god appearing under different names and in different aspects or attributes. The common people thought that each of his different attributes was a different god (Bray, p.157).

One authority on the gods and goddesses of the Greeks concluded that while the ancient Greeks came in time to worship many gods, many of these gods were only different names for what was originally one and the same deity. "There later developed a larger number of significant figures which we meet with in Greek religious myths. In my opinion, their multiplying variety depends to a very considerable degree on the different invocating names of originally one and the same deity". (Persson, p.124)

Herodotus "attributes to Homer and to Hesiod, the various names and distinctions of the gods and that endless polytheism which prevailed. This blindness in regard to their own theology, and to that of the countries from whence they borrowed, led them to misapply the terms which they had received and to make a god out of every title". (Bryant, p.307)

Likewise, there came to be in Egypt a multitude of deified objects. Plutarch was a Greek who lived from 46 A.D. till 120 A.D. He was a famous historian and a Roman citizen. He left us an illustration of how the Egyptians came to have many gods. Speaking regarding the worship of the crocodile, Plutarch tells us that as the crocodile had its eyes covered over by a thin transparent membrane, by means of which, though living in the water, it could see, and yet not be seen, it was "taken as a representation of the Invisible and all-powerful God . . . .

Professor Rawlinson speaks rightly when he says, 'The deity once divided, there was no limit to the number of His attributes of various kinds, and of different grades; and in Egypt everything that partook of the divine essence became a god. Emblems were added to the catalogue; and though not really deities, they called forth feelings of respect, which the ignorant could not distinguish from actual worship'". (Titcomb, pages 141-162, sections 18 & 20)

"The Egyptians . . . . being much addicted to refinement in their worship, made many subtle distinctions: and supposing that there were certain emanations of divinity, they affected to particularize each by some title; and to worship the deity by his attributes. This gave rise to a multiplicity of gods; for the more curious they were in their distinctions, the greater was the number of their substitutes. Many of them at first were designed for mere titles; others, as I mentioned before, were derivatives, and emanations, all of which in time were esteemed distinct beings". (Bryant, p.306)

When Sumerian tablets were translated, it came to light that there were a large number of false deities. This was as a result of the gradual misinterpretation of the various names and titles of a single Deity. A very famous British authority on early Mesopotamia, Theophilus Pinches, wrote that it was the custom of the Babylonians to deify the early rulers of their race. (We have already seen in a previous chapter how Nimrod was worshipped under the titles of Bel, Bal, Baal, Saturn and Kronos.)

Pinches mentioned a cuneiform tablet that told that the highest of the gods in the Babylonian pantheon were actually only manifestations of their chief god, Marduk. The different names used for the other highest gods were only descriptive titles of the different attributes of Marduk (Delitzsch, pp.144fn.). It was probable, Pinches wrote, that if we had more complete sources of information, other instances would be found of Babylonian gods being worshipped under more than one name. (Pinches, p.141)

The chief Sumerian god was Ea, but he was also known as "Shar Apsi." As Shar Apsi, he was "King of the Watery Deep," another instance of a new god arising from an attribute of an earlier one (Mackenzie, p.28). Ea had different names for the different things he was said to have instructed people in. "He was the artisan god--Nun-ura, 'god of the potter'; Kuski-banda, 'god of goldsmiths,' &c.--the divine patron of the arts and crafts." (Mackenzie, p.30). Ea was also "Enki," "lord of the world," or "lord of what is beneath"; Amma-ana-ki, "lord of heaven and earth;" Sa-kalama, "ruler of the land," as well as Engur, "god of the abyss," Naqbu, "the deep," and Lugal-ida, "king of the river,". (Mackenzie, p.31)

Even today, most people who read about ancient Sumer and its gods think that each of the gods named above were separate and distinct gods to the Sumerians, and perhaps to the average Sumerian in time they did come to be considered separate gods. Originally however, they simply represented different aspects or attributes of the one god Ea. "The attributes of a single God were differently emphasized by different people until those people in later years came to forget that they were speaking of the same person. Thus, attributes of a single deity became a plurality of deities". (Wiseman, p.24)

The same traces of alteration can be seen in Italy. An archaeologist by the name of Irene Rosenzweig, after researching the Iguvine tables, which date from Etruscan times, concluded that "deities are distinguished by adjectives, which in their turn emerge as independent divine powers". (Hanfmann, pp.170-171)

One theory on the evolution of religions claims that polytheism arose when people started to worship imagined spirits representing the powers of nature. Later, it is generally taught, as people in various parts of the world became more civilized and advanced, they came to a belief in a single god. But that is not a correct assumption. As we have seen in earlier articles, people first believed in one God and one alone. In the course of time, people developed different understandings of the various attributes of that one God. They also adopted gods and goddesses of other peoples and nations, changing the names into titles in their own language. These things eventually led to distortions in belief. The various attributes of the one God turned into the belief in several.

A third method by which new gods came to be worshipped in a country was when the same god, worshipped in different cities or countries under different names, would be adopted as a new god by a people who already worshipped him under another name. In other words, Nimrod was worshipped in Canaan as the god Bal. In the city state of Tyre he was worshipped as Melkart, which means "King of the Walled City" (Hislop, pp.296-297). The people of Tyre might be impressed with the worship of Bal as carried on in Canaan, and might decide to begin the worship of Bal in their own city, not realizing that they already worshipped him under the name of Melkart. They would then begin to worship Nimrod under two titles, that of Bal and that of Melkart, thus unknowingly worshipping the same god as two separate gods.

Turning away from the God of their ancestors, early people repeatedly were fooled and repeatedly fooled themselves by going from the worship of one God to many gods, and then to even more. As we have seen however, the true God was never fully forgotten, and some ethnic groups continued to pray to him right down until He revealed Himself to them as the God of the Bible, the Father of Jesus Christ, the Savior of all who trust in Him.

## No King But Jesus

No king but Jesus, no king but Him alone.
No king but He who sits on the heavenly throne,
No king but Jesus, we do declare,
Him to Whom the righteous do eagerly repair,
Hail, glorious Jesus, dear king of our souls,
Bless us on earth while the rivers yet roll,
On us thy poor children bestow a great grace;
Look on us and bless us with the sight of Thy face,
Hail, glorious Jesus, Thy words are still strong
Against Satan's wiles and the heretic throng;
Not less is thy might than where in Heaven thou art;
Oh, come Thou to our aid, in our battles take part!

In the war against sin, when for victory we wait,
Dear God, may Thy children in patience resist as we wait,
May our strength be in meekness, in patience, and prayer,
Our banner Your Cross, which we glory to bear.

Thy people, though strangers on this earthly shore,
Shall love and revere You till time be no more;

And the fire You have kindled shall ever burn bright,
Its warmth undiminished, undying its light.


Ever bless and defend this great land of our birth,
Where hope still blooms of Thy return to the earth,
And our hearts shall yet burn, wherever we roam,
For You, Lord and Savior, and our heavenly home.

-    Dr. N. James Brooks, Jr. (2012)

# CONCLUSION

By now you have read and completed the book, "Adam and Eve Were Real."

You are aware how in the most ancient times up until today, people all over this earth knew and believed that all mankind are descended from one man and one woman.

You have seen that science itself bears out the truth that one man and one woman are indeed the forebears of us all.

You have read a very few of the many accounts of peoples and ethnic groups who knew of Adam and Eve though stories handed down from their forebears. Tribes and ethnic groups who knew about Creation, the fact that snakes could once talk, the flood, the Tower of Babel, and the fact that all mankind once spoke the same language.

They knew that Adam and Eve once walked the earth and that they were created by a good and all-powerful God who lives above the sky, a God who rewards those who please Him by taking them to be with Him when they die.

Even more important than believing those things is whether or not you, yourself, want to live in such a way that when you die, you will go, like Adam and Eve, to that place of reward far above the sky.

You will not go there by following any man-made religion or by following any rules for living that you make up for yourself.

If you want to go to that place of reward above the sky, you must go thru the way that God has provided. Having recognized that the things you have read in this book are true, turn from living for yourself and turn to the God of the Bible. In the Old Testament, the book of Isaiah, chapter 53, verse 6 says:

> *"All we like sheep have gone astray; we have turned everyone to his own way; and the Lord hath laid on him the iniquity of us all."*

We cannot come to God our way.

There is only one way.

That way is thru Jesus Christ, the way that God has provided.

One of the most familiar verses in the Bible is John 3:16. It says, "For God so loved the world that he gave his only begotten Son, that whosoever believeth in him should not perish, but have everlasting life."

A more complete translation from the original Greek shows that several of the words in this verse have more meaning than appears at first glance.

Translated more fully, this verse says, "whosoever believes in, relies on, and trusts in Him (Jesus) will not perish, but has an everlasting eternal existence of joy."

Your Creator does not only wait for you in His dwelling place above the sky, He waits for you down here on this earth, while you yet live here.

He wants you to get to know Him and the love that He has for you. Whether or not you get to know Him is up to you. There is only one way to know Him, that is thru Jesus.

# CHAPTER REFERENCES

## Chapter One

Černý, Jaroslav, "Paper and Books in Ancient Egypt": An Inaugural Lecture Delivered at University College London, 29 May 1947. London, H. K. Lewis. 1952.

Bullinger, E.W., Appendixes to the Companion Bible, http://www.therain.org/appendixes/ February 21, 2015.

Cusack, Mary Francis, 1868. "The Illustrated History of Ireland," facsimile reprint by Bracken Books, London, 1987.

Davidson, Basil, "The Lost Cities of Africa," Little, Brown. Boston, 1959.

Lee, Susan P., "Lee's New School History of the United States," 1899.

MacManus, Seumas, "The Story Of The Irish Race," Devin-Adair Co., copyright 1921, 32nd printing 1979.

Priest, Josiah, "American Antiquities and Discoveries in the West," 3rd ed. Hoffman and White, Albany, 1833.

Sayce, A.H., "Monumental Facts and Higher Critical Fancies," third edition, London, The Religious Tract Society, 1904.

https://archive.org/stream/monumentfacts00saycuoft#page/n5/mode/2up. January 27, 2015.

## Chapter Two

Banks, William D., "The Heavens Declare . . . ," Kirkwood, Missouri, Impact Books Inc., paperback, copyright 1985.


Bancroft, Hubert Howe, "The Native Races," vol. iii., San Francisco, A.L. Bancroft & Co., 1883. reprinted by Kessinger Publishing).

Beckwith, Martha, "Hawaiian Mythology," Univ. of Hawaii Press, Honolulu, 1976.

Bernatzik, Hugo, "Akha and Miao; Problems of applied ethnography in farther India," Human Relations Area Files Press, 1970. New Haven; citing F.M.I. Savina, Histoire de Miao.

Bullfinch, Thomas, "Bulfinch's Mythology," Grosset & Dunlap. New York. 1913.

Chang, Maria Hsia, "Return of the Dragon: China's Wounded Nationalism," Westview Press, Boulder, CO., 2001.

Deane, John Bathurst, "The Worship of the Serpent," 2nd edition, London, J.G. & F. Rivington, 1833. (http://www.sacred-texts.com/index.htm)

Dods, Marcus, "Handbooks For Bible Classes - Genesis," T. & T. Clark, Edinburgh, 1882.

Donnelly, Ignatius, "Atlantis, The Antediluvian World," Harper & Brothers, 1882, (http://www.sacred-texts.com/index.htm). January 12, 2011.

Dorit, R.L., Akashi, H. and Gilbert, W., "Absence of polymorphism at the ZFY locus on the human Y chromosome." Science 268, 1995).

Ellis, William, "Polynesian Researches," vol.1, Henry G. Bohn, London, 1859.

Fergusson, James, "History of Tree and Serpent Worship," India museum, W.H. Allen and co., publishers to the India office, 1868. (http://www.sacred-texts.com/index.htm)

Frazer, James G., "Folk-Lore in the Old Testament: Studies in Comparative Religion, Legend and Law," Macmillan, New York, 1923.

Gascoigne, Mike, "Forgotten History of the Western People," Anno Mundi Books, Camberley, England, copyright 2002.

Hesiod, "The Theogony," translated by Hugh G. Evelyn-White, 1914. http://www.sacred-texts.com/cla/hesiod/theogony.htm

Hesiod, "Works And Days," translated by Hugh G. Evelyn-White, 1914. http://www.sacred-texts.com/cla/hesiod/works.htm.

Hooke, Samuel A., "Middle Eastern Mythology," Dover Publications, Mineola, N.Y.,

Johnson, Robert Bowie, "Athena and Kain," Solving Light Books, Annapolis, Maryland, copyright 2007.

Jones, Sir William, Third Annual Discourse, taken from "The Works of Sir William Jones, With A Life of The Author," by Lord Teignmouth, London, 1807, vol. III.
http://www.archive.org/stream/worksofsirwillia03jone#page/n6/mode/1up  (July 7, 2010)

Josephus, "Works of Flavius Josephus," Antiquities of the Jews, vol.1, translated by William Whiston, Leary & Getz, Publishers, Philadelphia, 1854.

Kang, C.H., & Nelson, E.R., "The Discovery of Genesis," Concordia Publishing House, St. Louis, MO, 1979.

Kikawa, Daniel. I., "Perpetuated In Righteousness," Aloha Ke Akua Publishing, Kea'au, Hawai'i, 1994.

King James Version of the Bible, printed for Matthew Carey, No.113, Market Street, Philadelphia, October 20, 1801.

Kingsborough, Viscount, (King, Edward), "Mexican Antiquities," London. 1831-48.

Kramer, Samuel Noah, "History Begins at Sumer: Thirty-Nine Firsts in Recorded History," University of Pennsylvania Press, Philadelphia, 1981.

Lee, Susan P., "Lee's New School History of the United States," 1899. p.22.

Legge, James, "Notions of the Chinese Concerning God And Spirits," Hong Kong, Hong Kong Register Office, 1852. https://archive.org/details/notionsofchinese00legg June 2, 2013.

Lenormant, Francois, "The Beginnings of History," Scribner's Sons, 1893. Reprinted by General Books, 2009.

Martill, David M., Tischlinger, Helmut, Longrich, Nicholas R. A four-legged snake from the Early Cretaceous of Gondwana, "Science." 24 Jul 2015: Vol. 349, Issue 6246, pp. 416-419.

Merriam Webster's Collegiate Dictionary, tenth edition.

Ovid, "Metamorphoses," Wordsworth Classics, Ware, England, copyright 1998.

Prescott, William H., "History of the Conquest of Mexico," John Foster Kirk, editor, J.B. Lippincott, Philadelphia, 1891.

Rafinesque, C.S., "The American Nations, Or, Outlines of A Natural History of the Ancient and Modern Nations of North and South America," Published by C.S. Rafinesque, Philadelphia, London, Paris. https://archive.org/stream/americannations02rafigoog#page/n160/mode/2up, January 28, 2015).

Rawlinson, George, "The Testimony of the Truth of Scripture: Historical Illustrations of the Old Testament," Henry A. Sumner & Co., Chicago, 1880. Reprinted by Kessinger Publishing.

Rawlinson, George, "The Origin of Nations," Scribner, N.Y., 1878.

Richardson, Don, "Eternity In Their Hearts," Regal Books, Ventura, California, copyright 1981.

Sayce, A.H. "Monumental Facts and Higher Critical Fancies," Third Edition, The Religious Tract Society, London, 1904. https://archive.org/stream/monumentfacts00saycuoft#page/n5/mode/2up. January 29, 2015

Science Daily, August 17, 2010. 'Mitochondrial Eve': Mother of all humans lived 200,000 years ago. http://www.sciencedaily.com/releases/2010/08/100817122405.htm

Science Daily, March 2, 2013. "X-rays reveal hidden leg of an ancient snake:" New hints on how snakes were getting legless. https://www.sciencedaily.com/releases/2011/02/110207142619.htm

Smith, George, "The Chaldean Account of Genesis," Thomas Scott, London, 1876.

Stefansson, Jon, "On Iceland, It's History and Inhabitants," Journal of Transactions of the Victoria Institute, vol. XXXVIII. London, published by the Institute, 1906.

Titcomb, J.A., "British-Israel ; How I Came To Believe It," Re-edited from the 2nd edition, The Covenant Publishing Co., LTD., London, 1875, 1878, this edition was probably published in 1928.

Titcomb, J.A., On Ethnic Testimonies, found in "Faith and Thought," Journal of the Transactions of the Victoria Institute," vol. 6, Robert Hardwicke, London, 1873. Reprinted by Google books.

Truax, Edgar, "Genesis According to the Miao People," Impact Article #214, April 1991. Institute for Creation Research. P.0. Box 2667. El Cajon. California 92021. http://www.icr.org/index.php?module=articles&action=view&ID= 341 September 2, 2005).

Wilford, Francis, On the Chronology of the Hindus, "Asiatic Researches," vol. 5, London, 1799. http://www.archive.org/details/workssirwilliam01jonegoog (July 8, 2010).

## Chapter 3

Baugh, Carl, "Panorama of Creation," Bible Belt Publishing, Bethany, Oklahoma.

Boyle, Rebecca,    http://www.popsci.com/science/article/2012-02/russian-scientists-resurrect-pleistocene-era-plants-buried-siberian-permafrost-30000-years, Popular Science, June 10, 2014.

Cranfill, S.A., 'They Came From Babel," The Write House, Limited., Tioga, Texas, 1994.

Digby, George Bassett, "The Mammoth and Mammoth Hunting in North-east Siberia," H.F. & G. Witherby, London, 1926.

Dillow, J.C., "The Waters Above: Earth's Pre-flood Vapor Canopy," Moody Press, Chicago, 1981.

Dukert, Joseph M., "This Is Antarctica," Coward, McCann & Geoghegan, New York. 1972.

Farrand, William R., "Frozen Mammoths and Modern Geology," Science, Vol.133, No. 3455, March 17, 1961.

Frazer, James George, "Folk-Lore in the Old Testament: Studies in Comparative Religion, Legend and Law," Macmillan, New York. 1923.

Hibben, Frank C., "The Lost Americans," New York, Apollo Editions, 1961.

Hooker, Dolph Earl, "Those Astounding Ice Ages," Exposition Press, New York, 1958.

Josephus, "The Works of Flavius Josephus, Antiquities of the Jews, vol.1," translated by William Whiston, Leary & Getz, Publishers, Philadelphia, 1854.

Kerr, Richard A., Fossils Tell of Mild Winters in an Ancient Hothouse, Science, vol. 261, August 6, 1993.

King James Version of the Bible, printed for Matthew Carey, No.113, Market Street, Philadelphia, October 20, 1801.

Lippman, Harold E., Frozen Mammoths, Science, Vol. 137, August 10, 1962.

McGee, J. Vernon, "Thru the Bible with J. Vernon McGee," Volume 1, Thomas Nelson Publishers, Nashville, 1981

Morris, Henry, "Scientific Creationism," El Cajon, Master Books, 1984.

Nelson, Bryon, C., "The Deluge Story In Stone," Augsburg Publishing House, Minneapolis, 1958.

Raymond, Chris, "Discovery of Leaves in Antarctica Sparks Debate over Whether Region Had Near-Temperate Climate," Chronicle of Higher Education, March, 1991,

Sanderson, Ivan T., Riddle of The Quick Frozen Giants, Saturday Evening Post, Jan. 16, 1960.

Science News, magazine published by Society for Science and the Public, August 31st, 1985.

"Sonic Bloom," Creation Illustrated, Vol. 7, No. 2, 2000.

Starr, Victor P., The General Circulation of the Atmosphere, Scientific American, Vol. 195, December 1956.

Stone, Richard, "Mammoth: The Resurrection of an Ice Age Giant," Perseus Publishing, Cambridge, Massachusetts, 2001.

## Chapter Four

Anderson, Ian, "Dinosaurs Breathed Air Rich in Oxygen," New Scientist, vol.116, 1987.

Baugh, Carl, "Panorama of Creation," Bible Belt Publishing, Bethany, Oklahoma, 1992.

Berner, Robert, & Landis, Gary, Discover, February, 1988. Catalano, Peter. Insight on the News. "New Treatment May Awaken Patients from Severe Comas." Volume: 11. Issue: 41. October 30, 1995. copyright 1995. News World Communications, Inc.; copyright 2002 Gale Group.

Cory, I.P., and Hodges, Raymond, "Cory's Ancient Fragments," 1876. Reprinted by Kessinger Publishing.

Custance, Arthur, C., "The Virgin Birth And The Incarnation," vol. 5 in The Doorway Papers Series, published by Zondervan Press, 1977.

Dods, Marcus, "Handbooks For Bible Classes – Genesis," T. & T. Clark, Edinburgh, 1882.

Felker, Clay, "The Best American Magazine Writing 2000," Public Affairs, New York, 2000.

Gilmore, Elaine, "Sunflower over Tokyo," Popular Science, May 1988.

Hesiod, "Works And Days," translated by Hugh G. Evelyn-White, Dover Pub. Mineola, N.Y., 2006.

Hess, Richard, and Tsumura, David (editors), "I Studied Inscriptions from Before the flood," Ancient Near Eastern, Literary, and Linguistic Approaches to Genesis 1-11, (Sources for Biblical and Theological Study, Vol. 4), Eisenbrauns, 1994.

Humphreys, Russel D., "Starlight and Time," Master Books (paperback), 2004.

Jacobsen, Thorkild, "The Sumerian King List," University of Chicago Press, Chicago, 1939.

Jones, F.A., "The Dates of Genesis," Kingsgate Press, London, 1912.

Josephus, "The Works of Flavius Josephus, Antiquities of the Jews, vol.1," translated by William Whiston, Leary & Getz, Publishers, Philadelphia, 1854.

King James Version of the Bible, printed for Matthew Carey, No.113, Market Street, Philadelphia, October 20, 1801.

Langdon, Stephen H., "Semitic Mythology," vol. v. of Mythology of All Races, Archaeological Institute of America, 1931.

Lenormant, Francois, "The Beginnings of History," New York, C. Scribner's Sons, 1893. Facsimile reprint by General Books, 2009.

Morris, Henry, "Scientific Creationism," Master Books, Green Forest, Arkansas, 1984.

Ovid, "Metamorphoses," Wordsworth Classics, Ware, England, copyright 1998.
Pritchard, James B., "Ancient Near Eastern Texts Relating to the Old Testament," (editor), Princeton Univ. Press, Princeton, New Jersey, 1969. (3rd Ed).

Rawlinson, George, and Hackett, Horatio B., "The Testimony Of The Truth of Scripture: Historical Illustrations Of The Old Testament," Hastings, Boston, 1898. Reprint by Kessinger Publishing.

Rawlinson, George, "The Origin of the Nations," New York, Charles Scribners' Sons, 1881. Reprint byKessinger Publishing.

Soden, Wolfram von, "The Ancient Orient," (translated by Schley), Grand Rapids, MI., Eerdmans Publishing Company, 1994.

Health Canada (Canadian Government), http://www.hc-sc.gc.ca/iyh-vsv/med/hyper_e.html, December 30, 2005.

Whole Health, http://www.wholehealthmd.com/refshelf/substances_view/1,1525, 725,00.html, December 30, 2005.


## Chapter Five

Baugh, Carl, "Panorama of Creation," Bible Belt Publishing, Bethany, Oklahoma

Ceram, C. W. "Gods, Graves, And Scholars," New York, Alfred Knoff, 1951

Cory, Preston, & Hodges, E. Richmond, "Cory's Ancient Fragments," Reeves and Turner, London, 1876. reprinted by Kessinger Publications

Custance, Arthur C., "The Genealogies of the Bible," Doorway Paper #24," Ottawa, Author, 1967

Daniken, Erich von, "Chariots of the Gods," New York, Bantam, 1969

Fleure, Herbert John, & Peake, Harold, "Priests & Kings," Yale University Press, New Haven, CT. 1927

Gascoigne, Mike, "Forgotten History of the Western People," Anno Mundi Books, Camberley, England. Copyright 2002

Gordon, Cyrus, "Before Columbus," Turnstone Press, Ltd., London, 1972

Heffner, John W. and Marvilyn E, and Baugh, Martha, "What Was It Like At The Beginning?" Oklahoma City, Hearthstone Publishing, Ltd., copyright 2001

Jacobsen, Thorkild, "The Sumerian King List," University of Chicago Press, Chicago, #11, 1939

Jerome, "Saint Jerome's Hebrew Questions on Genesis," Robert Hayward, translator, Clarendon Press, Oxford, 199

Josephus, "The Works of Flavius Josephus, Antiquities of the Jews, vol.1" translated by William Whiston, Leary & Getz, Publishers, Philadelphia, 1854.

King James Version of the Bible, printed for Matthew Carey, Philadelphia, October 20, 1801

Kramer, Samuel N., "History Begins at Sumer: Thirty-Nine Firsts in Recorded History," University of Pennsylvania Press, Philadelphia. 1981

Kramer, Samuel N., "Sumerian Mythology," Philadelphia, University of PA Press, 1972

Landsberg, Alan & Sally, "In Search of Ancient Mysteries," New York, Bantam Books, 1974

Moran, Hugh A., and Kelley, David H., "The Alphabet and the Ancient Calendar Signs," Palo Alto, Calif., Daily Press, copyright 1969

Neusner, Jacob, "Genesis Rabbah, The Judaic Commentary to the Book of Genesis, A New American Translation," Vol. III, Atlanta, Scholars Press, 1985

Noorbergen, Rene, "Secrets of the Lost Races," New York, Harper & Row, 1977

Rawlinson, George, "The Origin of the Nations," New York, Charles Scribners' Sons, 1881. Reprint by Kessinger Publishing

Ripley, William Z., "The Races of Europe," New York, D. Appleton & Company, 1899

Seiss, Joseph, "The Gospel In The Stars," 1882, reprinted by Kregel Publications, Grand Rapids, MI., 1972

Seyffarth, Gustavus. "The Literary Life of Gustavus Seyffarth," New York, E. Steiger & Co., 1886

Sitchin, Zecharia, "The Wars of Gods and Men," New York, Avon Books, 1985

Tomas, Andrew, "We Are Not The First," London, Souvenir Press, 1971

Traux, Edgar, "Genesis According to the Miao People," Impact Article #214, April 1991. Institute for Creation Research, El Cajon. California 92021 http://www.icr.org/index.php?module=articles&action=view&ID=341.

Victoria Institute, "Faith And Thought," vol. 3, 1869. Reprint by General Books

Victoria Institute, 23:303 as cited by Erich A. von Fange, Spading Up Ancient Words, @1984, http://www.creationism.org/vonfange/, January 25, 2005

## Chapter Six

Baugh, "Panorama of Creation," Bible Belt Publishing, (paperback), Bethany, Oklahoma, copyright 1989, 1992.

Bernatzik, Hugo, "Akha and Miao; Problems of applied ethnography in farther India," Human Relations Area Files Press, 1970. New Haven; citing F.M.I. Savina, Histoire de Miao.

Bryant, Jacob, "A New System, of an Analysis of Ancient Mythology," Vol. I, London, 1774. (reprint by Kessinger Publishing).

Bryant, Jacob, "A New System, of an Analysis of Ancient Mythology," Vol. II, London, 1775. (reprint by Kessinger Publishing).

Bryant, Jacob, "A New System, of an Analysis of Ancient Mythology," Vol. III, London, 1776. (reprint by Kessinger Publishing).

Campbell, Joseph, "The Masks of God - Oriental Mythology," Penguin Books (paperback), 1976, citing E. T. C. Werner, c.f., "A Dictionary of Chinese."

Ceram, C.W., "Gods, Graves, And Scholars," New York, Alfred A. Knopf, pub., 1967.

Dang, Nghiem Van, "The flood Myth and the Origin of Ethnic Groups in Southeast Asia," Journal of American Folklore, Vol.106, Issue 421, 1993.

Ellis, William, "Polynesian Researches," vol.1, Henry G. Bohn, London, 1859.

Fairbridge, Rhodes, W., "The Changing Level of the Sea," Scientific American, Vol.202, No.5, May 1960.

Frazer, Sir James G., "Folklore in the Old Testament," Macmillan and Co., (1919), Vol. 1,

Jones, William, "Discourse on the Chinese: Asiatic Researches," as cited in Sacred Annals: Or Researches Into the History and Religion of Mankind, vol.1, 4th Edition, George Smith, Carlton & Porter, New York, 1856.

https://books.google.com/books?id=utRCAAAAIAAJ&printsec=frontcover&source=gbs_ge_summary_r&cad=0#v=onepage&q&f=false. January 27, 2015.

Josephus, Flavius, "Antiquities of the Jews, vol. 1," Works of Flavius Josephus, translated by William Whiston, Leary & Getz, Publishers, Philadelphia, 1854.

Lang, Andrew, "The Making of Religion," originally published in 1898. Reprinted by BIBLIOLIFE.

Lenormant, Francois, "The Beginnings of History,"1893. Republished by General Books, 2009.

Montgomery, John W., "The Quest For Noah's Ark," copyright 1972, Bethany Fellowship, Minneapolis.

Nelson, Byron C., "The Deluge Story In Stone," Augsburg Publishing House, Minneapolis, Minnesota, 5th printing, 1958.

Ovid, "Metamorphoses," translated by Melville, A.D., (Oxford World's Classics), Oxford University Press, Oxford, 1986.

Peet, Stephen D., "The Story of the Deluge," American Antiquarian, Vol. 27, No. 4, July–August 1905.

Perloff, James, "Tornado in a Junkyard: The Relentless Myth of Darwinism," Arlington, MA., Refuge Books, 1999.

Prescott, William Henry, "History of the Conquest of Mexico," J.B. Lippincott, Philadelphia, 1891.

"The Popul Vuh," translated by Delia Goetz and Sylvanus Griswold Morley, Plantain Press, Los Angeles, 1954.

Truax, Edgar A., "Genesis According to the Miao People," An Impact article.

http://www.icr.org/index.php?module=articles&action=view&ID= 341, April 5, 2005.

## Chapter Seven

Bancroft, H.H., "The Works of Hubert Howe Bancroft," vol. 3, The Native Races, Myths and Languages, A.L. Bancroft & Co., San Francisco, 1883. Kessinger Publishing Reprint

Bancroft, H.H., "The Works of Hubert Howe Bancroft," vol. 5, The Native Races, Myths and Languages, A.L. Bancroft & Co., San Francisco, 1882. Kessinger Publishing Reprint

Berlitz, Charles, "The Lost Ship of Noah," W.H. Allen, London, 1987

Bryant, Jacob, "A New System, or an Analysis of Ancient Mythology," vol. I, London, 1807 edition http://www.annomundi.co.uk/history/bryant.pdf, October, 5, 2005

Bryant, Jacob, "A New System, or an Analysis of Ancient Mythology," vol. III, London, 1807 edition,

http://www.annomundi.co.uk/history/bryant.pdf, October 5, 2005

Donnelly, Ignatius, "Atlantis, the Antediluvian World," Harper & Brothers, 1882. http://www.sacred-texts.com/index.htm. January 12, 2011

Frazer, James G., "Folk-Lore in the Old Testament: Studies in Comparative Religion, Legend and Law," Macmillan, New York, 1923

Gaster, Theodor H., "Myth, Legend, and Custom in the Old Testament," Harper & Row, New York, 1969

Hislop, Alexander, "The Two Babylons," Life Line, Pasig City, Philipines, no date given

Homberg, Uno. Finno-Ugric, Siberian, in "The Mythology of All Races," MacCulloch, C. J. A., editor, vol. IV, Marshall Jones Co., Boston, 1927

Jones, William, "Discourse on the Chinese; Asiatic Researches," vol. ii. quoted in Sacred Annals: Or Researches Into the History and Religion of Mankind, vol.1, 4th Edition, George Smith, Carlton & Porter, New York, 1856,

https://books.google.com/books?id=utRCAAAAIAAJ&printsec=frontcover&source=gbs_ge_summary_r&cad=0#v=onepage&q&f=false. January 27, 2015

King James Version of the Bible, printed for Matthew Carey, No.113, Market Street, Philadelphia, October 20, 1801

Lenormant, Francois, "The Beginnings of History," 1893. Reprinted by General Books, 2009

Lucian, "The Syrian Goddess," translated by Herbert A. Strong and John Garstang, Constable & Co., Ltd., London, 1913

Mackenzie, Donald A., "Myths Of Babylonia And Assyria," The Gresham Publishing Co., London, 1915; Kessinger Reprint, 2004

Nelson, Byron, "The Deluge Story in Stone," Augsberg Publishing House, Minneapolis, MN. 1931

Prescott, William Henry, "The Conquest of Peru," Book League of America, 1945

Prescott, William Henry, "History of the Conquest of Mexico," John Foster Kirk, editor, J.B. Lippincott, Philadelphia, 1891

Prichard, James Cowles, "Researches Into the Physical History of Mankind," vol. 5, Sherwood, Gilbert and Piper, London, 1847. Reprinted by ULAN Press

Rawlinson, George, & Hackett, Horatio, "The Testimony of the Truth of Scripture," Boston, H.L. Hastings, 1898

Rohl, David, "The Lost Testament," Century-Random House, London, 2002

Titcomb, J.H., "Ethnic Testimonies To The Pentateuch,' Journal of 1872-73.

http://www.creationism.org/victoria/VictoriaInst1872_pg233.htm, September 2, 2005

## Chapter Eight

Albright, W.F., & Lambdin, T.O., The evidence of Language, (in) "The Cambridge Ancient History," Part 1, Cambridge University Press, Cambridge, UK, New York, N.Y., copyright Cambridge University Press, 1970.

Bodmer, Frederick, "The Loom of Language," Geo. Allen & Unwin Ltd, London, 1944.

Chadwick, H. Munro, "The Nationalities of Europe and the Growth of National Ideologies," Cambridge, University Press, 1966.

Chang, Tsung-tung, "Indo-European Vocabulary In Old Chinese," Sino-Platonic Papers, Victor H. Mair, editor, Department of East Asian Languages and Civilizations, University of Pennsylvania, Philadelphia, 1988. http://www.scribd.com/doc/211901228/Indo-European-Vocabulary-in-Old-Chinese-Tsungtung-Chang-1988 March 2005

Delitzsch, Franz, "Genesis" in Commentary of the Holy Scriptures, editor, Peter Lange, translated by Tayler, Lewis, and Gosman, A., New York. Charles Scribner's Sons, 5th edition, 1899.

Edkins, Joseph, "China's Place in Philology, an Attempt to show that the Languages of Europe and Asia have a Common Origin," Kegan, Paul, Trench, Trubner & Co., London, 1893, reprinted by Elibron Classics Replica Edition, copyright 2005, Adamant Media Corp.

Gordon, Cyrus, "Forgotten Scripts: Their Ongoing Discovery and Decipherment," Basic Books, New York, 1982.

Hannas, William C., "Asia's Orthographic Dilemma," University of Hawaii Press, Honolulu, 1997.

Itzkoff, Seymour, "The Road to Equality: Evolution and Social Reality," Praeger, Westport, CT. 1992.

Kramer, Samuel Noah, "The Babel of Tongues: A Sumerian Version," Journal of the American Oriental Society vol. 88, 1968.

Muller, Max, "The Science of Language," founded on lectures delivered at the Royal institution in 1861 and 1863, London, Longmans Green, 1899.

Nehru, Jawaharlal, "Discovery of India," New York, John Day, 1946.

Robinson, Orrin, W., "Old English and Its Closest Relatives: A Survey of the Earliest Germanic Languages," Routledge, London, 1993.

Van Ordt, J.F., "The Origin of the Bantu," Cape Town, South Africa, Government Printers, 1907.


## Chapter Nine

Barnes, Jonathan, "Early Greek Philosophy," Penguin Classics, England, paperback, 1987.

Budge, E.A. Wallis, "The Book of The Dead," 1895. http://www.sacred-texts.com/egy/ebod/ June, 2012.

Bulfinch, Thomas, "Bulfinch's Mythology: The Age of Fable; The Age of Chivalry; Legends of Charlemagne," Grosset & Dunlap, New York, 1913.

Cicero, "The Nature of the Gods," trans. by Horace McGregor, England, Penguin Classics, paperback, copyright 1972, 1988.

Cooper, Bill, quoting Lao-tzu, Tao-te-ching, tr. Leon Wieger. English version by Derek Bryce. 1991. Llanerch Publishers, Lampeter. p.13.

Custance, Arthur C., "Evolution or Creation," vol. 4 of The Doorway Papers, Zondervan Publishing House, 1976.

Deane, John Bathurst, "The Worship of the Serpent," 2nd Edition, J.G. & F. Rivington, London, 1833.

Donnelly, Ignatius, "Atlantis, The Antediluvian World," Harper & Brothers, 1882, (http://www.sacred-texts.com/index.htm). January 12, 2011.

Goetz, Delia, Morley, Sylvanus G., & Recinos, Adrian, "Popol Vuh: The Sacred Book of the Ancient Quiche Maya," University of Oklahoma Press, 1950.

Herrman, Paul, "Conquest By Man," Harper & Brothers, New York, 1954.

Hislop, Alexander, "The Two Babylons,"originally published in full in 1838. Reprint by Lifeline, Philippines.

James, E.O., "Prehistoric Religion: A Study in Prehistoric Archaeology," Frederick A. Praeger, publisher, New York, 1957.

Kang, C.H. & Nelson, Ethel R., "The Discovery of Genesis," Concordia Publishing House, St. Louis, Missouri, paperback, copyright 1979.

Kristensen, W. Brede, "The Meaning of Religion: Lectures in the Phenomenology of Religion," translated by John B. Carman, published by Martinus Nijhoff, The Hague, 1960.

Lang, Andrew, "The Making of Religion," Longmans, Green, and Co., London, New York, Bombay, 1898. https://archive.org/details/makingofreligion00languoft, April 24, 2015.

Langdon, Stephen H., "Semitic Mythology," cited in "Evolution or Creation?" The Doorway Papers, vol. 4, Custance, Arthur C., Zondervan Publishing House, Grand Rapids, 1976.

Legge, James, "The Notions of the Chinese Concerning God and Spirits," https://archive.org/details/notionsofchinese00legg June 2, 2013.

Lukar, Manfred, "The Routledge Dictionary of Gods and Goddesses, Devils and Demons," Routledge, New York, 2004.

Muller, Max, "History of Sanskrit Literature," London : Williams and Norgate, 1859.

https://catalog.hathitrust.org/Record/011983903 January 24, 2015.

Peters, Larry, "Mystical Experience in Tamang Shamanism," Journal Title: Re-vision. Volume: 13. Issue: 2. 1990.

Prescott, W.H., "The History of the Conquest of Peru," originally published in 1847. Mass market reprint by Signet Books, paperback, 1966.

Prichard, James Cowles, "Researches Into the Physical History of Mankind, vol. 5. London, Sherwood, Gilbert, and Piper, 1847. Reprinted by Ulan Press.

Rawlingson, George, "History of Phoenicia," Longmans, Green. London, 1889.

Richardson, Don, "Eternity In Their Hearts," Regal Books, Ventura, California, 1984.

Rolleston, Francis, "Mazzaroth," Rivington, London, 1862. reprint of Kessinger Publications

Rose, H.J., "Religion in Greece and Rome," Harper & Row, New York, 1959.

Saunder, Kenneth, "Epochs in Buddhist History: The Haskell Lectures," University of Chicago Press, Chicago, 1924.

Sturluson, Snorri., "Edda," trans. & edited by Anthony Faulkes, publisher, Everyman Library, J.M. Dent, London; Charles Tuttle, Vermont, 1987.

Titcomb, J.A., "British-Israel ; How I Came To Believe It," Re-edited from the 2nd edition, The Covenant Publishing Co., LTD., London, 1875, 1878, this edition was probably published in 1928.

Titcomb, J.A., Prehistoric Monotheism, "Faith and Thought," vol.6, Victoria Institute, published by the Institute, London. 1873.

Toy, Crawford Howell, "Introduction to the History of Religions," Ginn and Company, Boston, 1913.

Waddell, L.A., "The Phoenician Origin of Britons, Scots & Anglo-Saxons," Williams & Norgate, 1924; 2nd ed., 1925.

## Chapter Ten

Abydenus, quoted by Eusebius, Praeparatio Evangelica Book 9, Translated by E.H. Gifford, Oxford, Clarendon, 1903.

Bancroft, Hubert H., "The Native Races," vol. iii, San Francisco, 1882. Kessinger Reprints

Bancroft, Hubert H., "The Native Races," vol. v, San Francisco, 1888. Kessenger Reprint

Charles, R.H., "The Book of Jubilees," Society for Promoting Christian Knowledge, London, 1917.

Cory, Preston, and Hodges, E. R. "Cory's Ancient Fragments," London, Reeves & Turner, 1876.

Donnelly, Ignatius, "Atlantis, The Antediluvian World," Harper and Brothers, N.Y. 1882. (http://www.sacred-texts.com/index.htm). January 12, 2011.

Ellis, William, "Polynesian Researches," vol.1, Henry G. Bohn, London, 1859.

Eusebius, "Theophilus To Autolycus,"Book II, chapter XXXI. Anti-Nicene Fathers, Volume 2, edited by Alexander Roberts and James Donaldson, reprint by Hendrickson Publishers, Inc., copyright 2004.

Goetz, Delia & Morley, Sylvanus, from the translation by Adrian Recinos, "Popul Vuh, The Sacred Book of the Quiche Maya," Univ. of Oklahoma Press, Norman, OK.,@1950.

Halley, Henry H., "Halley's Bible Handbook," Zondervan. Minneapolis, 1972.

Josephus, Flavius, "The Works of Flavius Josephus, Antiquities of the Jews, vol.1," translated by William Whiston, Leary & Getz, Publishers, Philadelphia, 1854.

Kang, C.H. & Nelson, Ethel R., "The Discovery of Genesis," Concordia Pub., St. Louis. copyright 1979.

King James Version of the Bible, printed for Matthew Carey, No.113, Market Street, Philadelphia, October 20, 1801.

Kramer, Samuel N., "The Babel of Tongues: A Sumerian Version," Journal of the American Oriental Society 88, 1968.

Legge, James, "The Notions of The Chinese Concerning God And Spirits," Printed at the "Hongkong Register" office, Hong Kong, 1852. https://archive.org/details/notionsofchinese00legg June 2, 2013.

Traux, Edgar, "Genesis According to the Miao People," Impact Article #214, April 1991. Institute for Creation Research, El Cajon. California, http://www.icr.org/index.php?module=articles&action=view&ID=341.

Velikovsky, Immanuel, Worlds In Collision, New York: Doubleday & Co., Inc., 1950.

Wenham, Gordon, "Genesis 1-15," Waco, Texas, Word Biblical Commentary, 1987.

Williamson, R.W., "Religious and Cosmic Beliefs of Central Polynesia," Cambridge, 1933.

## Chapter Eleven

Catholic Encyclopedia on-line. http://www.catholic.org/encyclopedia/ 2003.

Ceram, C.W., "Gods, Graves, And Scholars," New York, Alfred A. Knopf, 1967.

Charles, R.H., (editor), "Apocrypha and Pseudepigrapha of the Old Testament," vol. 2, Clarendon Press, Oxford, London, 1913.

Ferrar Fenton's translation of the Bible, Destiny Publishers, Merrimac, Massachusetts., 1966. Reprint of the 1903 original. Halley, H., "Halley's Bible Handbook," Zondervan. Minneapolis, 1972.

Herodotus, author, William Beloe, translator, Henry Colburn and Richard Bentley, publishers, London, 1830.

Hilprecht, H.V., Benzinger, Hommel, Jensen, Steindorff, authors. "Explorations in Bible Lands during the 19th Century," A. J. Holman, publisher, Philadelphia, 1903.

Jewish Encyclopedia (The), New York, Funk & Wagnalls, vol.9, 1908.

Jones, A. "The Empires of the Bible," Review and Herald Publishing Association, Washington D.C., 1904.

Josephus, Flavius, "The Works of Flavius Josephus, Antiquities of the Jews, vol.1," translated by William Whiston, Leary & Getz, Publishers, Philadelphia, 1854.

King James Version of the Bible, printed for Matthew Carey, No.113, Market Street, Philadelphia, 1801.

Lenormant, François, "Records of the Past," Old Series, Vol. VII., 1873.

Pinches, Theophilus, G., "The Old Testament: In the Light of the Historical Records and Legends of Assyria and Babylonia," Society for Promoting Christian Knowledge. London. 1908.

Pinches, Theophilus G., "The Religion of Babylonia and Assyria," London, Archibald Constable and Co., 1906.

Sayce, A.H., "Lectures on the Origin and Growth of Religion As Illustrated by the Religion of the Ancient Babylonians," Williams and Norgate, London and Edinburgh, 1898.

Smith, William, Dr. "Entry for 'Tongues, Confusion of," "Smith's Bible Dictionary," 1901.
http://www.biblestudytools.com/dictionaries/smiths-bible-dictionary/abaddon.html 2012.

Verbrugghe, Gerald, and Wickersham, John, editors, "Berossos and Manetho, Introduced and Translated: Native Traditions in Ancient Mesopotamia and Egypt," Univ. of Michigan, 2001.

## Chapter Twelve

Bryant, Jacob, "Bryant's Mythology," 1807, Volume 4, Kessinger reprint.

Bryant, Jacob, "New System or an Analysis of Ancient Mythology," Vol. 1, facsimile reprint of original edition of 1774. Kessinger Publishing's Rare Reprints.

Bryant, Jacob, "New System or an Analysis of Ancient Mythology," Vol. 3, facsimile original edition of 1776. Kessinger Publishing's Rare Reprints.

Bullinger, Ethelbert W., "Commentary On Revelation," Kregel Classics, Grand Rapids, Michigan, 1984.

Cicero, "On the Nature of the Gods," translated by P.G. Walsh, Oxford University Press, Oxford, New York, copyright 1997, 1998. 2015.

Clarke, Adam, "Clarke's Commentary, vol.1," Abingdon Press, New York/Nashville, 1930.

Clement of Alexandria, Ante-Nicene Fathers, vol. 2, "Theophilus To Autolycus," vol. II, Sacred Texts, CD Rom, and also at http://www.sacred-texts.com/chr/ecf/002/0020000.htm, April 28, 2012.

Clement, "Recognitions of Clement," Chapter XXIX, Ante-Nicene Fathers, Sacred Texts, CD Rom, and also at http://www.sacred-texts.com/chr/ecf/008/index.htm, April 24, 2012.

Cory, Preston, and Hodges, E. Richmond, "Cory's Ancient Fragments," 1876. Kessinger Publishing's Rare Reprints.

Diodorus Siculus, Library of History, Book XVII, translated by Welles, C. Bradford, Harvard University Press, London, Cambridge, 1963.

Gill, John, "An Exposition of the Old Testament," Vol. 1, 1763. facsimile reprint by ECCO.

Hislop, Alexander, "The Two Babylons," first published in 1853 in pamphlet form, printed in full in 1858. Reprinted by Life Line, Pasig City, Philipines, no publication date given.)

"Jewish Encyclopedia" vol. 9, Funk and Wagnalls, New York, 1906. http://www.jewishencyclopedia.com/

Josephus, "Works of Flavius Josephus," Antiquities of the Jews, vol.1, translated by William Whiston, Leary & Getz, Publishers, Philadelphia, 1854.

Kautzsch, Emil, ed., "Genesis' Hebrew Grammar," Oxford, Clarendon, 1910.

Keating, Geoffrey, "The History of Ireland," vol. II, (styled by Keating as Book 1, section XV), written in the early 1600s, compiled from books written centuries earlier, NABU Domain facsimile reprint of 1902 edition of Keating's History.

Kiel, C.F., & Delitzsch, F., "Kiel and Delitzsch's Old Testament Commentary," reprinted by Hendrickson Publishers, 1996.

Murray, K. C., "Nigerian Bronzes," Antiquity (England), March 1941. http://antiquity.ac.uk/ant/015/Ant0150071.htm, March 2, 2015.

Paterculus, Velleius, "Roman History," Book 1, http://www.scribd.com/doc/27178780/Velleius-Paterculus-Roman-History-Vol-1, April 26, 2012.

Pinches, Theophilus, G., "The Old Testament: In the Light of the Historical Records and Legends of Assyria and Babylonia," Society for Promoting Christian Knowledge. London. 1908.

Rawlinson, George, "Egypt and Babylon from sacred and profane sources," New York, Charles Scribner's Sons, 1885.

Rolleston, Frances, "Mazzaroth," reprint by Kessinger Publishing. Originally published at Edinburg in 1862.

St. Jerome, "Saint Jerome's Hebrew Questions on Genesis," Robert Hayward – translator, Clarendon Press, Oxford, 1995.

Young, Robert, "Young's Literal Translation of the Bible," 1898. Reprint by Baker Book House, Grand Rapids, Michigan.

## Chapter Thirteen

Bryant, Jacob, "Bryant's Mythology," 1807, Volume 4, Kessenger Reprint.

Bryant, Jacob, "New System or an Analysis of Ancient Mythology," vol. I, 1774, reprinted by Kessinger Publishing

Bryant, Jacob, "New System or an Analysis of Ancient Mythology," vol. III, 1776, reprinted by Kessinger Publishing. Cicero, "On The Nature of The Gods," translated by P. G. Walsh, Oxford University Press, copyright 1997, 1998.

Clarke, Adam, "Clarke's Commentary, vol.1," Abingdon Press, New York/Nashville, 1930.

Clement of Alexandria, Ante-Nicene Fathers, vol. 2, "Theophilus To Autolycus", Book II, Translations of the Writings of the Fathers down to A.D. 325, Alexander Roberts, D.D., and James Donaldson, LL.D., editors, American reprint of the Edinburgh Edition, arranged with notes by A. Cleveland Coxe, D.D. vol. II, Sacred Texts, CD Rom, and also at http://www.sacred-texts.com/chr/ecf/002/0020000.htm, April 28, 2012.

Clement, "Recognitions of Clement," Chapter XXIX, Ante-Nicene Fathers, vol.8, Sacred Texts, CD Rom, and also at http://www.sacred-texts.com/chr/ecf/008/index.htm, April 24, 2012.

Cory, Isaac Preston, & Hodges, Richmond, "Cory's Ancient Fragments," Reeves and Turner, London, 1876. reprinted by Kessinger Publishing.

Cumberland, Richard, "Sanchoniatho's Phoenician History," London, 1720. Reprinted by NABU.

Diodorus Siculus, "Library of History," (available from the Loeb Classical Library)

Donnelly, Ignatius, "Atlantis: The Antediluvian World," Harper & Brothers, 1882, (http://www.sacred-texts.com/index.htm). January 12, 2011.

Eusebius, "Preparation For The Gospel," Vol. I, translated by Edwin Hamilton Gifford, published by Clarendon Press, 1903, reprinted by Wipf and Stock Publishers, Eugene, Oregon, 2002.

Fell, Barry, "America B.C.," Quadrangle, the New York Times Book Company, 4th printing, 1977.

Fell, Barry, "Bronze Age America," Little, Brown and Company, copyright 1982.

Frazier, James G., "The Golden Bough," MacMillan, N.Y., 1922.

Garnier, J., "The Worship of the Dead," Chapman & Hall, Limited, London, 1909. Reprinted by Kessinger Publishing.

Gascoigne, Mike, "Forgotten History of the Western People," Anno Mundi Books, Camberly, England, copyright 2002.

Gill, John, "An Exposition of the Old Testament," Vol. 1, 1763. facsimile reprint by ECCO.

Grey, Sir George, "Polynesian Mythology & Ancient Traditional History of the New Zealanders," 1854. http://www.sacred-texts.com/pac/grey/grey00.htm, December 4, 2013).

Hilprecht, H.V., contributors: J. Benzinger, F. Hommel, P. Jensen, and G. Steindorff, "Explorations in Bible Lands during the 19th Century," A. J. Holman, publisher, Philadelphia, 1903.

Hislop, Alexander, "The Two Babylons," reprinted by Life Line, Philippines, publication date not given.

"Jewish Encyclopedia" vol. 9, Funk and Wagnalls, New York, 1906. http://www.jewishencyclopedia.com/

Josephus, "The Works of Flavius Josephus, Antiquities of the Jews, vol.1," translated by William Whiston, Leary & Getz, Publishers, Philadelphia, 1854.

Rouse, Martin, Bible Pedigree of the Nations of the World, "Journal of the Transactions of the Victoria Institute," vol. XXXVIII, published by the Institute, London. 1906.

Kautzsch, Emil, ed., "Genesis' Hebrew Grammar," Oxford, Clarendon, 1910.

Keating, Geoffrey, "The History of Ireland," vol. II, (styled by Keating as Book 1, section XV), written in the early 1600s, compiled from books written centuries earlier, NABU Domain facsimile reprint of 1902 edition of Keating's History.

Kiel and Delitzsch's Old Testament Commentary,

MacManus, Seumas, "The Story of the Irish Race," Devin-Adair Company, Old Greenwich, Connecticut, copyright 1921. 32nd printing, October 1979.

Mendenhall, George E., "The Tenth Generation: The Origins of the Biblical Tradition," Baltimore: The Johns Hopkins University Press, 1973.

Murdoch, John, Huxley, Thomas H. "Papers on Great Indian Questions of the Day,' Christian Literature Society for India, London, Madras, 1903).

Murray, K.C., "Nigerian Bronzes," Antiquity (England), Volume:15, number 57, March 1941. http://antiquity.ac.uk/ant/015/Ant0150071.htm, March 2, 2015.

Paterculus, Velleius, "Roman History", Book 1, http://www.scribd.com/doc/27178780/Velleius-Paterculus-Roman-History-Vol-1, April 26, 2012.

Pinches, Theophilus, G., "The Old Testament: In the Light of the Historical Records and Legends of Assyria and Babylonia," Society for Promoting Christian Knowledge. London. 1908.

Prescott, William Henry, "History of the Conquest of Mexico," John Foster Kirk - editor,   J. B. Lippincott, Philadelphia, 1891.

Quigley, Carroll, "The Evolution of Civilizations," Liberty Fund, Indianapolis, copyright 1979.

Robbins, Eliza, "Elements of Mythology,"Eldredge & Brother, Philadelphia, 35th edition, copyright 1830.

Robinson, David M., "Baalbek, Palmyra," published by J. J. Augustin, New York, 1946.

Rolleston, Francis, "Mazzaroth," On the Original Language, Kessinger Reprint.

Rolleston, Francis, "Mazzaroth," On The Signs of The Zodiac, Kessinger Reprint.

St. Augustine, "The City of God," translators - Grace Monahan & Gerald Walsh, Catholic University of America Press. Washington, DC., 1952. Books VIII-XVI.

St. Jerome, "Saint Jerome's Hebrew Questions on Genesis," Robert Hayward – translator, Clarendon Press, Oxford, 1995.

Unger, Merrill F., "Unger's Bible Hand Book," Chicago, Moody Press, 1967.

Waddell, L.A., "The Phoenician Origin of Britons, Scots & Anglo-Saxons," Williams & Norgate, 2nd ed., 1925.

Wright, William, "Empire of the Hittites," Scribner & Welford, New York, 1884.

Wylie, Alexander, "History of The Scottish Nation," Hamilton Adams and Company, London; Andrew Elliot, Edinburgh, 1886, Vl. 1.

Young, Robert, "Young's Literal Translation of the Bible", 1898. Reprint by Baker Book House, Grand Rapids, Michigan.

## Chapter Fourteen

Beckwith, Martha. "Hawaiian Mythology," Honolulu, Hawaii, University of Hawaii Press, 1970

Bryant, Jacob, "New System or an Analysis of Ancient Mythology," Vol. 1, 1874 edition

Cicero, "On the Nature of the Gods," translated by P.G. Walsh, Oxford University Press, Oxford, New York, copyright 1997, 199

Cumberland, Richard, "Sanchuniathon's Phoenician History," London, 1720

Cory, I.P. & Hodges, Richmond, "Cory's Ancient Fragments, A New and Enlarged Edition," Reeves & Turner, London, 1876. Facsimile reprints from Kessinger Publishing, Kila, MT

David, Antony E. & Rosalie, "A Biographical Dictionary of Ancient Egypt," Seaby, London, 1992

Davidson, Basil "The Lost Cities of Africa," Little & Brown, Boston, 1959.

Diodorus Siculus (Diodorus the Sicilian), "The Library of History," Book VI of the Loeb Classical Library, translated by C. H. Oldfather, volume 3, Harvard Univ. Press, Cambridge, Mass., London, 1970

Diodorus Siculus (Diodorus the Sicilian), "Library of History," Book I, 27, translated by C. G. Frazer, Loeb Classical Library, Harvard Univ. Press, Cambridge, Massachusetts, London, 1954

Du Chaillu, Paul B., "The Viking Age: The Early History, Manners, and Customs of the Ancestors of the English-Speaking Nations," London, John Murray, 1889

Encyclopedia Britannica, Ninth Edition (1894), vol. 2

Eusebius, "Preparation For The Gospel," Vol. I, translated by Edwin Hamilton Gifford, published by Clarendon Press, 1903, reprinted by Wipf and Stock Publishers, Eugene, Oregon, 2002

Fleure, Herbert John, and Peake, Harold, "Priests & Kings," Yale University Press, New Haven, CT., 1927

Hislop, Alexander, "The Two Babylons," First published in full in 1858. 3rd edition, reprinted in the Philippines by Lifeline

King, Leonard W., Legends of Babylon and Egypt in Relation to Hebrew Tradition," Oxford University Press, H. Milford, London, 1918.

Landsburg, Alan and Sally, "In Search of Ancient Mysteries," Bantam Books, (paperback), 1974.

MacManus, Seumas, 'The Story of the Irish Race," Devin-Adair Company, Old Greenwich, Conn., 1979

Paterculus, C. Velleius, "Roman History," Book One, translated by Frederick W. Shipley, Loeb Classical Library, University of Chicago, 1924

Pinches, Theophilus G., "The Old Testament: In the Light of the Historical Records and Legends of Assyria and Babylonia," Society for Promoting Christian Knowledge, London, 1908

Rawlinson, George, "History of Phoenicia," Longmans, Green and Company, London, 1889.

Tertullian, "Apology," American Edition of the Ante-Nicene Fathers, Vol. 3, edited by Alexander Roberts and James Donaldson, reprint by Hendrickson Publishers, Inc., copyright 2004

Tertullian, "Ad Nationes," Vol. 3, American Edition of the Ante-Nicene Fathers, Vol. 3, edited by Alexander Roberts and James Donaldson, reprint by Hendrickson Publishers, Inc., copyright 2004

Tertullian, "The Divine Institutes," chapter 15; see also Volume 7 of the Anti-Nicene Fathers, edited by Alexander Roberts and James Donaldson, reprint by Hendrickson Publishers, Inc., copyright 2004

Sturluson, Snorri, "Edda," (sometimes called the Prose Edda), translated and edited by Anthony Faulkes, London, 1987

Virgil, "The Aeneid," translated by W.F. Jackson Knight, Penguin Classics (paperback), 1958.

Waddell, L.A., "The Phoenician Origin of Britons, Scots & Anglo-Saxons," Williams & Norgate, 1924; 2nd ed., 1925.

## Chapter Fifteen

Bray, Warwick, "Everyday Life of the Ancient Aztecs," Dorset Press, New York, 1987.

Bryant, Jacob, "New System or an Analysis of Ancient Mythology," Part One. London, 1774. reprint by Kessinger Publishing, Kila, MT.

Cumberland, Richard, Bishop of Peterborough, "Sanchoniatho's Phoenician History," London, 1720. Reprinted by Nabu Public Domain Reprints, no date given.

Delitzsch, Friedrich, "Babel and Bible," Williams and Norgate, London, 1903.

Hanfmann, George M.A., "Review of Irene Rosenzweig's Ritual and Cults of Pre-Roman Iguvium," American Journal of Archaeology, Vol. 43, No. 1, Jan.-Mar. 1939.

Hislop, Alexander, "The Two Babylons," reprint of the 1838 edition. Reprinted by Life Line, Pasig City, Philippines, no date given.

King James Version of the Bible, printed for Matthew Carey, No.113, Market Street, Philadelphia, October 20, 1801.

Mackenzie, Donald, A., "Myths of Babylonia and Assyria," The Gresham Publishing Company, London, 1915.

McCrady, Edward, "Genesis and Pagan Cosmogonies," Transactions of the Victoria Institute, Vol. 72, 1940.

Persson, Axel W., "The Religion of Greece in Prehistoric Times," University of California Press, 1942.

Pinches, Theophilus G., "The Old Testament: In the Light of the Historical Records and Legends of Assyria and Babylonia," Society for Promoting Christian Knowledge, London, 1908.

Titcomb, Rev. J.H., "Prehistoric Monotheism," Journal of 1872-73 of the Victoria Institute-- pages 141 to 162. http://www.creationism.org/victoria/VictoriaInst1872_pg141.htm June, 2011

Wiseman, P.J., "New Discoveries in Babylonia about Genesis," Marshall, Morgan, and Scott, London, 1936. Citing Henri Frankfort, "Third Preliminary Report on Excavations at Tell Asmar."

CPSIA information can be obtained
at www.ICGtesting.com
Printed in the USA
LVOW13s1925290717
542936LV00003B/4/P